I0799861

IMAGES
of America

JEWISH COMMUNITY OF CHATTANOOGA

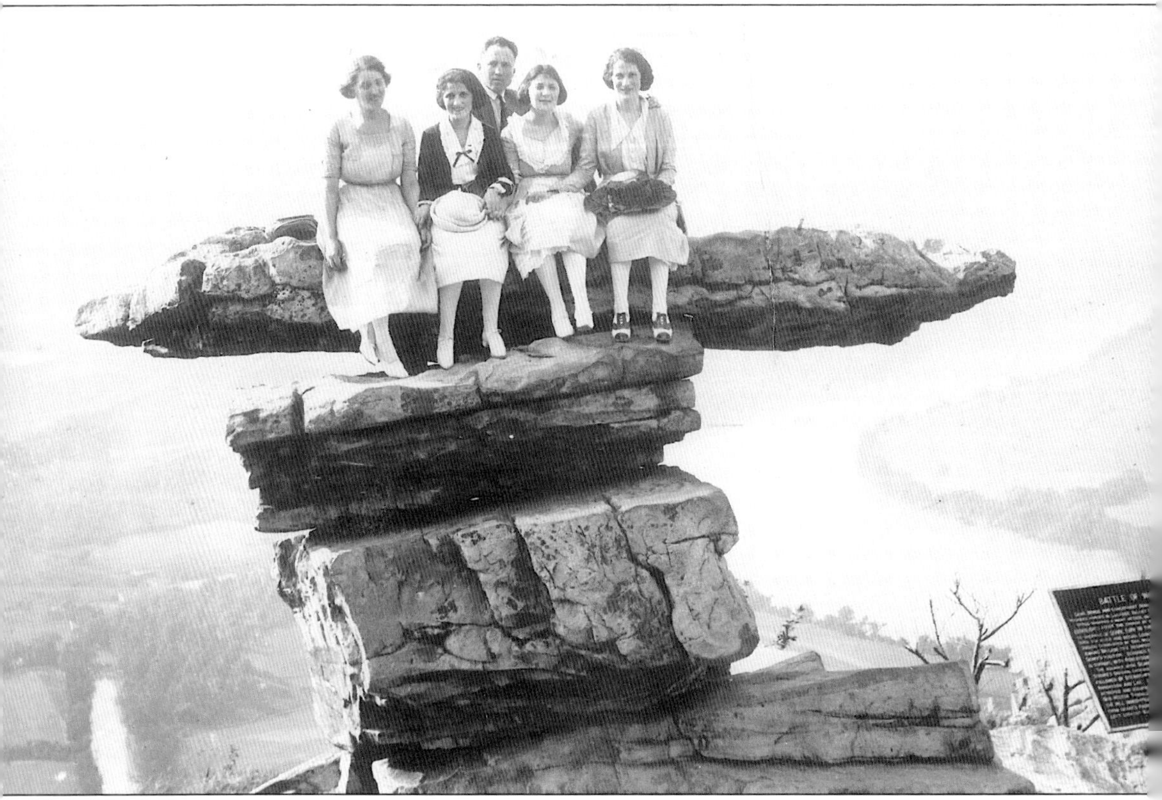

A favorite place for taking family pictures was Umbrella Rock at Lookout Point, Lookout Mountain, overlooking the Tennessee River in Chattanooga. No one has been able to explain how this series of huge rocks became stacked and balanced in such a way. It is an extremely dangerous overlook and has been fenced off and nearly covered over by the observation deck at the Ochs Museum, which was built there in 1939. Since that time, no one has been allowed to climb the structure. In this picture, taken in 1921, a group of young people can be seen on a June outing. They are, from left to right, Lena Diamond, Lillie Rittenbaum, Jake Abelson, his sister Lena, and Belle Levy. The two Lenas and Jake were born in Chattanooga, while Lillie and Belle are Atlantans.

IMAGES
of America

JEWISH COMMUNITY OF CHATTANOOGA

Joy Effron Abelson Adams

ARCADIA
PUBLISHING

ISBN 978-0-7385-0120-8

Published by Arcadia Publishing
Charleston, South Carolina

Printed in the United States of America

Library of Congress Catalog Card Number: 99-62336

For all general information contact Arcadia Publishing at:
Telephone 843-853-2070
Fax 843-853-0044
E-Mail sales@arcadiapublishing.com
For customer service and orders:
Toll-Free 1-888-313-2665

Visit us on the Internet at www.arcadiapublishing.com

This book is dedicated to my parents,
Lou and Lucille Heymann Effron.

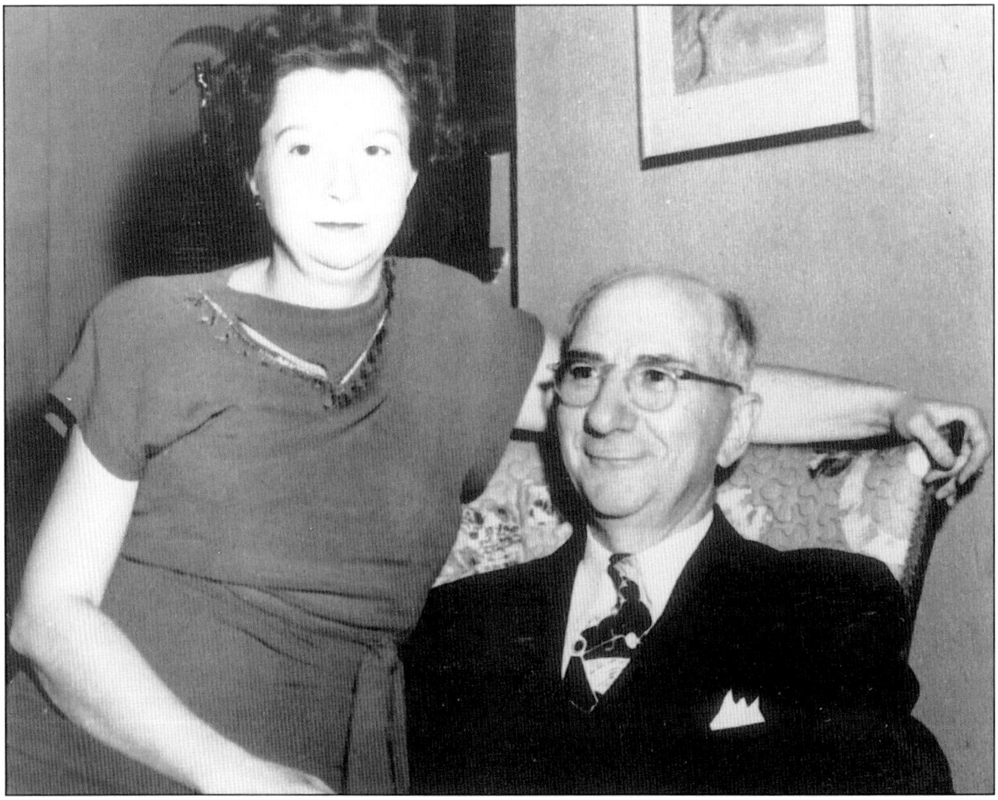

Contents

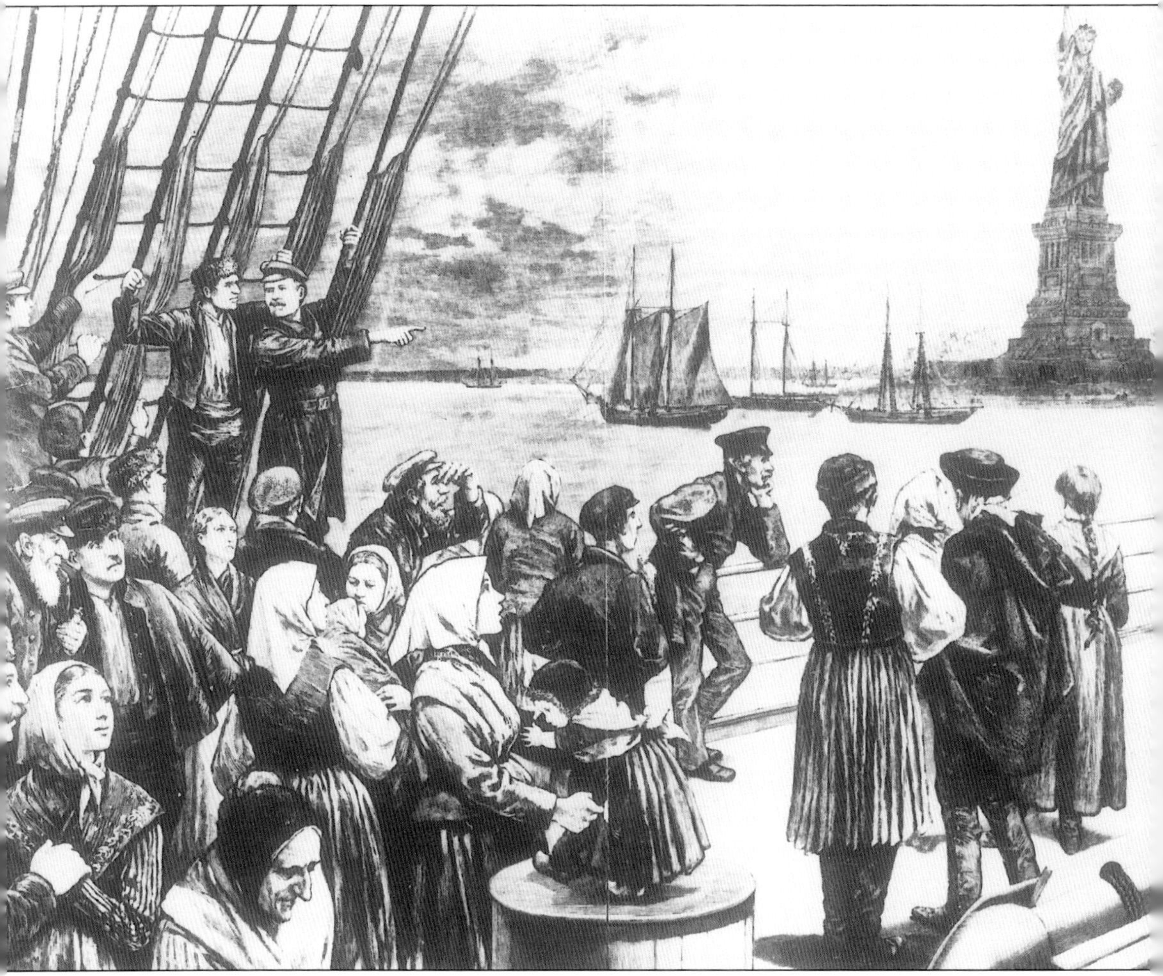

A group of immigrants arrives in New York Harbor and gazes for the first time at the Statue of Liberty. After their long voyage, this was a welcome and most dreamed of site for the newcomers entering the United States for the first time.

Introduction

Dreams do come true! In 1993, the Chai Steppers Seniors Club of the Chattanooga Jewish Community Federation traveled to Atlanta's Emory University to view a pictorial exhibit on loan from the Museum of Southern Jewish Experience of Utica, Mississippi. The group was so impressed with this display that they vowed they would somehow collect and create a pictorial exhibit for their hometown, Chattanooga, Tennessee. In 1996, the Chattanooga Jewish Reflections Exhibit opened at the Chattanooga-Hamilton County Regional History Museum. This author is the curator of the exhibit. The dream did come true.

"The most important theme in the exhibit shows that the Jewish Community has always been an integral part of the greater community," said Rabbi Joseph Klein of the Mizpah Congregation. "We have never been a small pocket within the population, but have always been involved with an active presence." The pictorial exhibit has become a part of a permanent "Jewish Heritage Collection" in Chattanooga.

This book, *Jewish Community of Chattanooga,* is an outgrowth of the Reflections Exhibit, but it is in no way an exact copy of it. It begins with families immigrating to the United States from Europe and depicts how the newcomers established themselves in worship, work, and play, finally becoming volunteers in building institutions for themselves and all the citizens of Chattanooga and the surrounding area.

The newcomers came to Chattanooga during what is called the Second Wave of Jewish immigration from Western Europe (1865–1880) and the Third Wave of Jewish immigration from Eastern Europe (1881–1928). The Holocaust years (1930–1948) brought another group of freedom-seeking survivors. Finally, new residents came from Russia in the 1970s and again in the 1990s, with the fall of the Iron Curtain.

Chattanooga was always a transportation crossroads. The Tennessee River connected it to other parts of the country. Then, in 1849, the railroads came and assured Chattanooga industrial and business growth. The Jewish newcomers came here to join in the free enterprise movement that they had been denied in Europe.

Although there is some reference to a Jewish settlement in Chattanooga as early as 1858, the first documented evidence of Jewish activity in Chattanooga started after the close of the War between the States, when Western European and German Jews arrived in 1865. A year later they established the Reform Mizpah Congregation. After this initial group came the Eastern European Russian, Polish, Latvian, and Lithuanian Jews, who established the Orthodox B'nai Zion Congregation in 1888 (which became a Conservative Congregation in 1960). The Shaari Zion Orthodox Congregation (1904–1956) was formed later by a group from the B'nai Zion Congregation. The Beth Sholom Orthodox Synagogue opened its doors in 1959. Thirty miles south of Chattanooga is Dalton, Georgia, the carpet center of the world, where Jewish families founded the Beth El Congregation in 1941. The families observed events dear to them in freedom such as weekly Shabbat and the Jewish holidays. Also, they observed life cycle events: birth, bar/bat mitzvah, confirmation, marriage, birthdays, wedding anniversaries, and, through their cemeteries, death.

Opportunities for economic success abounded. Jewish organizations and clubs were formed. Jews became active in politics, the arts, the military, social welfare, and charitable endeavors. Recognition came to Jewish individuals as well as Jewish institutions. From 1906 to 1935, Chattanooga boasted a Young Men's Hebrew Association. From 1945 until 1991, there was a Chattanooga Jewish Community Center. Both of these early institutions have been replaced in the 1990s with the Jewish Community Federation of Greater Chattanooga, and a new building is on the drawing board.

The Jewish presence has been reflected throughout the community during the more than 130 years that Jews have lived in the Chattanooga area. The images presented herein are a sampling of happenings, persons, and places, and are not meant to form a chronological history. As the 20th century comes to a close, one becomes aware that changes are inevitable and that the time period presented in this book is gone forever, as are many of the places and people.

One

Beginning in Chattanooga: *Immigration, Cemeteries, and Synagogues*

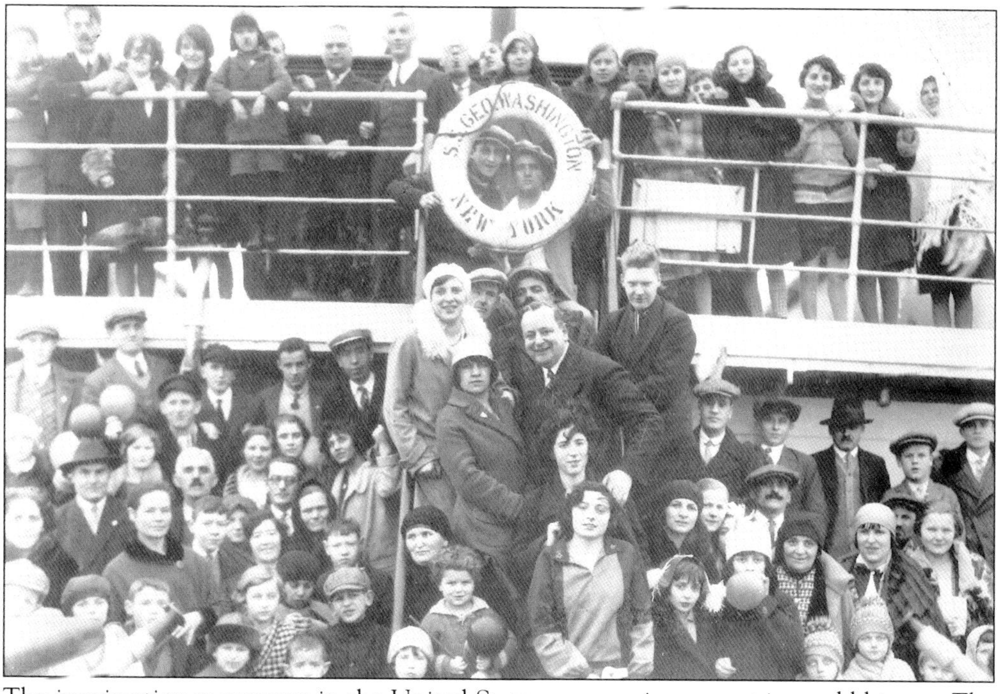

The immigration movement in the United States was a unique event in world history. The Jewish community of Chattanooga is made up of settlers from many towns in Europe. Sol Freedman and his bride, Lillian (Liffy) Freedman (top row, sixth and seventh from the right), arrived on a boat in New York harbor in 1928. Sol originally settled in Chattanooga and opened a grocery store in 1910. He returned to Poland to marry and to bring his sweetheart to America. Their children are Clara Shoenig of Chattanooga and Anita Eidex of Atlanta. (Courtesy of the Ida Pearle and Joseph Cuba Community Archives of the William Breman Jewish History Museum.)

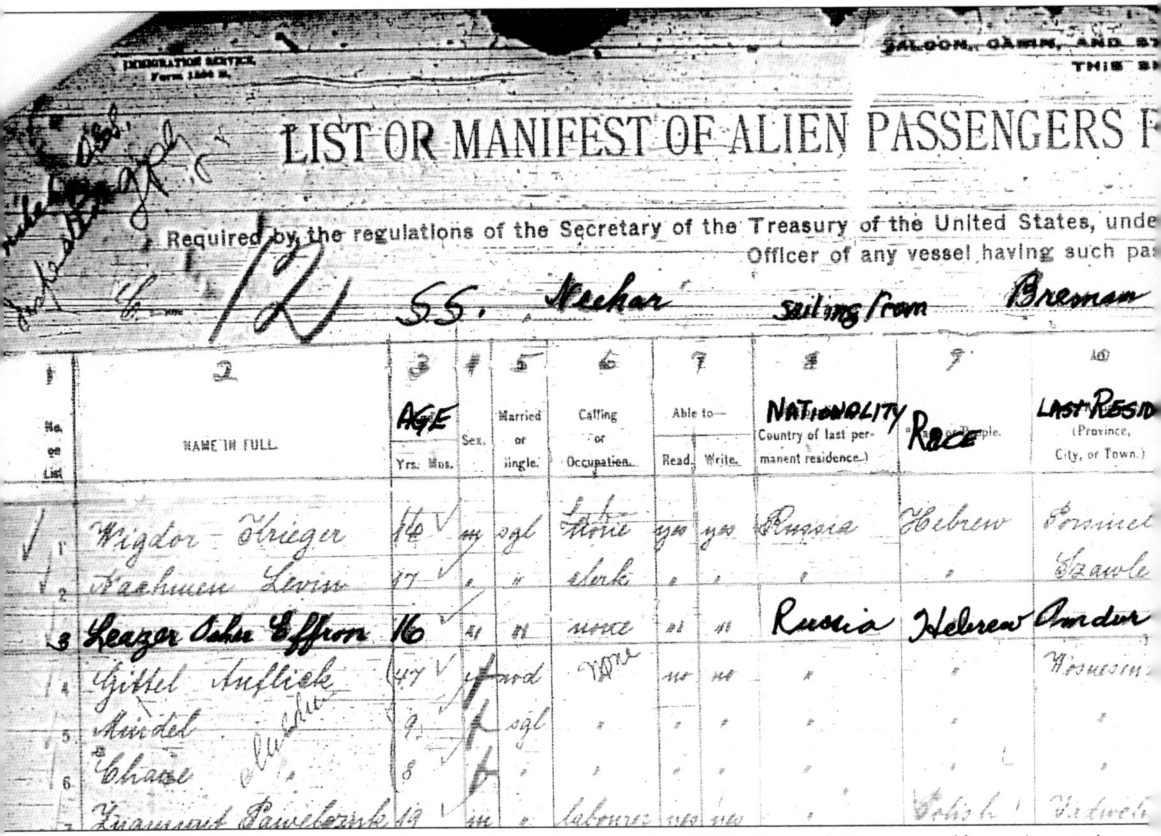

IMMIGRATION SERVICE.

SALOON, CABIN, AND ST…

LIST OR MANIFEST OF ALIEN PASSENGERS F…

Required by the regulations of the Secretary of the Treasury of the United States, unde…

Officer of any vessel having such pa…

(12) S.S. Neckar sailing from Bremen

No. on List	NAME IN FULL.	AGE Yrs. Mos.	Sex.	Married or Single.	Calling or Occupation.	Able to— Read.	Write.	NATIONALITY (Country of last permanent residence.)	RACE or People.	LAST RESIDENCE (Province, City, or Town.)
1	Wigdor Krieger	16	m	sgl	none	yes	yes	Russia	Hebrew	
2	Nachmen Levin	17	"	"	clerk	"	"	"	"	
3	Leazer Osher Effron	16	"	"	none	"	"	Russia	Hebrew	
4	Gittel Auflick	47	f	wd		no	no	"	"	
5	Mindel	9	f	sgl	"	"	"	"	"	"
6	Chaie	8	f		"	"	"	"	"	"

Ships' manifests record early arrivals to America. In 1853, Samuel Hiemann (from Austria) arrived at the port of New York aboard the SS *Heidelberg* from L'Harve, France, with his wife and eight children. They settled in Philadelphia. His grandson, Joseph Heymann, and his great-

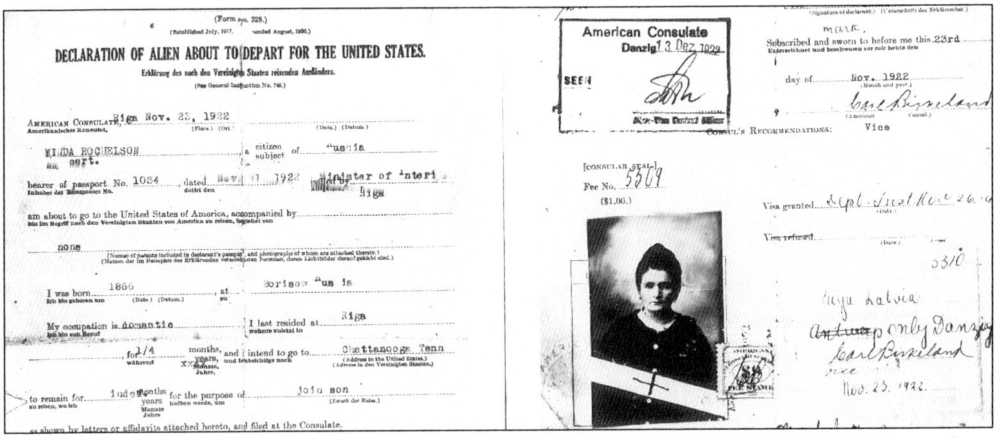

DECLARATION OF ALIEN ABOUT TO DEPART FOR THE UNITED STATES.

Erklärung des nach den Vereinigten Staaten reisenden Ausländers.

American Consulate, Riga Nov. 23, 1922

MINDA ROCHELSON … citizen / subject of Russia

bearer of passport No. 1034, dated … 1922 … Minister of Interior … Riga

am about to go to the United States of America, accompanied by none

I was born 1866 at Borisov Russia

My occupation is domestic. I last resided at Riga

for 1/4 … and I intend to go to Chattanooga Tenn

to remain for indefinitely for the purpose of join son

as shown by letters or affidavits attached hereto, and filed at the Consulate.

American Consulate Danzig 13 Dez 1922 SEEN

Subscribed and sworn to before me this 23rd day of Nov. 1922

Vice Consul.

Consul's Recommendations:

[Consular Seal] Fee No. 5569 ($1.00.)

Visa granted

Visa refused

Riga Latvia

only Danzig

Nov. 23. 1922.

Another document that each immigrant had to apply for when they decided to leave their European homes and come to America was the Declaration of Alien about to Depart for the United States. Pictured here are Hilda (Minda) Richelson's papers to leave Riga, Russia, to come to Chattanooga. Her son Louis sent for her to join him in America in 1922. The Richelson family was involved in Chattanooga in the iron and steel business. Louis and Rosa Richelson had six children: Issy, Ida, David, Mary, Maurice, and Alvin.

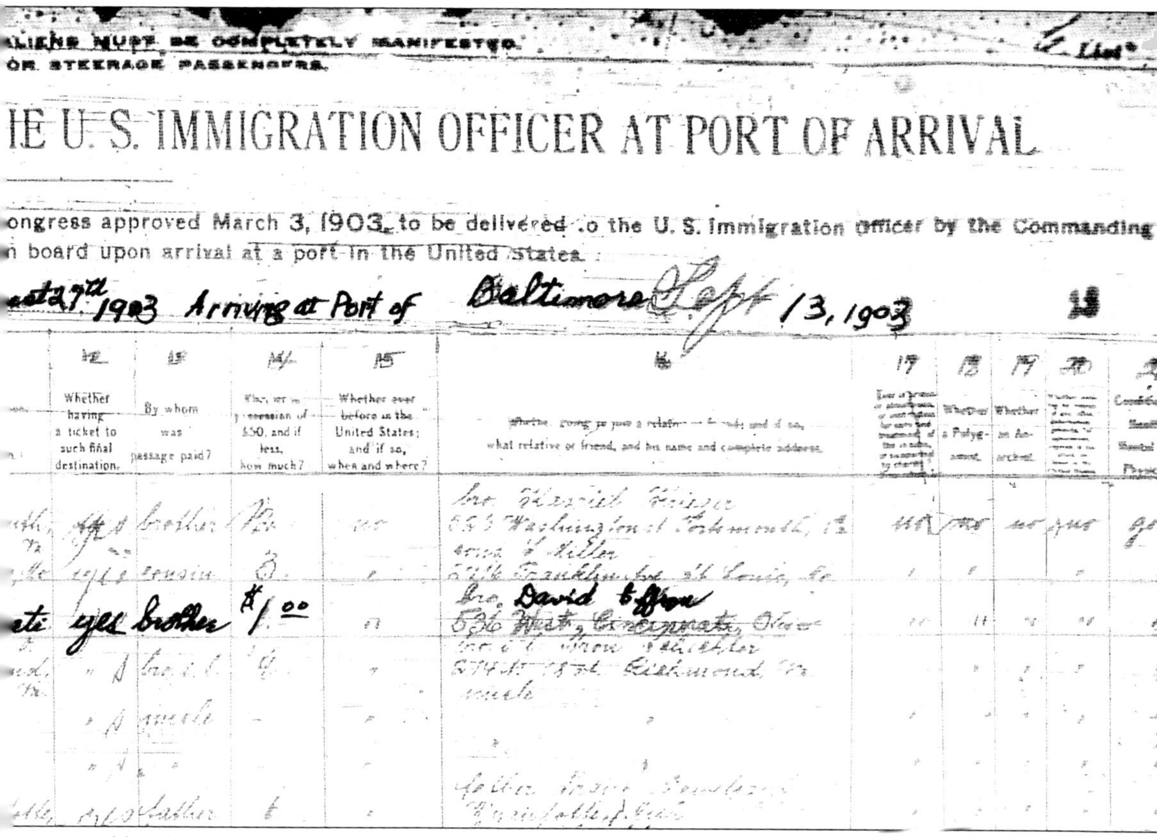

ALIENS MUST BE COMPLETELY MANIFESTED.
OR STEERAGE PASSENGERS.

HE U. S. IMMIGRATION OFFICER AT PORT OF ARRIVAL

ongress approved March 3, 1903, to be delivered to the U. S. Immigration officer by the Commanding
n board upon arrival at a port in the United States.

27th 1903 Arriving at Port of Baltimore Sept 13, 1903

12	13	14	15	16
Whether having a ticket to such final destination.	By whom was passage paid?	Whether in possession of $50, and if less, how much?	Whether ever before in the United States; and if so, when and where?	Whether going to join a relative or friend, and his name and complete address.
yes	brother	$1.00		Bro. David Effron 536 West, Cincinnati, Ohio

granddaughter, Lucille Heymann, from Fayetteville, Tennessee, settled in Chattanooga in 1918. Lou Effron debarked at the port of Baltimore (from Amdur, Poland/Russia) in 1903, listing his Yiddish name of Lazer Usher Effron. He arrived in Chattanooga in 1918, after serving in World War I at Fort Oglethorpe, Georgia. Lou and Lucille were married in 1920.

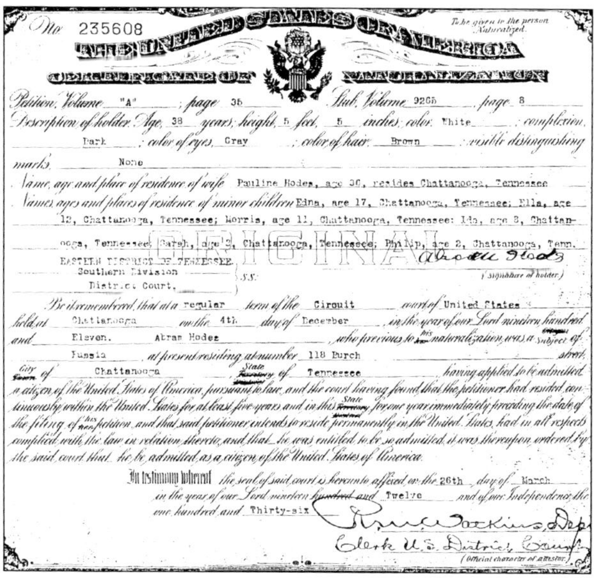

No 235608

To be given to the person Naturalized.

THE UNITED STATES OF AMERICA

CERTIFICATE OF NATURALIZATION

Petition, Volume "A" page 35 Stub, Volume 9265 page 8

Description of holder: Age, 38 years; height, 5 feet, 5 inches; color, White; complexion, Dark; color of eyes, Gray; color of hair, Brown; visible distinguishing marks, None

Name, age and place of residence of wife Pauline Hodes, age 36, resides Chattanooga, Tennessee

Names, ages and places of residence of minor children Edna, age 17, Chattanooga, Tennessee; Ella, age 12, Chattanooga, Tennessee; Morris, age 11, Chattanooga, Tennessee; Ida, age 8, Chattanooga, Tennessee; Sarah, age 5, Chattanooga, Tennessee; Philip, age 2, Chattanooga, Tenn.

ORIGINAL

EASTERN DISTRICT OF TENNESSEE
Southern Division
District Court, } SS:

Abram Hodes (Signature of holder.)

Be it remembered, that at a regular term of the Circuit court of United States held at Chattanooga on the 4th day of December in the year of our Lord nineteen hundred and Eleven. Abram Hodes who previous to his naturalization was a subject of Russia at present residing at number 118 Burch street, City of Chattanooga State of Tennessee having applied to be admitted a citizen of the United States of America, pursuant to law, and the court having found that the petitioner had resided continuously within the United States for at least five years and in this State for one year immediately preceding the date of the filing of his petition, and that said petitioner intends to reside permanently in the United States, had in all respects complied with the law in relation thereto, and that he was entitled to be so admitted, it was thereupon ordered by the said court that he be admitted as a citizen of the United States of America.

In testimony whereof the seal of said court is hereunto affixed on the 26th day of March in the year of our Lord nineteen hundred and Twelve and of our Independence the one hundred and Thirty-six

Clerk U.S. District Court
(Official character of attestor.)

Abram Hodes' naturalization papers indicate that he became a U.S. citizen in 1912. Other Chattanooga newcomers who became U.S. citizens included Phillip Poss from Austria in 1859; Max Diamond and family from Poland in 1892; Ephraim Mennen and family in 1911; Ben Hasden and family in 1921; and Herman Cohen from Poland in 1928.

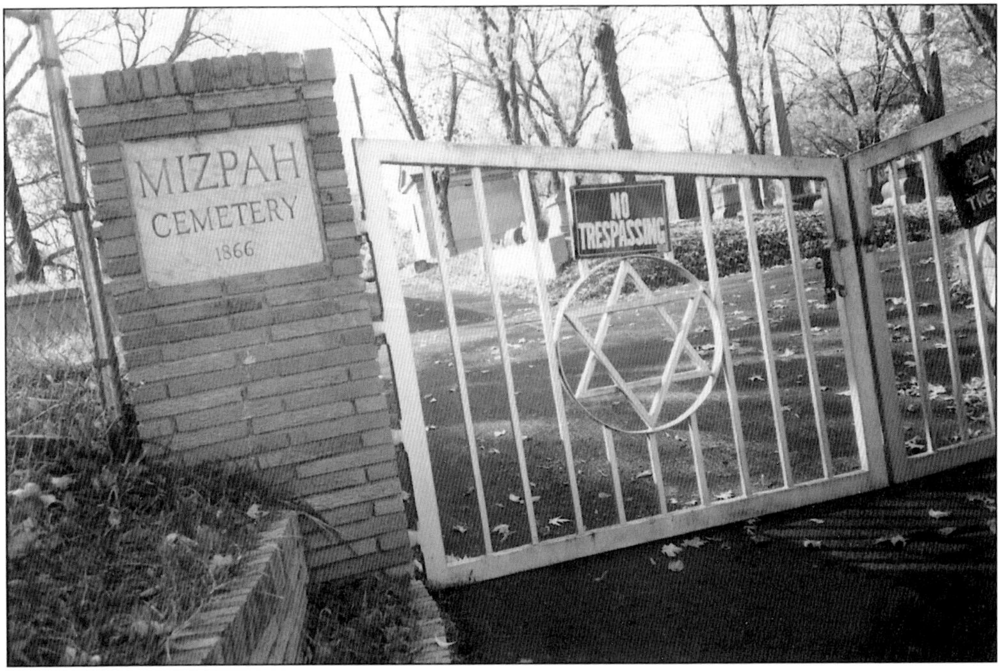

Most of the new arrivals to America felt it their first order of business to buy land for a sacred burial ground for the dead. Thus, in 1866, land was bought at East Third and Collins Streets, and the Mizpah Congregation Cemetery (Reform) was established. The first burial in Mizpah Cemetery was Adolph Deutch in 1867.

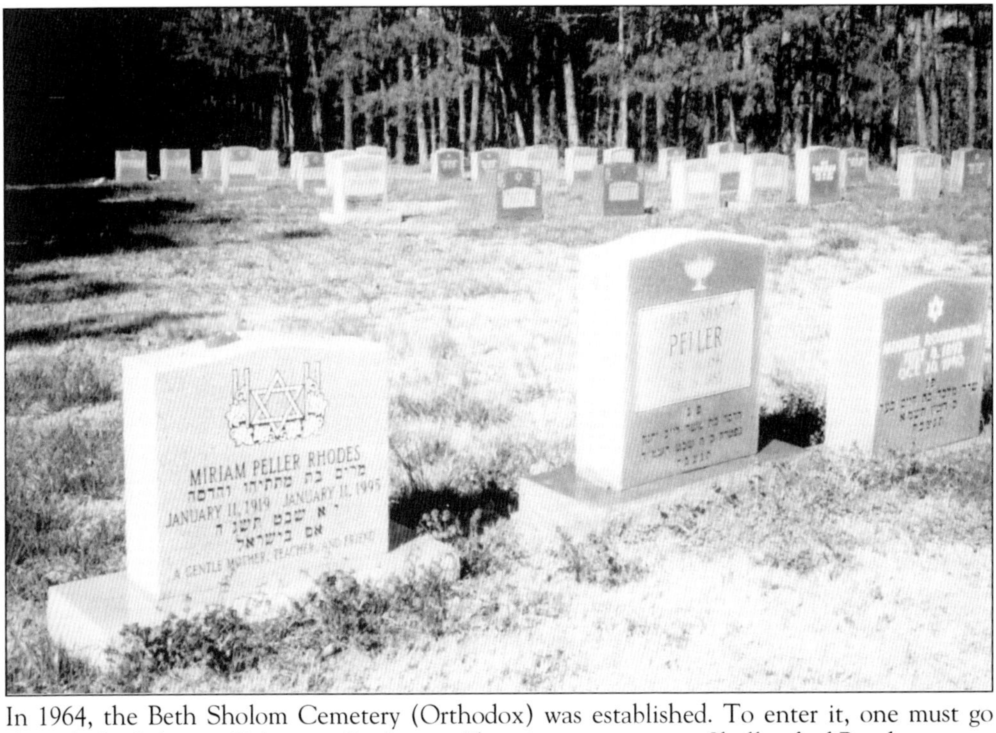

In 1964, the Beth Sholom Cemetery (Orthodox) was established. To enter it, one must go through the Lakewood Memory Gardens, a Christian cemetery, on Shallowford Road.

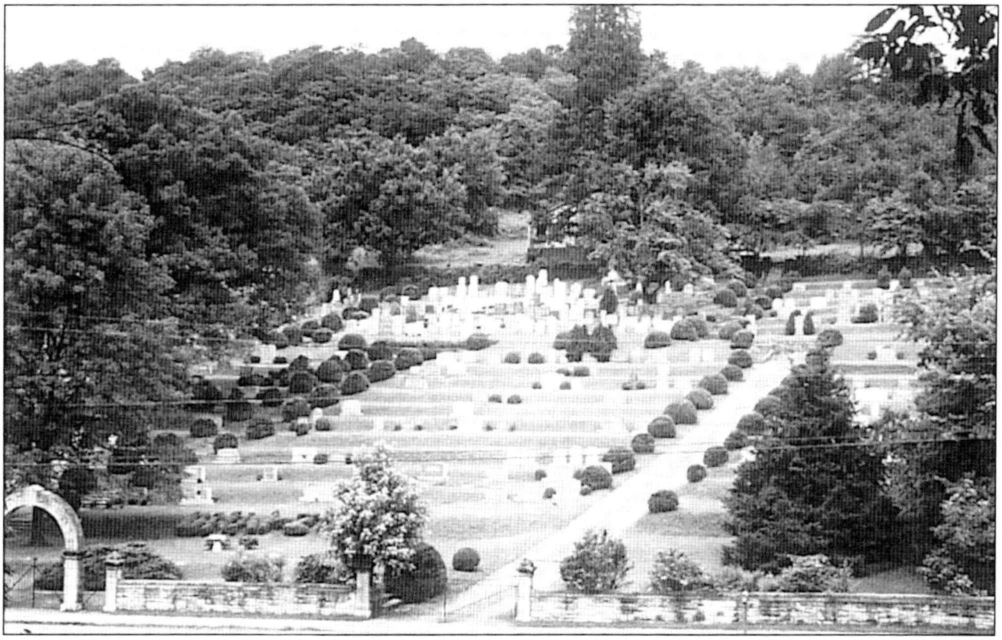

This is an aerial view of the beautiful B'nai Zion Cemetery (Conservative). It was established in 1890 on Hedgewood Drive in North Chattanooga, after the Mizpah Congregation Cemetery adopted a policy of not accepting any more non-member burials.

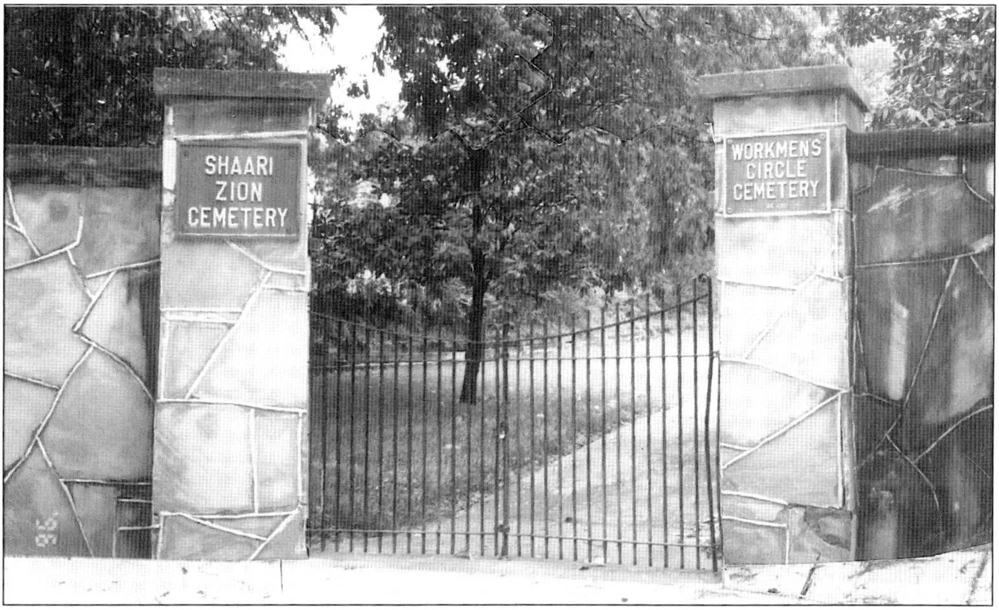

About 1905, the Shaari Zion Cemetery (Orthodox) was established together with the Chattanooga Branch #495 of Workman's Circle Cemetery (Yiddish culture). A concrete walk separates the two. The cemetery is located on Rowe Road, just outside of the Shepherd Hills Community in Brainerd.

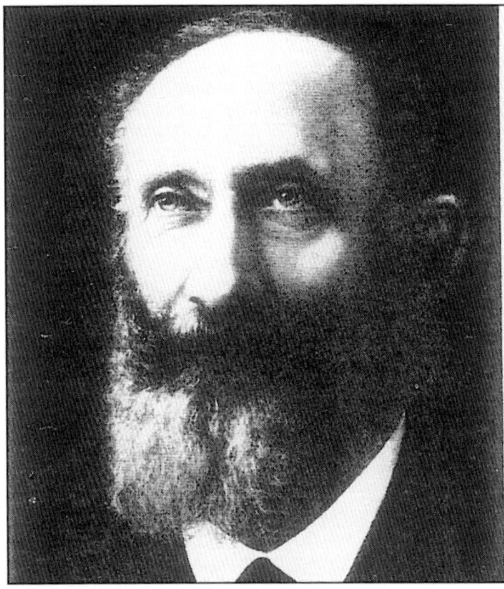

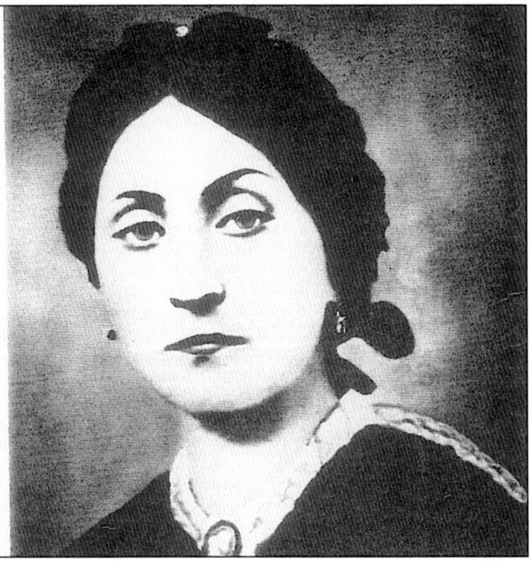

The Mitzpah Congregation (Reform) was founded in 1866 by a group of 21 young men under the Hebrew name of Chebra Gamias Chased, which translates into English as the "Hebrew Benevolent Association." Jacob and Fannie Bach, who came from Germany, held the first religious services in their home, with Jacob Bach serving as lay rabbi, hazzen (a cantor), shohet (a ritual animal slaughterer), and mohel (a skilled person who performs circumcisions). The Mitzpah Religious School was established in 1870, and the Hebrew Ladies Aid Society was organized in 1877 with Mrs. Delphine Block as its first president. It later became the Sisterhood of Mitzpah Congregation and was the oldest Jewish philanthropic organization in Chattanooga. By 1878, Julius and Bertha Ochs, pictured here, moved to Chattanooga, and Julius became spiritual head of the Hebrew Benevolent Association, which met in Concordia Hall on Market Street. Joseph B. Spitzer and Morris Bradt were prime movers in the organization. By 1888, the name had been changed to the Mitzpah Congregation. In 1902, the spelling was changed to Mizpah (omitting the "t").

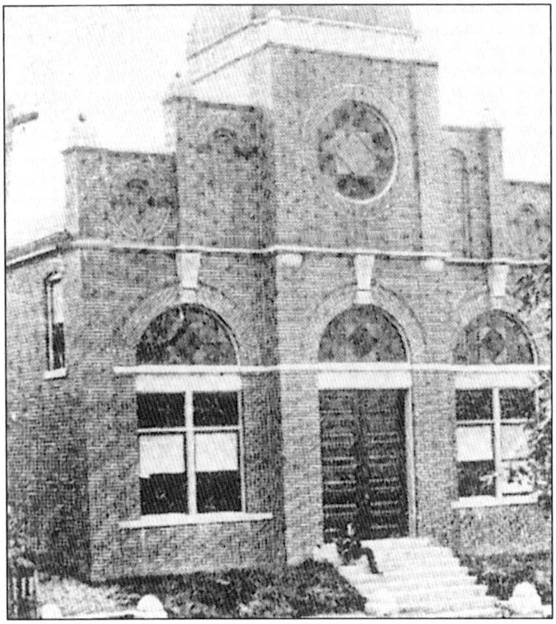

In 1882, the first Jewish Reform Temple was built and dedicated at 429 Walnut Street, between Fourth and Fifth Streets. This Mizpah Temple was occupied for 22 years. In 1888, a charter was secured by Joseph Wassman, Joe Simpson, Julius Ochs, and Herman Goodman Jr., giving official status to the congregation.

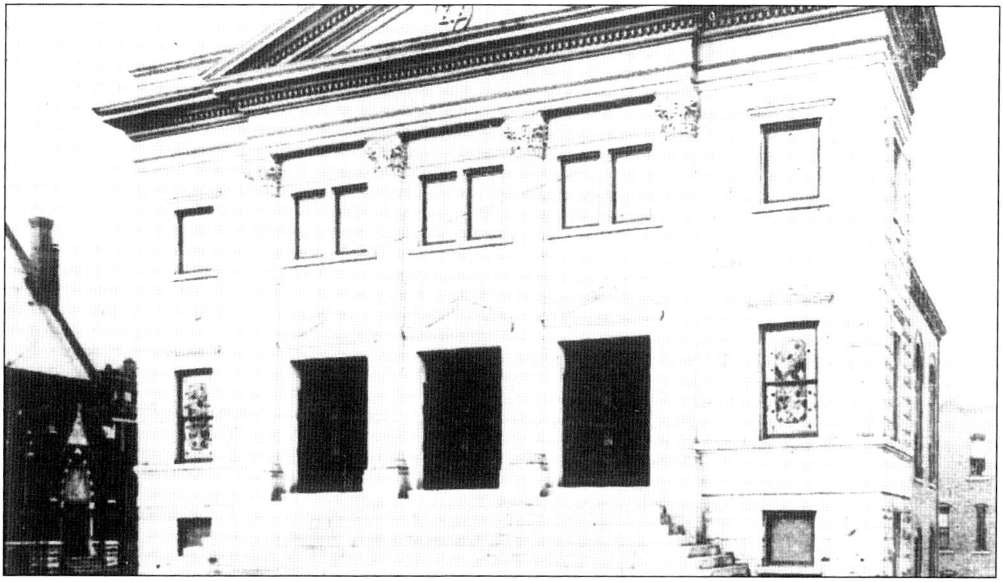

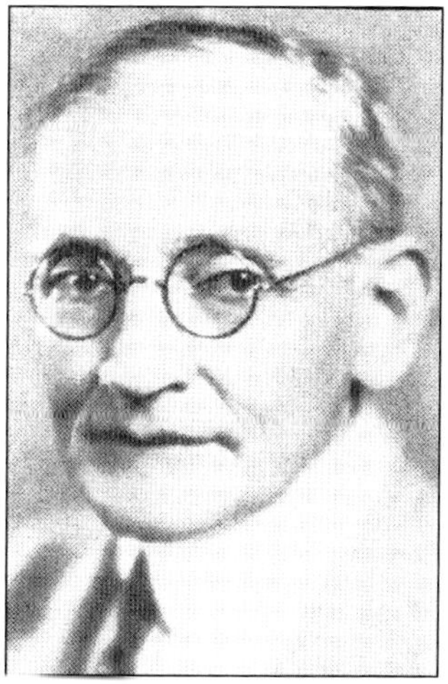

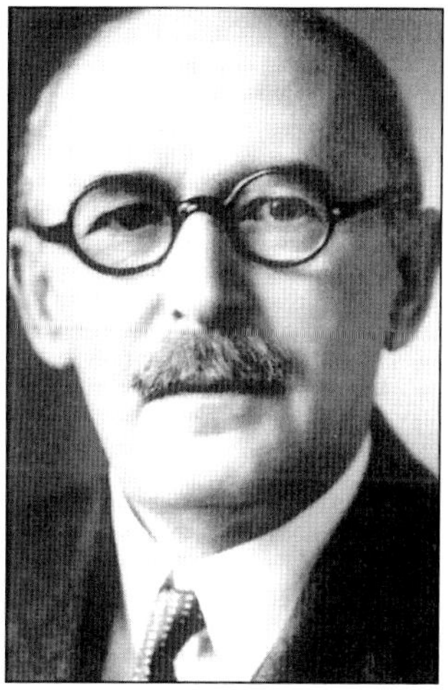

Above: The second Mizpah Sanctuary, on the corner of Lindsay and Oak Streets, was built in 1904 and served the congregation until 1928. Former presidents of the Mizpah Congregation include Joseph Wassman, E.K. Fisher, Dr. Max Bloch, Harry Wise Sr., L. Rosenau, Prosper Lazard, Harry C. Adler, Simon Geismar, Lige B. Werteimer, Sol Moyses, H. Goodman Jr., Emil Wassman, Adolph Mathis, Sidney Marks, Phil Angel, Lester Cohn, Harry Wise Jr., Wolfe Lefkoff, M.C. Poss, H.H. Michelson, Harry Miller, Felix Diamond, Harry Weill, Lawrence Rubenstein, Ira Trivers, Jay Silverstein, Dr. Ed Reisman Jr., Dr. Harold Schwartz Sr., Alvin Blumberg, Lawrence Levine, Norman Moore, Herbert Stoloff, Howard Levine, Carolyn Henning, Dr. Max Brener, Harold Schwartz Jr., Paul Lefkoff, Warren Dropkin, Melvin Young, David Diamond, Myron Kushner, and Marcia Krosner.

Upper Right: Harry Wise Sr., the son of Isaac Meyer Wise of Cincinnati (who founded Reform Judaism in America), came to Chattanooga in 1888. He was married to Sarah (Landa), and they had one child, Harry Jr. Harry Sr. was president of Mizpah in 1894, and from 1918 to 1931. Harry Jr. married Dorothy (Rose) and had one child, Harriet (Stern) of Memphis. Harry Wise Jr. was president of Mizpah from 1951 to 1953.

Lower Right: Herman Goodman was Mizpah's president from 1907 to 1911, and he served the congregation collecting and recording historical material. He also founded the Goodman Hide and Leather Company. Both Harry and Herman served the congregation for over 50 years and were elected honorary presidents for life. In 1926, Adolph S. Ochs, the son of Julius Ochs, offered to bear the cost of a new Mizpah Sanctuary and Activities Hall as a memorial to his father and mother, Julius and Bertha Ochs.

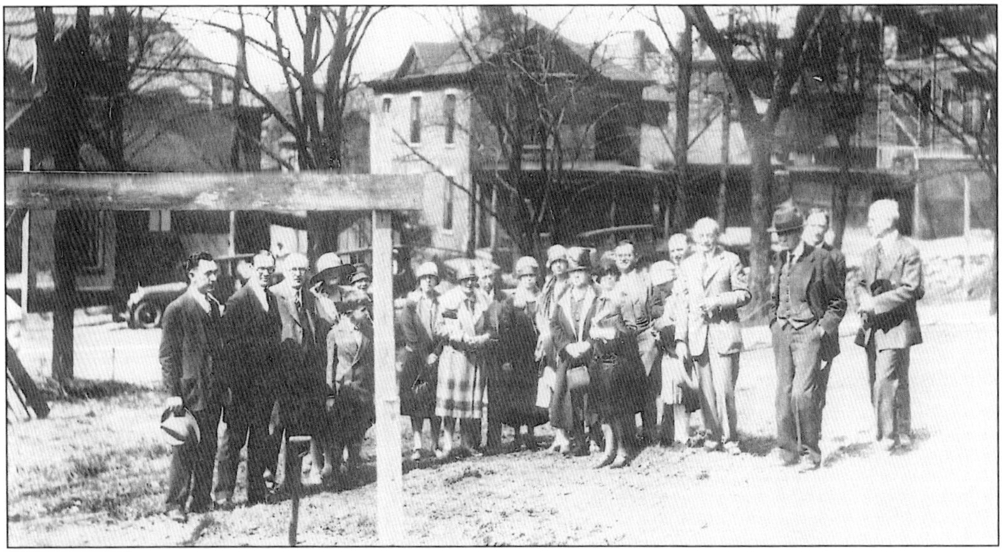

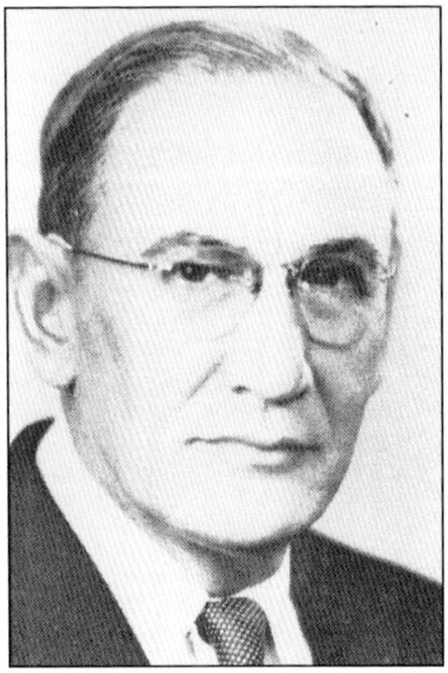

Above: The groundbreaking ceremony for the new Ochs Memorial Temple at 923 McCallie Avenue took place in 1926. Former Mizpah Sisterhood presidents include Mesdames Delphine Block, Herman Goodman, Simon Geismar, Cecile Tschopik, Anna Cohn, Harry Simpson, Gertrude Friedman, Celia Rose, Sarah Wise, Hazel Goodman, Soly Joseph, Heloise Schwartz, Blanche Eisendrath, Pearl Klaus, Addie Effron, Ida Gould, Esther Diamond Cohn, Ruth Poss, Roselyn Reisman, Muriel Mallen, Eleanor Schwartz, Carolyn Henning, Rosemary Weber, Joy Abelson Adams, Lillian Feinstein, Ceil Amsterdam, Rene Tepper, Peggy Moore, Ruth Rubenstein, Rita Speer, Gail Kirk, Marion Geismar Abrams, Lori Shalett, Judy Pressman, Ethel Rosenthal, M.J. Levine, Marilyn Center, and Cherie Monen.

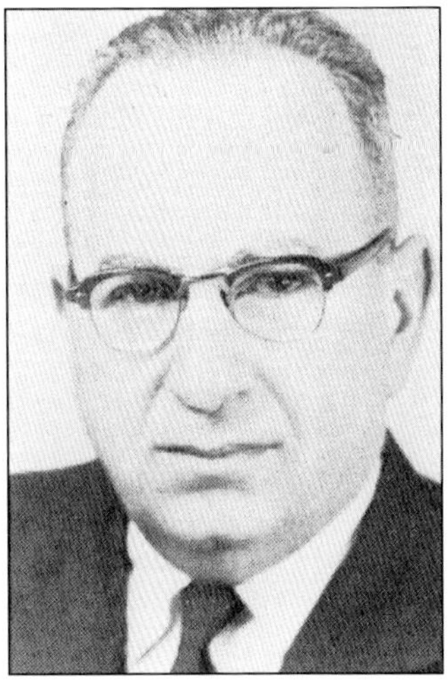

Upper Left: Rabbi Dr. Abraham Feinstein served the congregation from 1932 to 1966 and then was elected Rabbi Emeritus from 1966 to 1985. His period of service is the longest of any rabbi in the Mizpah Congregation's history. In 1955, his peers at the Hebrew Union College in Cincinnati, Ohio, bestowed on him the honorary degree of Doctor of Divinity. In 1984, Rabbi Feinstein was honored by the Patton family of Chattanooga with the Love of Chattanooga Award for his extraordinary contribution and deep devotion to the city of Chattanooga. His wife was Lillian (Brown), and they had one daughter, Dee (Mrs. Herman Shacter), and two grandsons, Jeffrey and Arnie Berman.
Lower Left: Lester Cohn served Mizpah beginning as a child in 1910. He was hired at $1 per month to take care of and distribute hymnbooks at services. He became president of the congregation from 1934 to 1941 and was then elected honorary president for life in 1966.

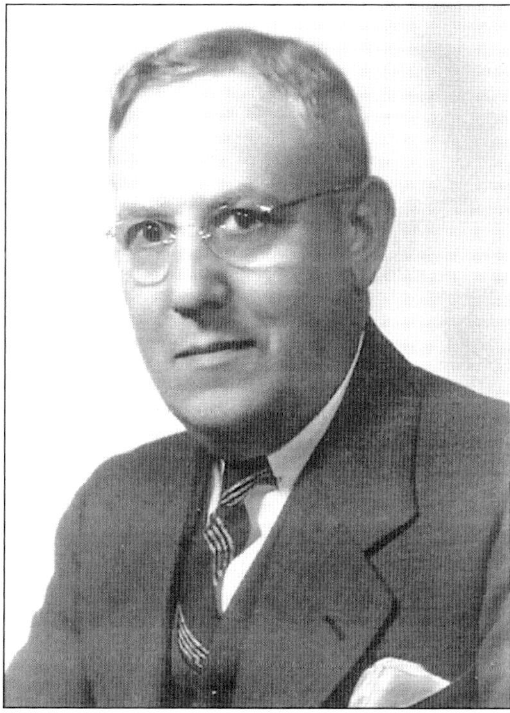

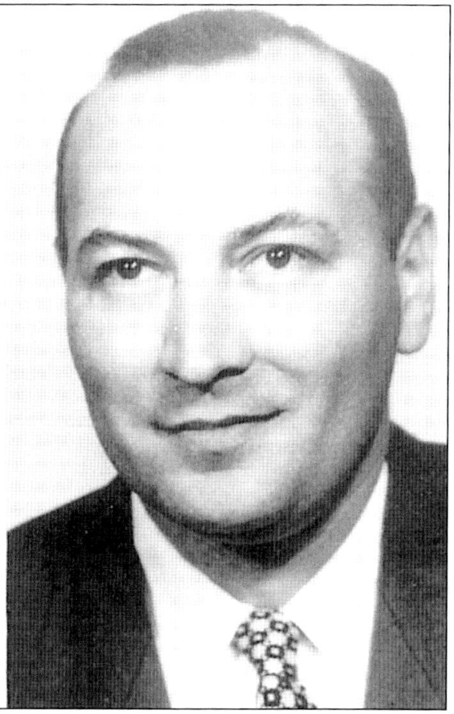

Upper Left: Sidney Marks served as Mizpah president in 1935 and again from 1947 to 1948. In 1954, he was elected honorary president for life.
Upper Right: Dr. Edward E. Reisman Jr. was president from 1965 to 1967. A lifelong supporter of the Mizpah Congregation, he gave freely of his time and money. There were other physicians who served Mizpah as president, including Dr. Max Block, Dr. Harold Schwartz Sr., and Dr. Max Brener.

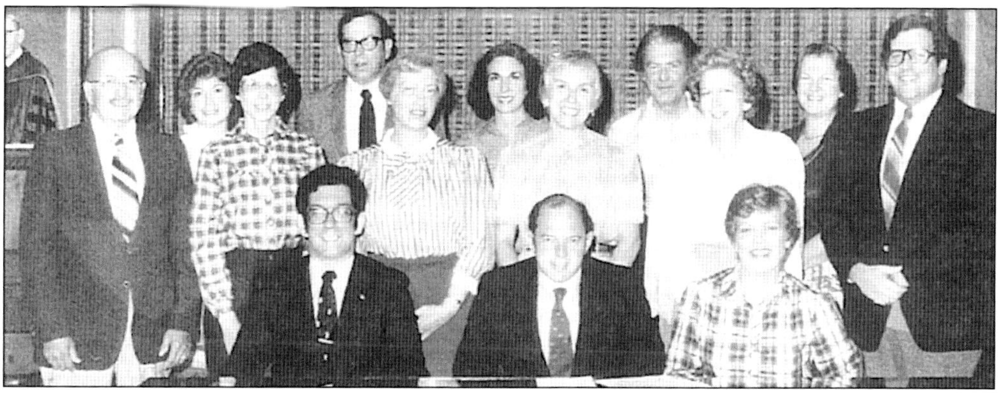

Pictured is part of the 1982–83 Mizpah Congregation Board with Max Brener, president. Shown here are, from left to right, Hal Schwartz Jr., Max Brener, Liz Hodes, Irving Schulman, Trudy Trivers, Pat Maner, Rabbi Goldman, Rita Speer, Marilyn Center, Marion Geismar, Norman Moore, Joy Adams, Peggy Moore, and Eric Blechner.

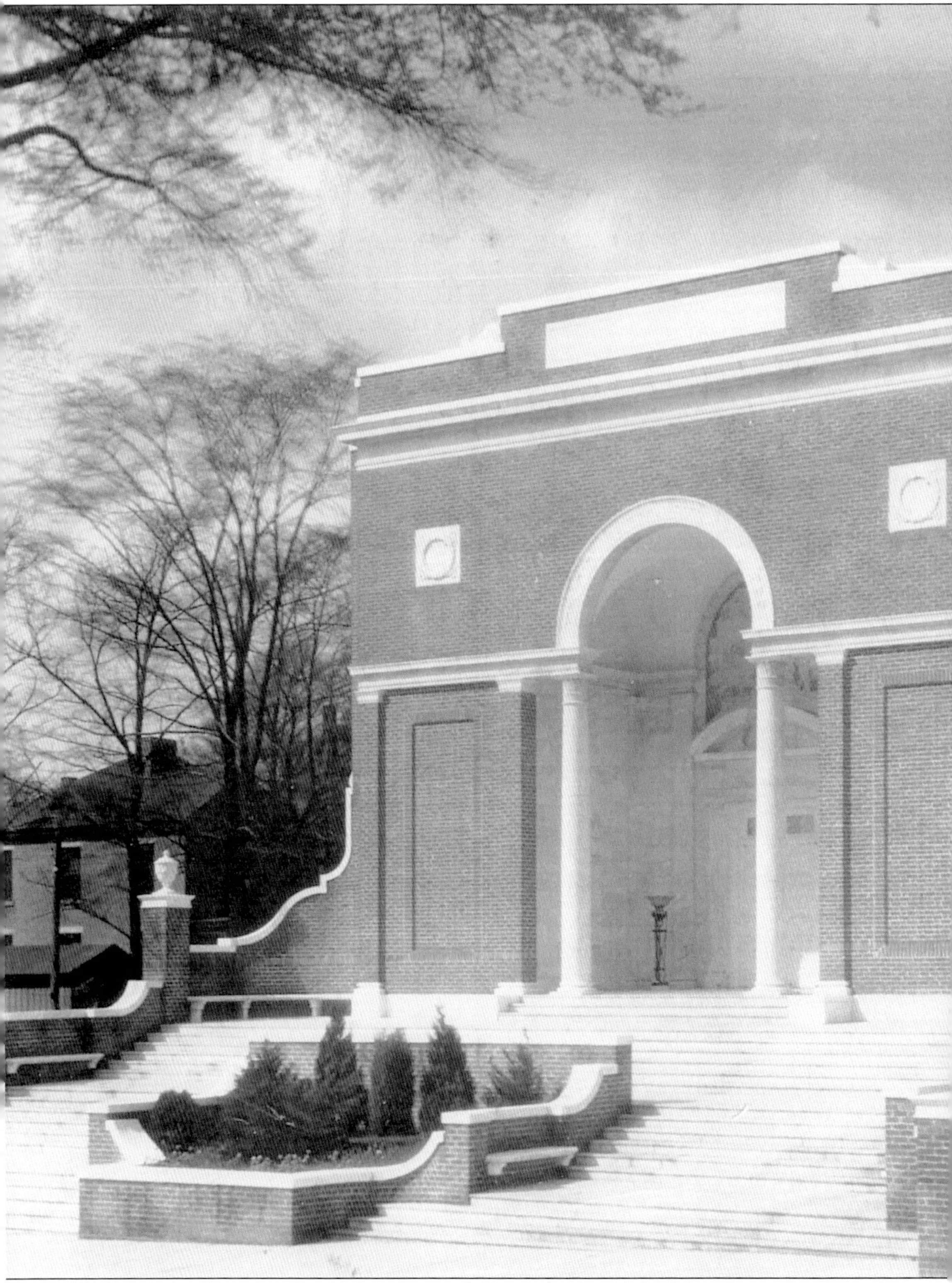

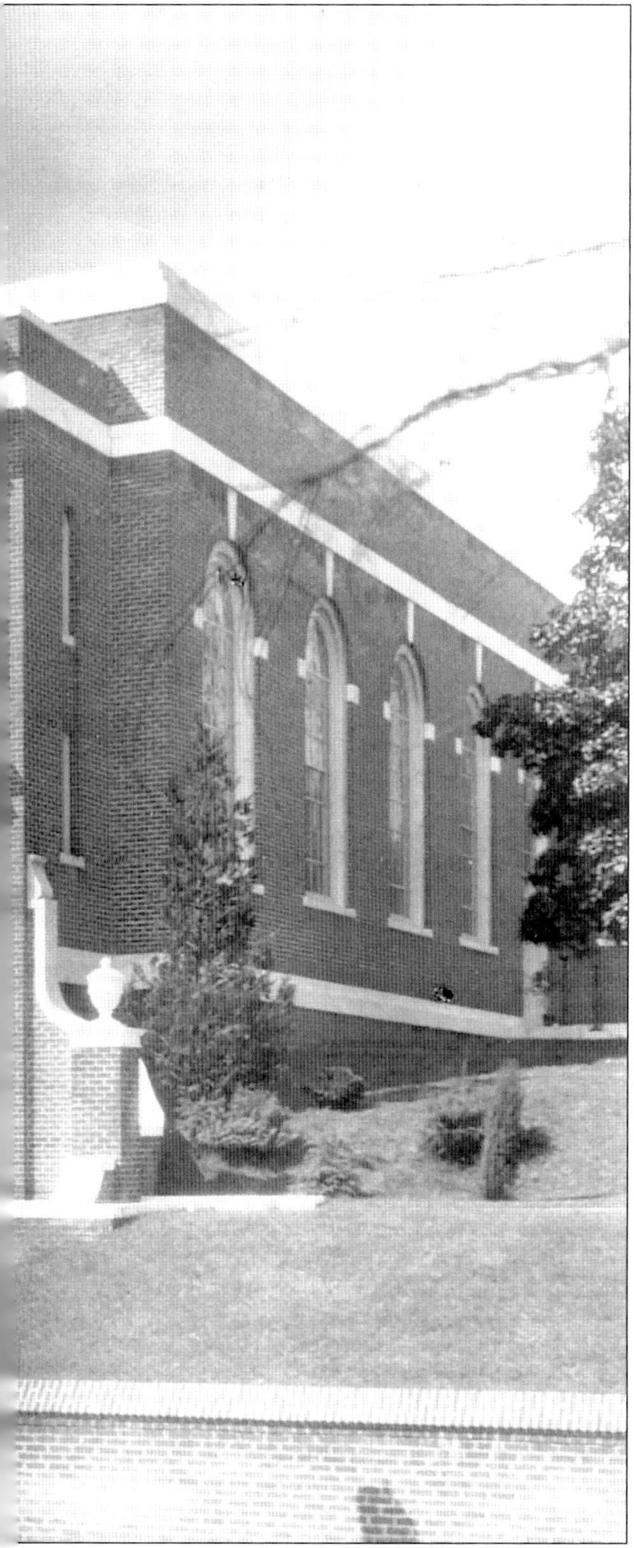

The Julius and Bertha Ochs Memorial Temple at 922 McCallie Avenue, a gift from Adolph S. Ochs, was dedicated in 1928. The building's design features Colonial and Georgian architecture with Georgian marble leading up to the entry. In the vestibule is a huge white marble statue of Moses, a copy of the work of Michaelangelo. The Temple Center had ten classrooms, a chapel with stained-glass windows, an auditorium, and offices. In 1979, the temple was designated a Tennessee Historical Preservation Site. A recent addition to the temple grounds was created in the late 1990s by Joe and Susan O'Hara Barack and Ruth Zachary. They designed, labored, and secured volunteer membership labor to transform a barren area into a gorgeous private garden, which was named "The Garden of Life." Services, parties, and weddings can now be held outside in utmost splendor.

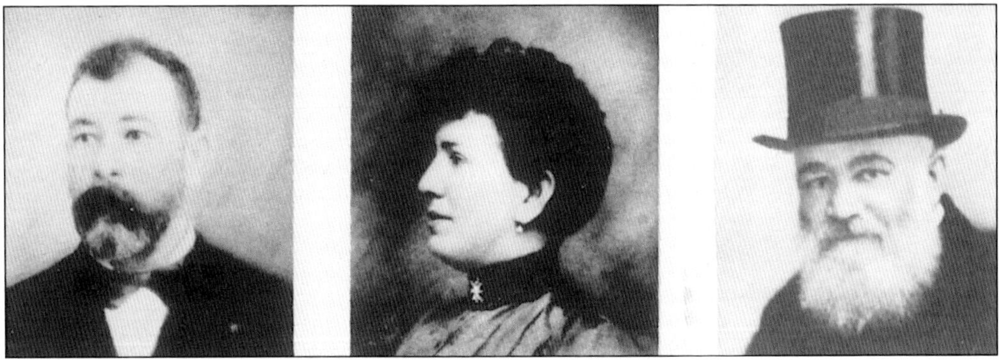

The B'nai Zion Congregation (Orthodox) was organized in 1888 as an outgrowth of Friday evening services held by Jewish merchants in the home of Wolfe and Dora Brody (pictured at left and center). She built a mitkvah in her backyard by digging a hole in the ground and inserting a large box. The B'nai Zion Congregation rented halls for services at 1208 Carter Street, 1027 Carter Street, and 1201 Chestnut Street during its developmental years. Pictured on the right is the Reverend Isaac Maisel, who served as lay rabbi, shohet, mohel, and chazen from 1919 until 1943.

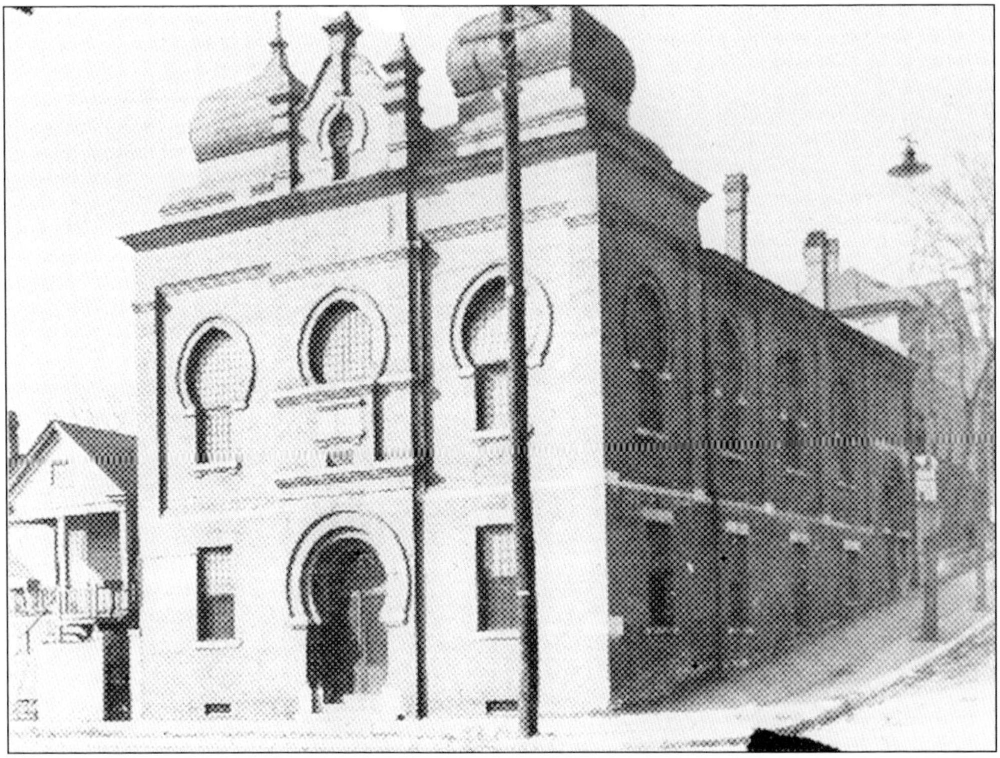

In 1902, the congregation erected a synagogue on the corner of Fourteenth and Carter Streets. The red-brick structure of modernized Romanesque architecture was occupied for about 30 years.

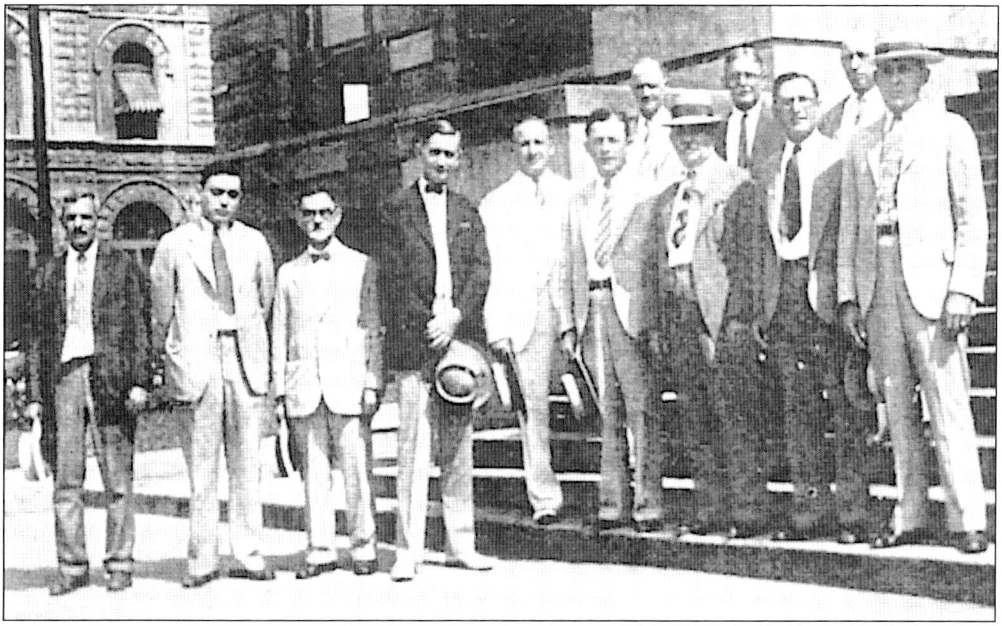

By the late 1920s, the B'nai Zion Congregation needed a new sanctuary. The building committee for the new structure consisted of, from left to right, L. Winer, L. Rubenstein, L. Koblentz, Mayor Ed Bass of Chattanooga, J. Kushner, A.J. Alper, H. Winer, S.H. Frank, S. Block, S. Goldstein, S. Raider, and S. Brody.

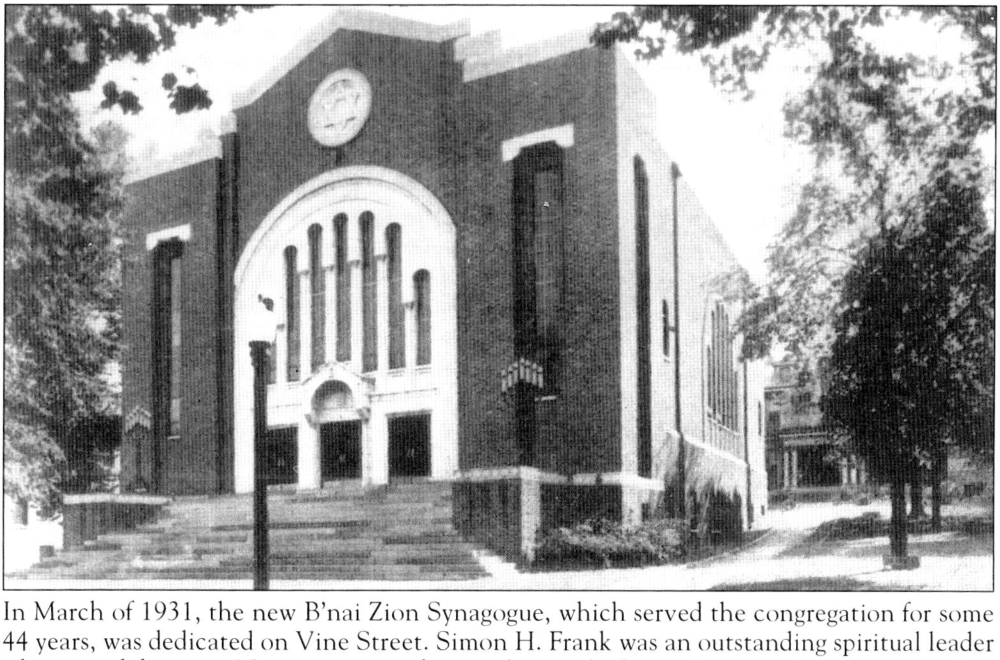

In March of 1931, the new B'nai Zion Synagogue, which served the congregation for some 44 years, was dedicated on Vine Street. Simon H. Frank was an outstanding spiritual leader who served for over 25 years as president and a total of over 34 years in numerous other positions. Ben Zion Hasden devoted over 30 years to the Vine Street Synagogue, serving as a shames (a caretaker).

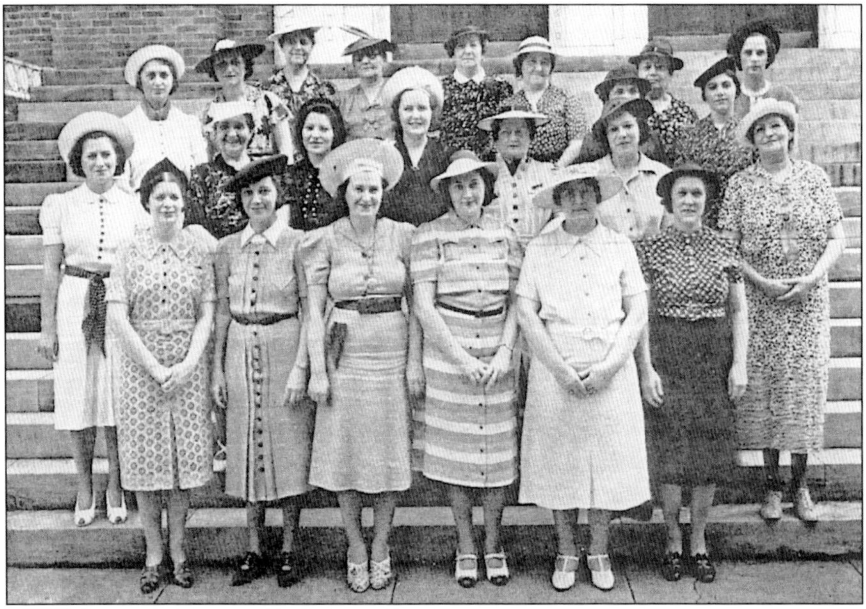

The Ladies Aid Society of B'nai Zion was organized in 1903 by Mrs. Max Silverman. Posing here in 1938 are the following officers and committee members, from left to right: (front row) Mesdames R. Abelman, B. Block, J. Sherman, Mose Siskin, E. Solomon, and H. Cure; (middle row) Mesdames L. Lebovitz, L. Koblentz, S. Pressman, P.D. Hodes, A.I. Fanburg, P. Kolodkin, and J. Berger; (back row) Mesdames H. Daneman, M. Alper, S. Baras, S. Hershfield, S.H. Frank, M. Brener, H. Rosenbloom, O. Frumin, I. Gerstein, and S. Deitch. In later years, the Ladies Aid Society became the Sisterhood of B'nai Zion Congregation.

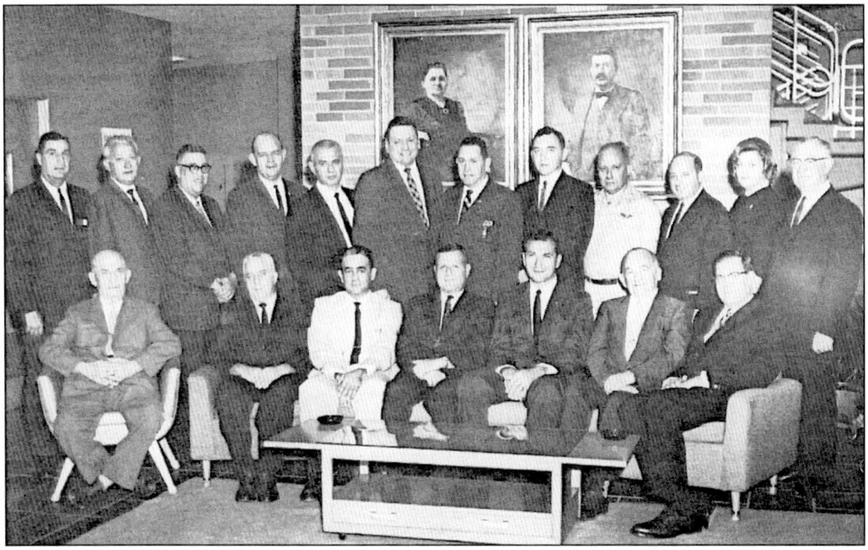

The 1963 Board of B'nai Zion consisted of the following men, from left to right: (front row) D. Alper, P.D. Hodes, D. Levy, A. Shoenig, M. Pregulman, P. Dubrow, and Dr. S. Binder; (back row) M. Bush, H. Trotz, I. Lander, M. Spector, Dr. S. Ulin, Dr. S. Speal, I. Richelson, Dr. R. Dubrow, B. Brody, A. Goldstein, Mrs. H.L. Collins, and N. Hofferman. Not pictured are Mose Siskin, Meyer Siskin, and H. Eidex. The pictures in the background on the wall are portraits of Anna Siskin and Robert Hyman Siskin.

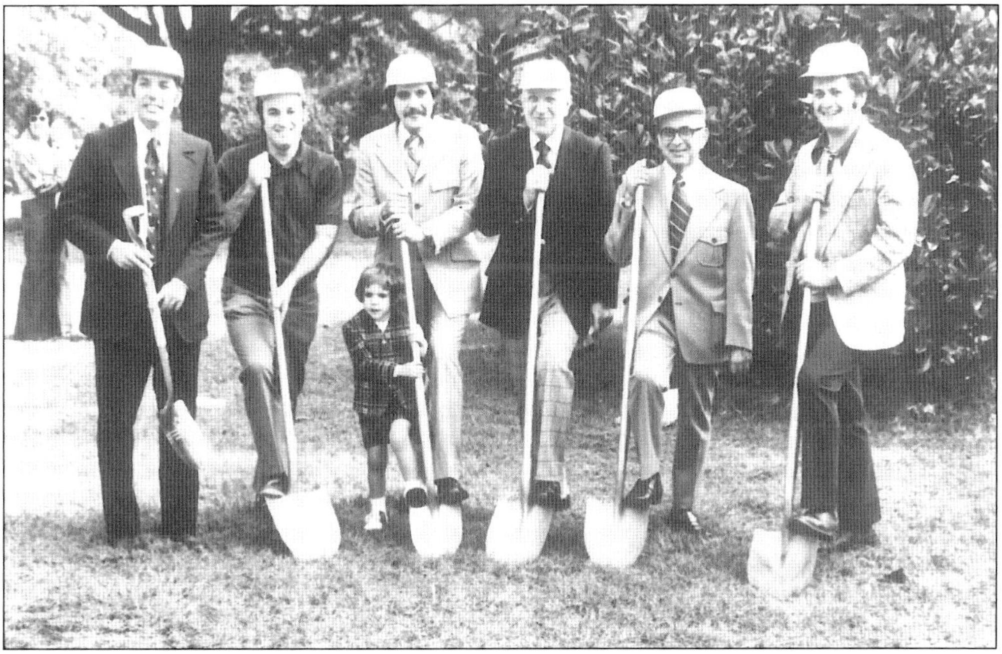

The 1973 groundbreaking committee for the proposed B'nai Zion McBrien Road Synagogue in Brainerd consisted of, from left to right, Charles Lebovitz, Paul Greenberg, Robert Siskin, little Jonathan Siskin, Mose Lebovitz, Billy Raider, and Colman Hochman.

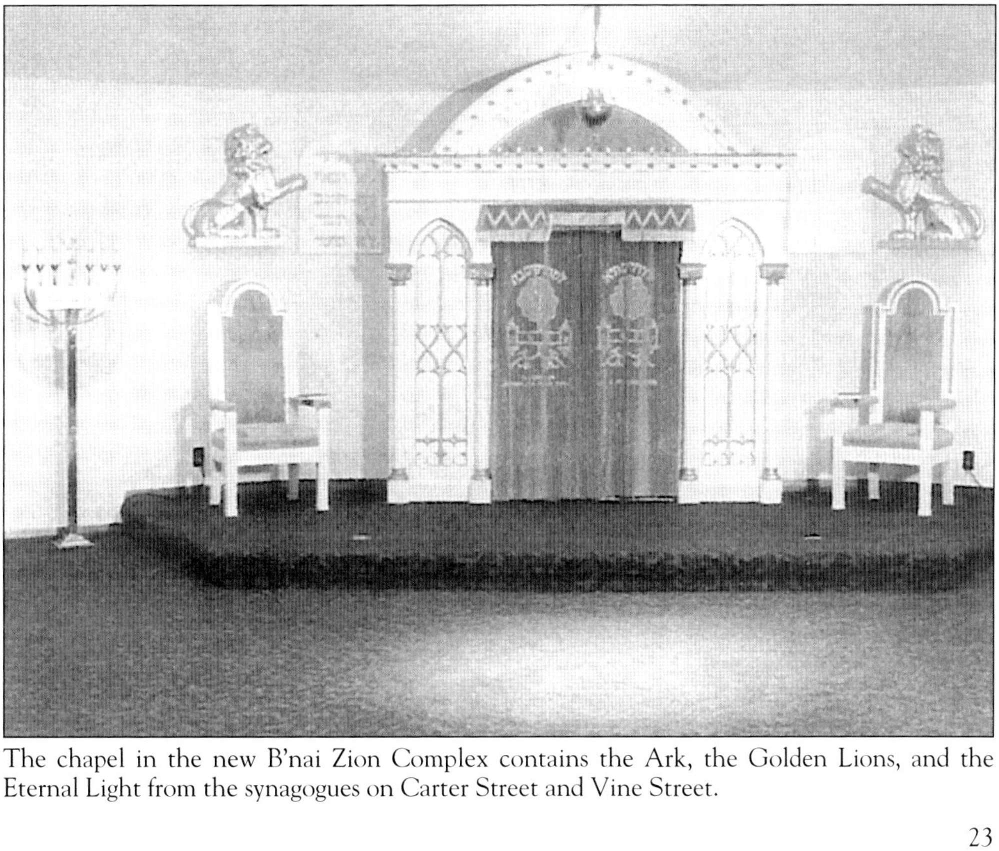

The chapel in the new B'nai Zion Complex contains the Ark, the Golden Lions, and the Eternal Light from the synagogues on Carter Street and Vine Street.

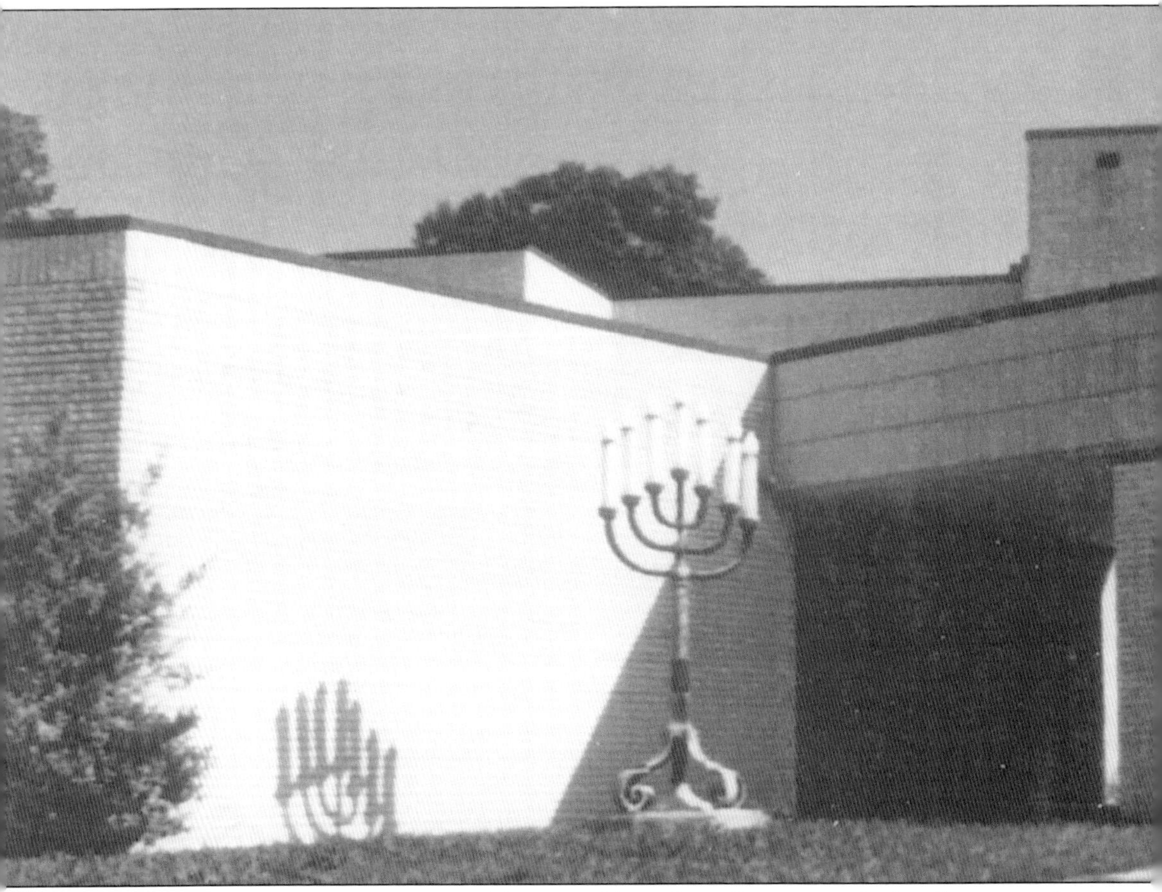

The new B'nai Zion Synagogue, built all on one level,

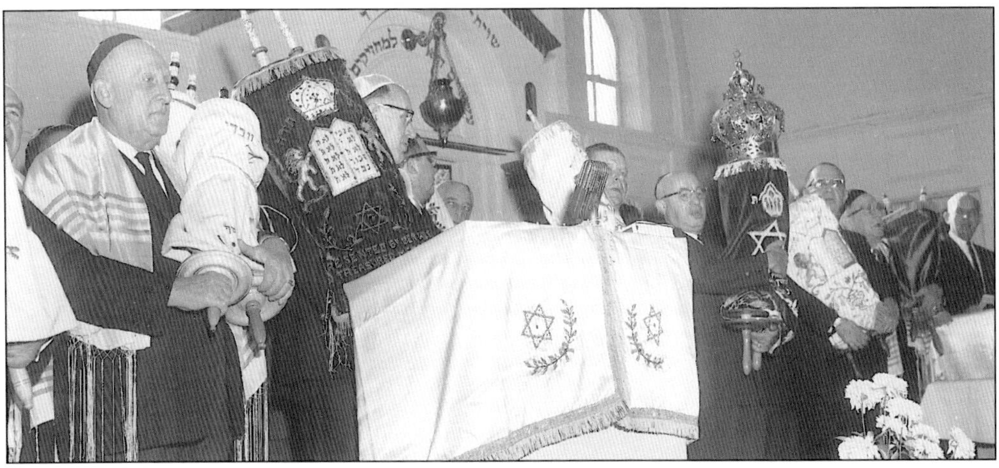

In 1963, the Diamond Jubilee Celebration marked 75 years of B'nai Zion's history. Mark Spector was the chairman of the weekend events, which included a Torah Procession and the presentation and inscription of a new Torah, given by the family of Sadye Pressman. The highlight of the celebration was a gala banquet at the Jewish Community Center auditorium. Pictured are the congregants with the Torahs. (Courtesy of Stanrich Studio.)

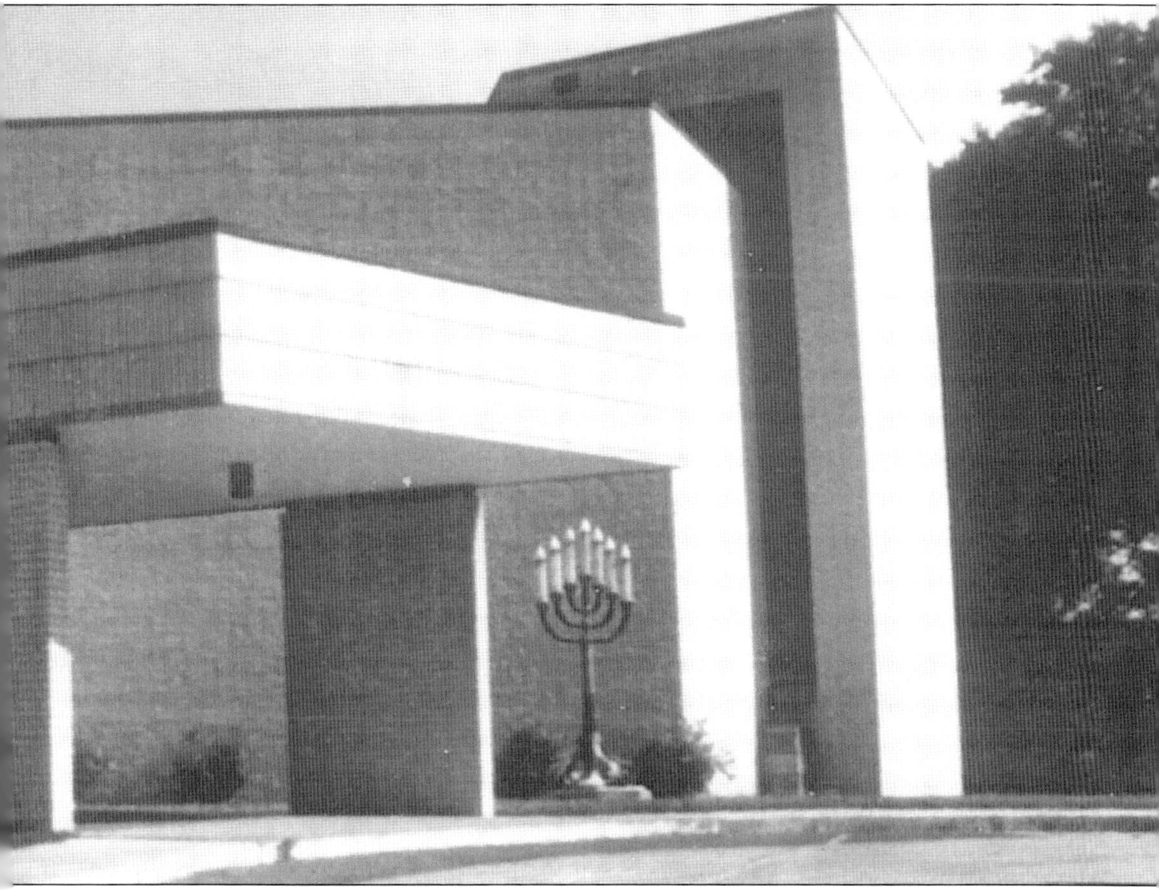

is located at 114 McBrien Road in Brainerd.

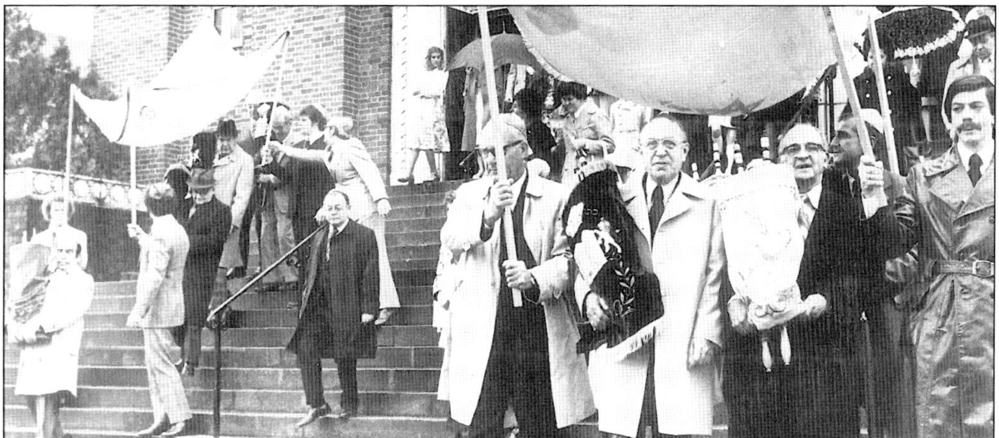

In 1975, the McBrien Road Synagogue was dedicated by a farewell service at the Vine Street Synagogue followed by a dedication service at the new building. Those honored by carrying the Torahs included past presidents H. Berke, S. Binder, M. Bush, P. Dubrow, R. Dubrow, A.J. Koblentz, M. Lebovitz, M. Pregulman, A. Shoenig, M.H. Winer, J.H. Eidex, A. Jacobs, H. Radin, J.L. Wise, P. Greenberg, C. Lebovitz, W. Raider, and R. Siskin.

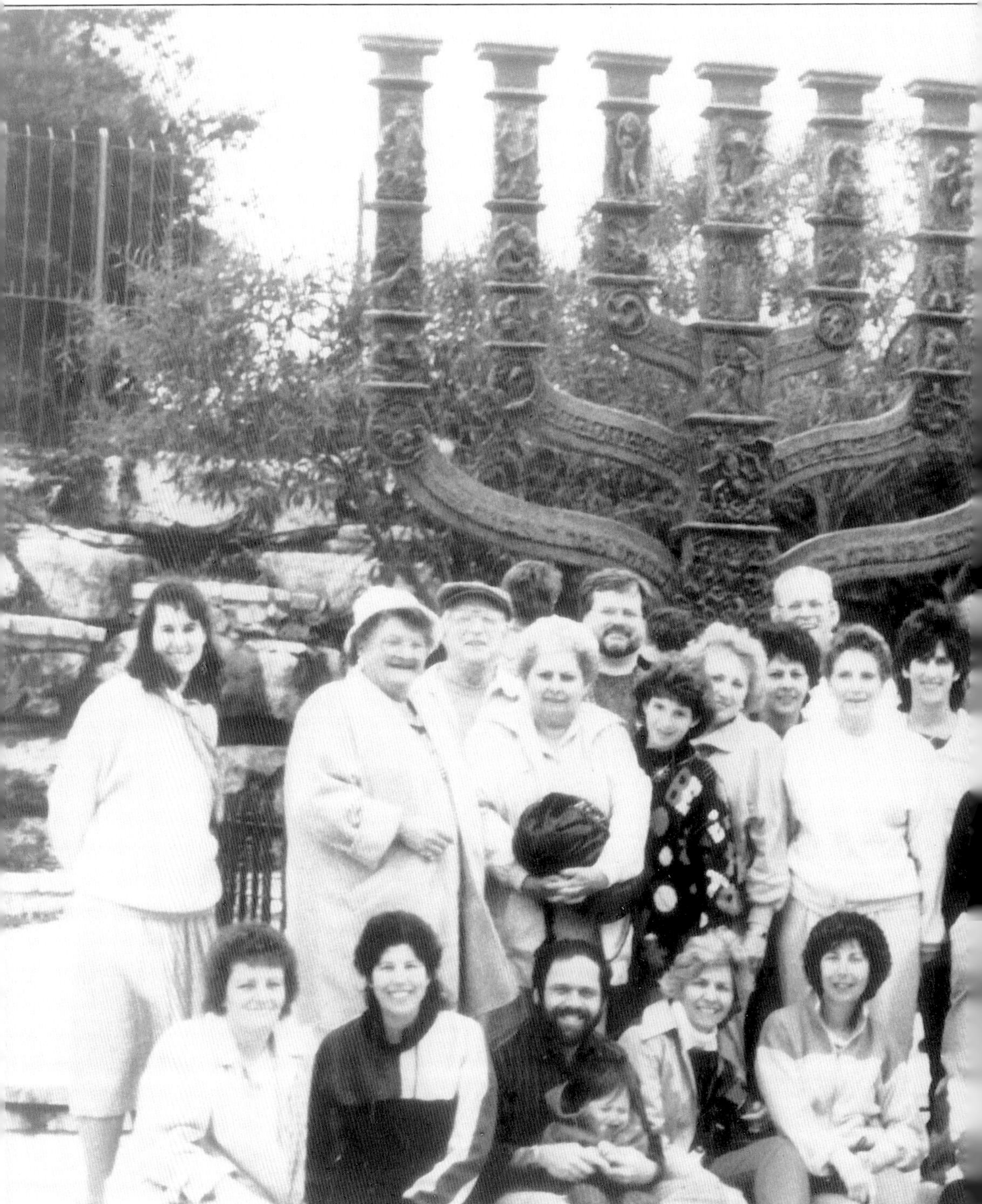

In 1988, B'nai Zion celebrated its centennial, a celebration that focused on the theme "For Our Ancestors, For Us, For Our Descendants." Climaxing the year-long festivities was a two-week congregational trip to Israel. Thirty-three people made the voyage; the travellers are

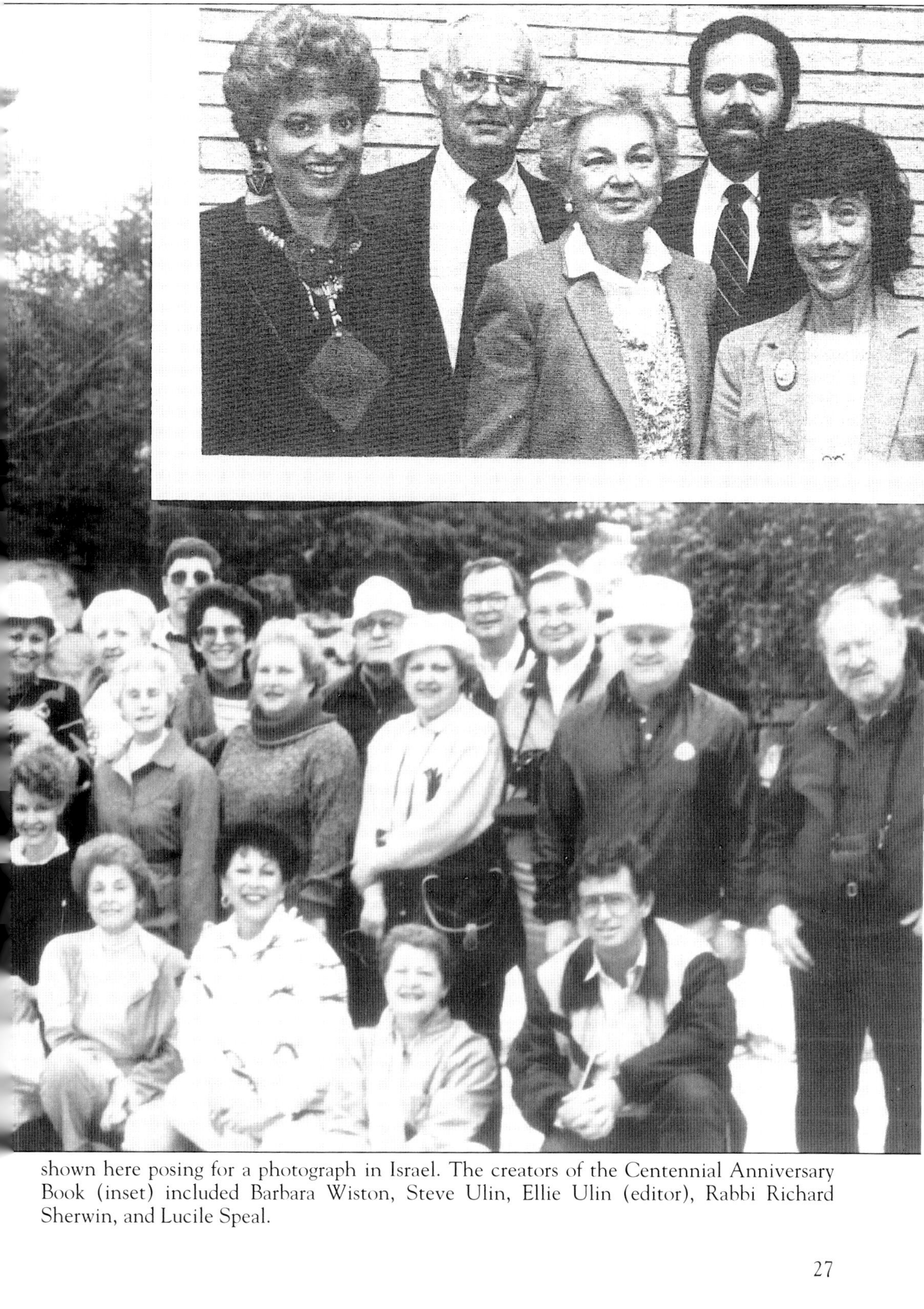

shown here posing for a photograph in Israel. The creators of the Centennial Anniversary Book (inset) included Barbara Wiston, Steve Ulin, Ellie Ulin (editor), Rabbi Richard Sherwin, and Lucile Speal.

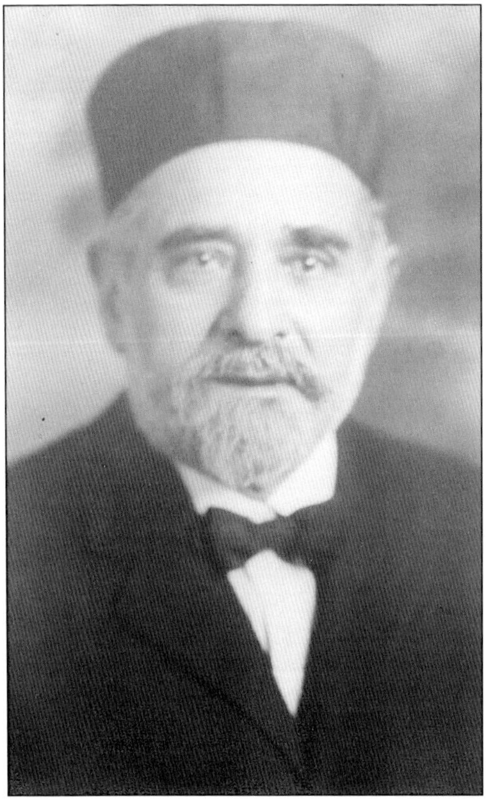

The Shaari-Zion Congregation was organized in 1904 by a small group of orthodox Jews with Lay Rabbi Herschel Contor (pictured) as leader. A charter was secured in 1907. Services were held in a rented hall on Poplar Street (they called it the Kleine Shule, meaning "the small synagogue"). In 1914, a two-story brick building at Carlisle and Cedar Streets was occupied. Like the cemetery, this building was shared with Workmans' Circle. The upper floor was converted into a synagogue, while the lower floor was used as a meetingplace. The building served as a synagogue for about 40 years until it was finally sold during the West Side urban renewal and freeway projects. Reverend Contor served from 1904 until his death in 1932. S.J. Rausen, one of the founders, succeeded him. Other leaders include Reverend Efraim Mennen (from 1913 to 1919), Barney Okin, Abraham Berke, Sol (Shlomo) Frumin, Louis Koblentz, Samuel Chawkin, S. Sacks, Sam Freeman, Harry Hyman, and Israel Saluk. The remaining families of this group are now members of the Beth Sholom or B'nai Zion Congregations.

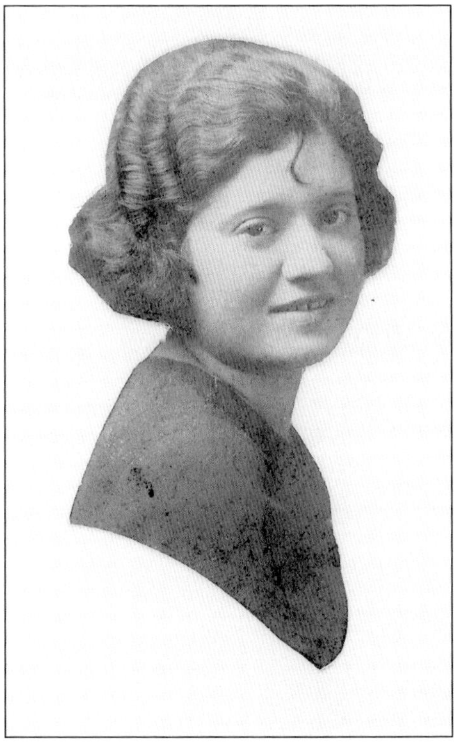

Lay Rabbi Herschel Contor came to Chattanooga from Grodno, Poland/Russia, about 1880. He had five children: Isaac, Max, Charles, Pearl, and Nelle. The three sons were merchants and had stores at 529 Market Street, North Chattanooga, East Chattanooga, and Ridgedale. Isaac (Ike) Contor married Elsie Dicker from Ithica, New York, and they had one son, Maurice. Pictured is Pearl Contor, who was very active in the Jewish community.

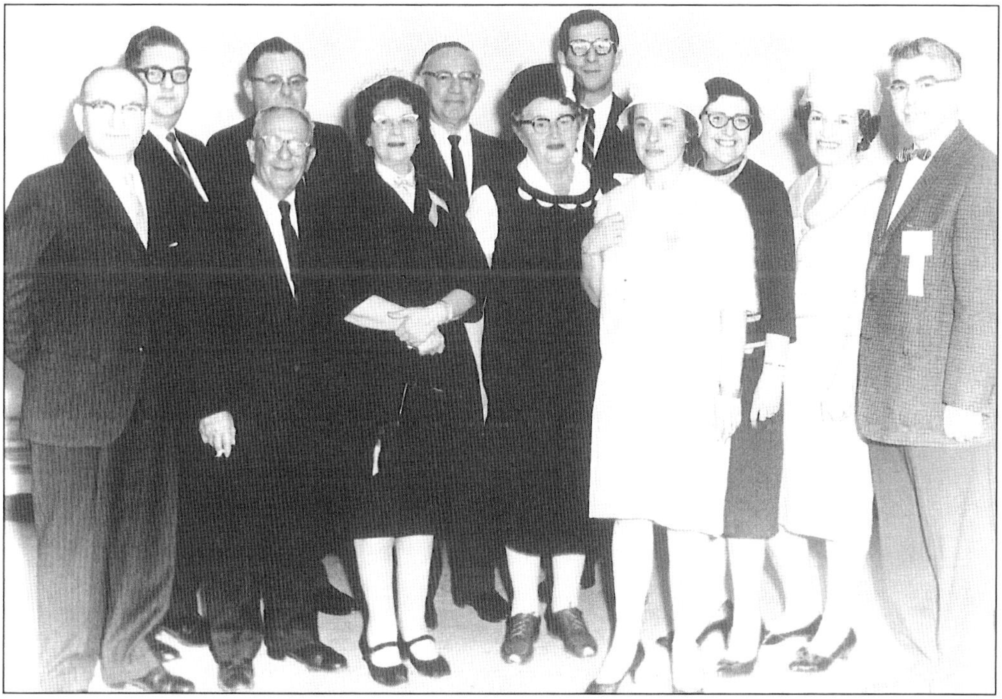

In 1959, after B'nai Zion became a conservative synagogue, a group consisting of mostly former B'nai Zion members, led by Morris Ellman, secured a charter for an Orthodox congregation under the name of Beth Sholom. A Hebrew and Sunday school were soon established and property was purchased at 20 Pisgah Avenue in Brainerd to serve as synagogue headquarters. Rabbi Meyer Horowitz was the first spiritual leader. The congregation is affiliated with the Union of Orthodox Congregations of America. In March of 1963, some of the founders of the Beth Sholom Congregation attended a meeting in Nashville. Pictured, from left to right, are as follows: (front row) M. Feintuch, N. Brouner, Leah Brouner, E. Gill, R. Ellman, I. Feintuch, D. Finkle, and A. Finkle; (back row) M. Ellman, H. Shoenig, M. Gill, and Rabbi Meyer Horowitz.

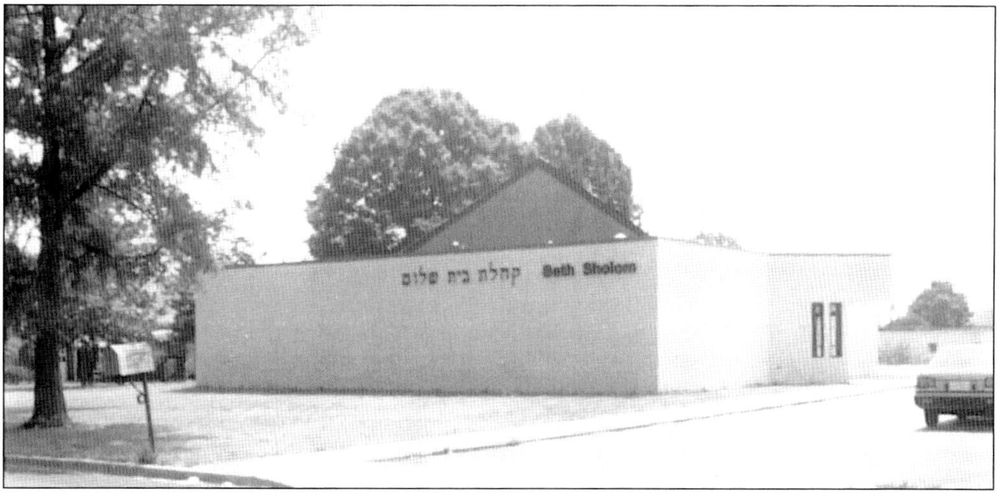

In 1977, Beth Sholom headquarters was bombed by a hate-crime terrorist and was reduced to splinters by the blast. The perpetrator was caught and is now in prison. A new synagogue (pictured) was constructed and dedicated in 1977.

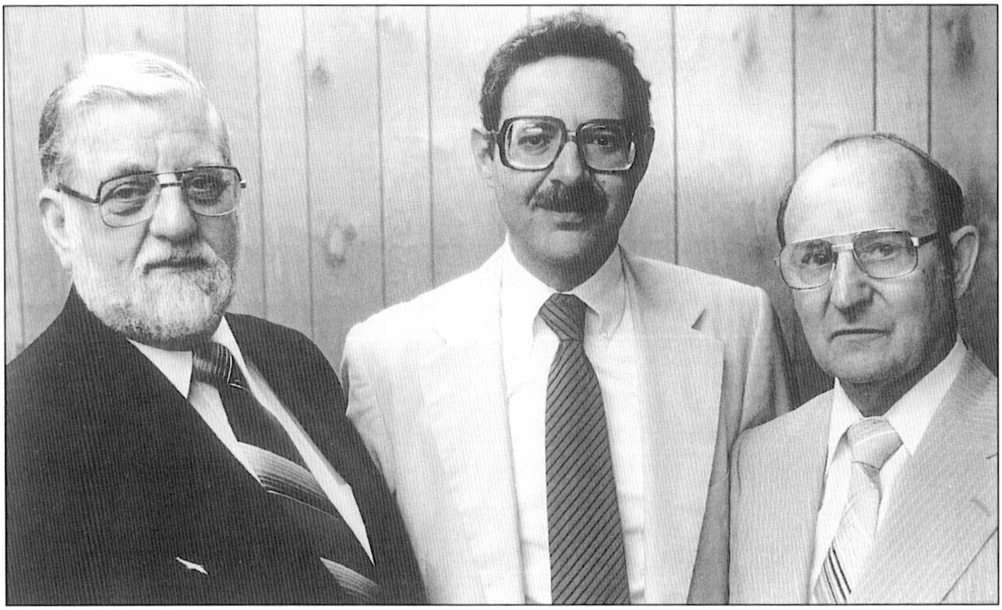

The 1980–1981 officers of Beth Sholom were Morris Ellman, Ted Feintuch, and Max Yagoda.

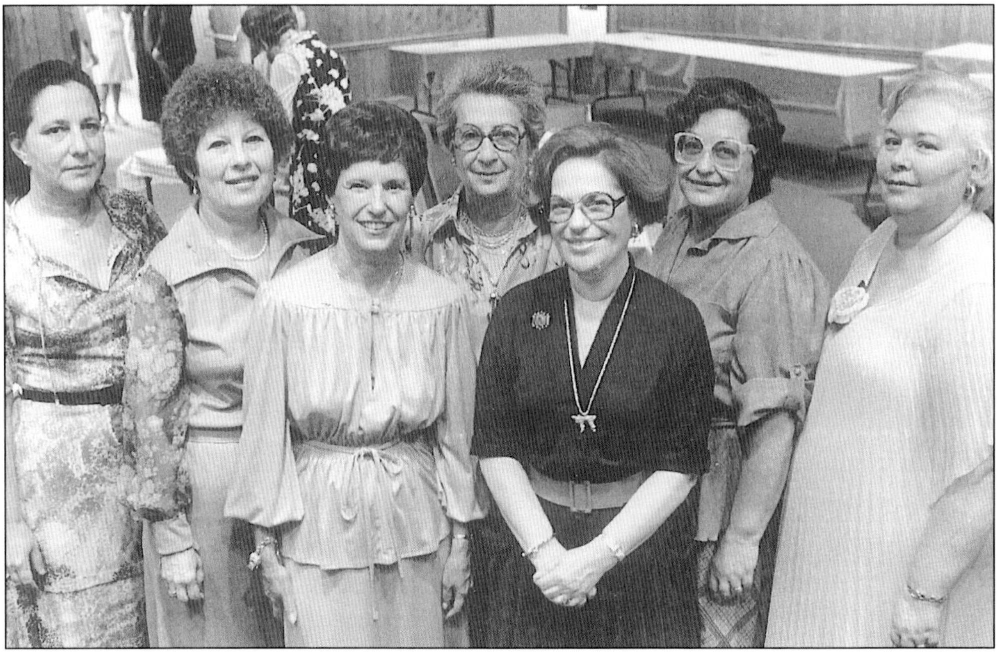

The 1980–1981 Sisterhood Board included Marsha Mogul, Millie Shapiro, Betty Hyman, Leah Yagoda, Sally Gordon, Muriel Porter, and Harriet Major.

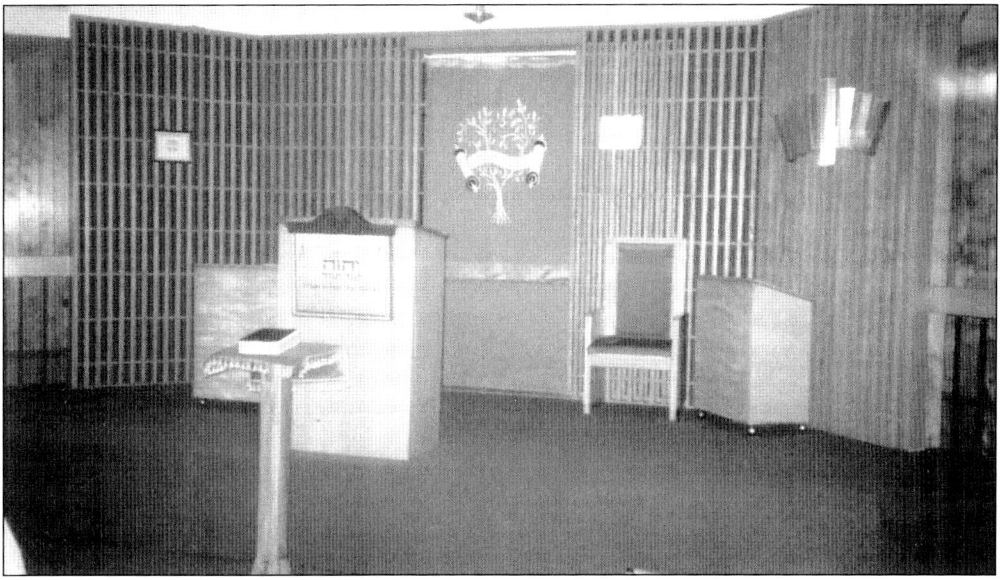

The interior and Bimah of the Beth Sholom Synagogue is shown here.

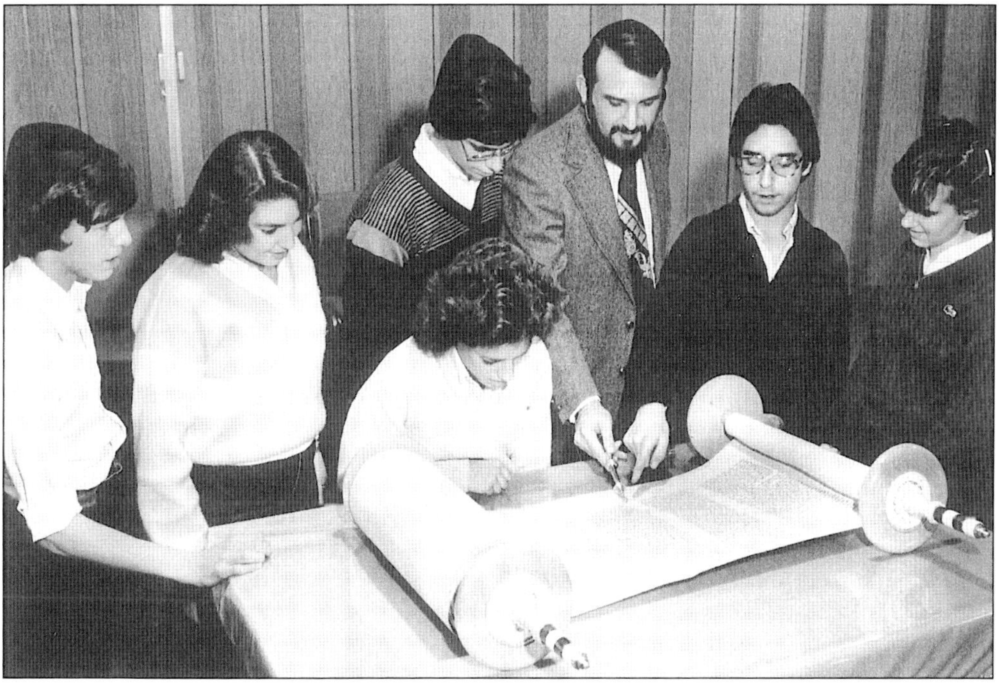

Rabbi Yitzchok Adler became a rabbi in 1979. Pictured here are some of his students reading the Torah. Among those present are John Stern, Marla Bell, Howard Andrews, and Charlene Andrews. The others remain unidentified.

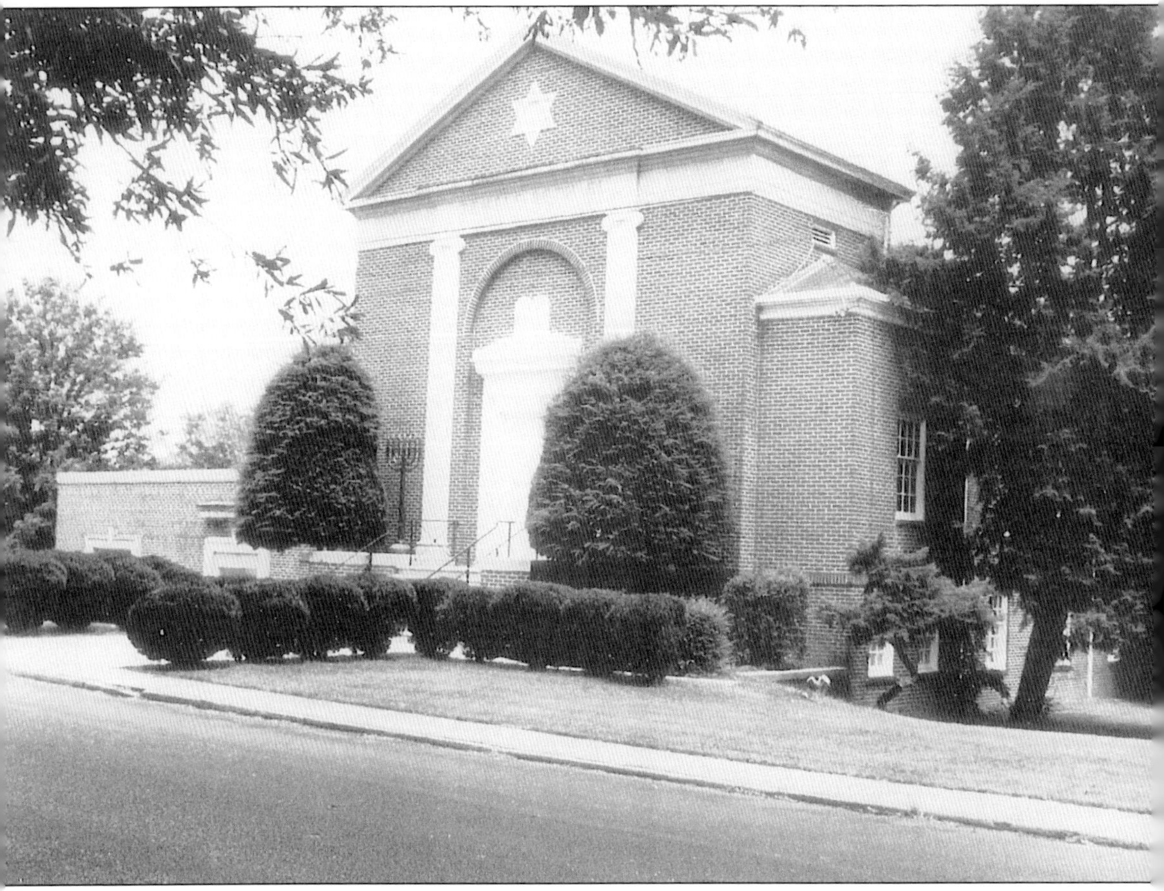

The first record of a Jewish resident in Dalton, Georgia, was the owner of Hirsch's Florist Shop in 1880. Then came the Loveman family, who opened their department store in Chattanooga but had their residence in Dalton. About 1900, Herman Fox established the Empty Stocking Fund, which evolved into the United Fund. In 1938, the Friendly Alliance was formed to hold weekly Shabbat services. In 1941, the Charter for Temple Beth El was received from the State of Georgia. A lot on Valley Drive was purchased to build a synagogue and a rabbi was elected to conduct services and start a Sunday school. The Temple Beth El Cemetery was established on Crawford Street in 1956. The temple affiliated with the Orthodox United Synagogue of America in 1962.

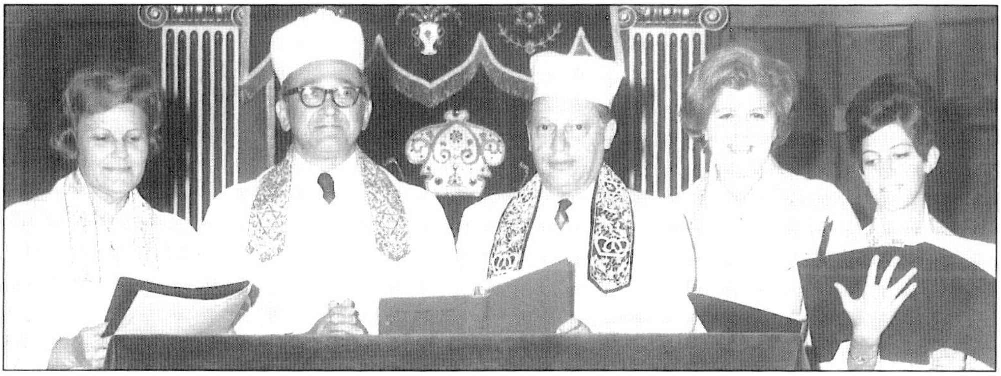

Dalton's Temple Beth El Choir included Minnie Koplan, Lou Meltzer, and Frances Lumiere. By the mid-20th century, Jewish life in Dalton had become an exceptional experience. Dalton's corporate and civic developments far surpassed those of other small Southern cities. Jewish families moved to Dalton to take advantage of the flourishing carpet industry and became owners and managers of many mills. Dalton was indeed "The Carpet Capital of the World."

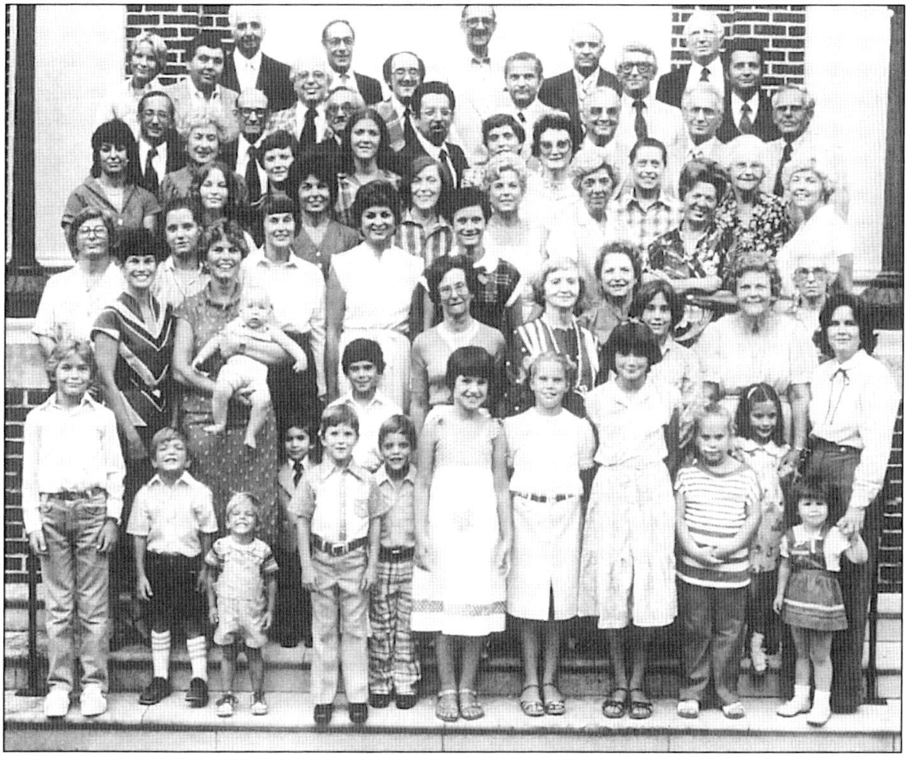

In 1981, the Temple Beth El Congregation celebrated its 40th anniversary. Pictured are some of the members during this celebration. The founders of Temple Beth El were Jack Braver, Joe Dubrof, Jack Frank, Irving Funk, Simon Ginsberg, Jerome Gold, Ben Goldman, Samuel B. Hurowitz, Leo Koplan, Seymour Lorberbaum, Simon Mendel, Sam Millender, A.H. Nicholas, Phil Phillips, Arthur Richman, Dr. Eli Rosen, Ira Rosen, Phil Rosenthal, Harry Saul, Bert Schulman, David Stein, Sam Stock, Abe Tenenbaum, M.W. Wisen, Ben Winkler, and all of their wives, who formed the Sisterhood. By the 1950s, Ira Nochumson, the Jack Lumieres, the Lester Goldbergs, the Jerry Shapiros, and the Barney Solomons were active in temple affairs.

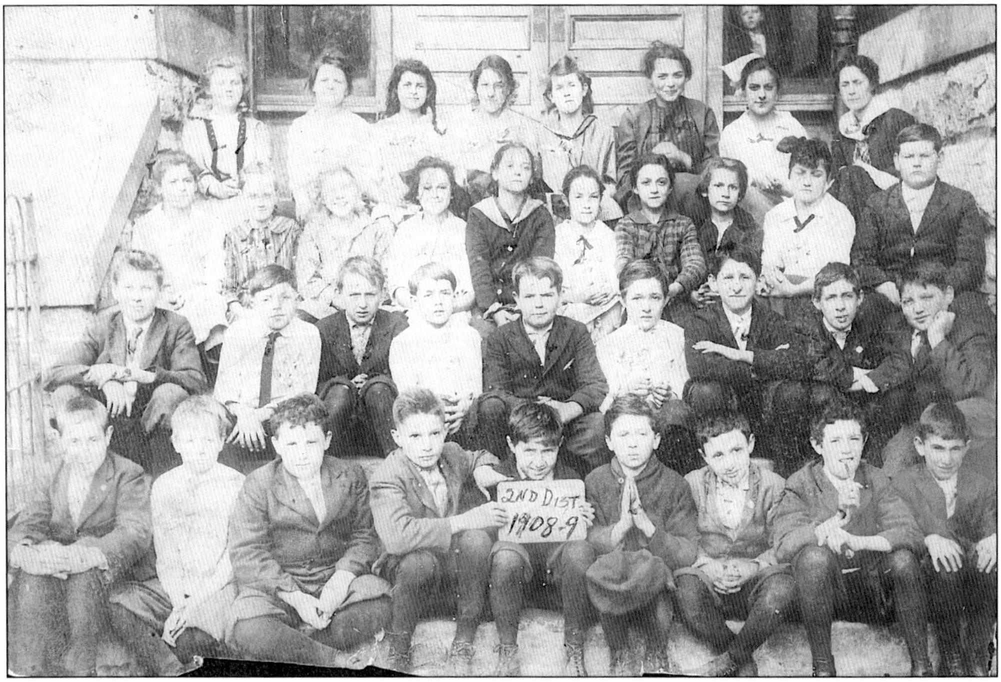

The Jewish people have always put a premium on education, and those in Chattanooga were no exception. In 1909, there were 19 Jewish children in one class at the Second District Grammar School—Meyer Winer, Willie Silverman, Harold Shalett, Benny Cash, Dave Slabosky, Louis Silverman, Philip Rubin, Felix Diamond, Lena D. Benkovitz, Ethel Rose Bergheimer, Esther Pearlman, Malvine Amster, Rae Frank, Pearl Contor, David Karr, Flora Bell Fine, Dora Frumin, Rae Lebovitz, and Annie Winer. The other children in the class were not Jewish.

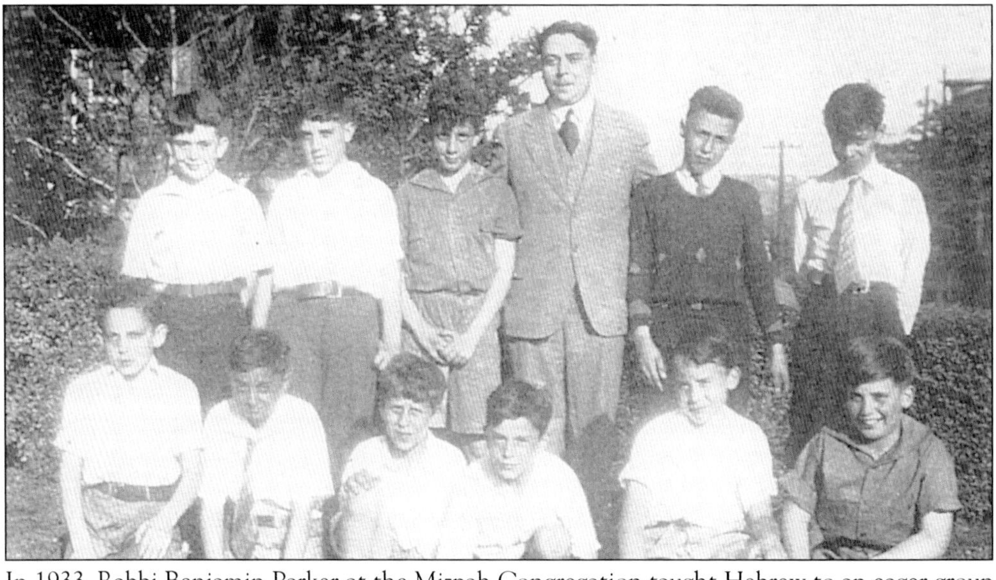

In 1933, Rabbi Benjamin Parker at the Mizpah Congregation taught Hebrew to an eager group of youngsters. From left to right are as follows: (front row) Joe Copland, Ervin Dolob, Joe Schwitzer, Norman Cassell, Paul Block, and Harry Edelstein; (back row) Leonard Leventhal, Lawrence Elson, Joel Solomon, Rabbi Parker, Robert Cassell, and Raymond Weitzner.

Two

TEACHING THE YOUNG: *Schools and Education*

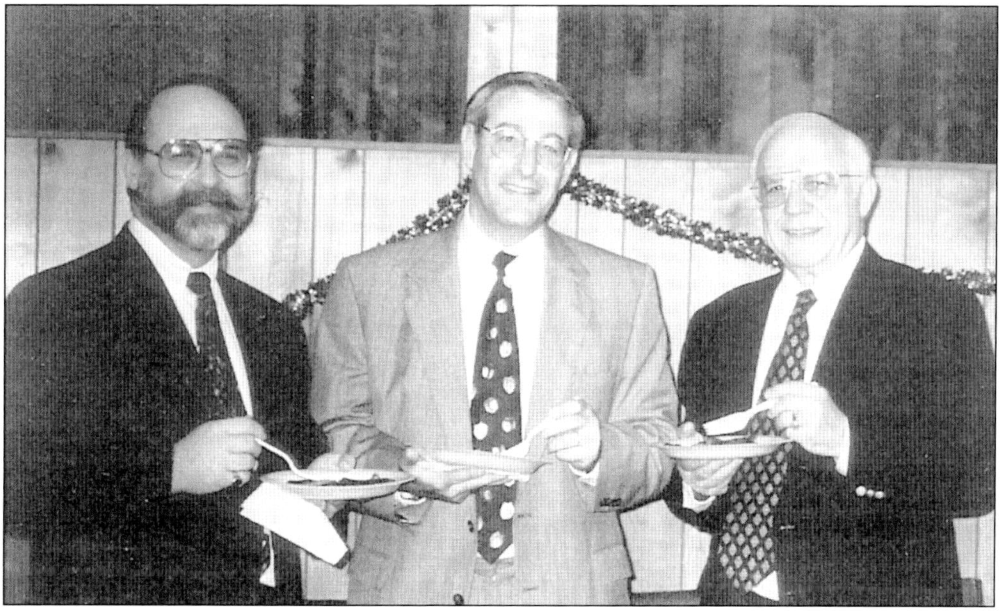

The rabbis serving Chattanooga in the mid-1990s were Rabbis Josef Davidson at B'nai Zion, Joseph Klein at Mizpah, and Maynard Hyman at Beth Sholom, shown at a reception at Beth Sholom. Chattanooga has also had its share of Jewish College professors at the University of Tennessee at Chattanooga, including Boris Belinsky, David Brodsky, Lawrence Ettkin, Stephen Lewinter, Robert Marlowe, Jay Menuskin, Richard Metzger, Alan Rabin, Irven Resnick, David Sachsman, and Sonia Young, the "Purple Lady," to name only a few. Ronni and Chaim Charyn have been teaching in secular schools as well as in the Day School and the Jewish religious schools of Chattanooga for many years.

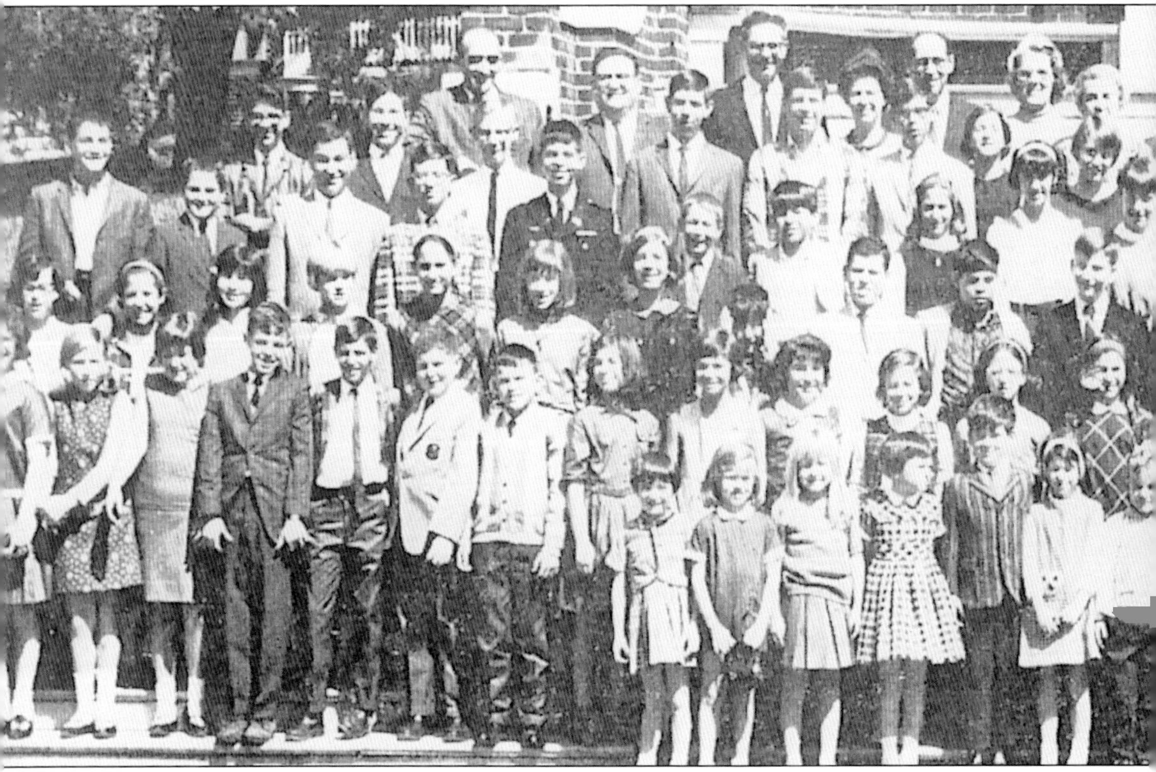

On the occasion of the Mizpah Congregation's centennial year in 1966, the teachers and religious schoolchildren from these families assembled on the steps in front of the temple for this group picture. Included among those shown here are members of the Stoloff, Kirk, Zurett, Lichtenstein, Wolff, Cohn, Baras, Abelson, Framm, Poss, Young, Kushner, Kass, Seretean,

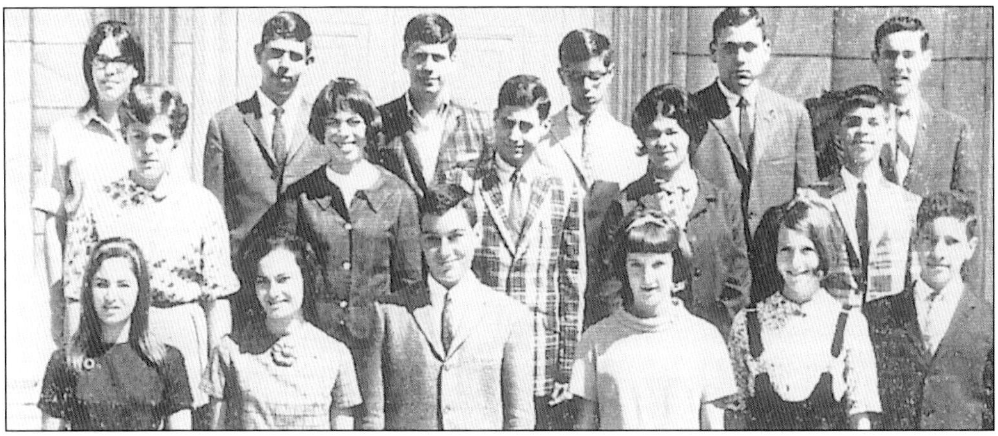

The 1966 Mizpah Youth Group consisted of the following, from left to right: (front row) Gloria Adler, Bonnie Adler, Robert Levine, Ellen Schwartz, Mathilde Silverstein, and David Shavin; (middle row) Sheryl Speer, Debbie Cohen, Eric Tepper, Patti Abelson, and Robert Henning; (back row) Yetta Levitt, Robert Marx, Randall Weber, Ronald Kaplan, David Miles, and William Blumberg. Alan Bergheimer, Bruce Gold, Ken Gordon, Steve Gordon, Steve Kaset, Joyce Olins, Kay Resiman, Steve Silver, Claire Weber, Marcy Weber, Flossie Weill, Donnie Wise, Eddie Wise, and Mark Wygoda were not present for the group photograph.

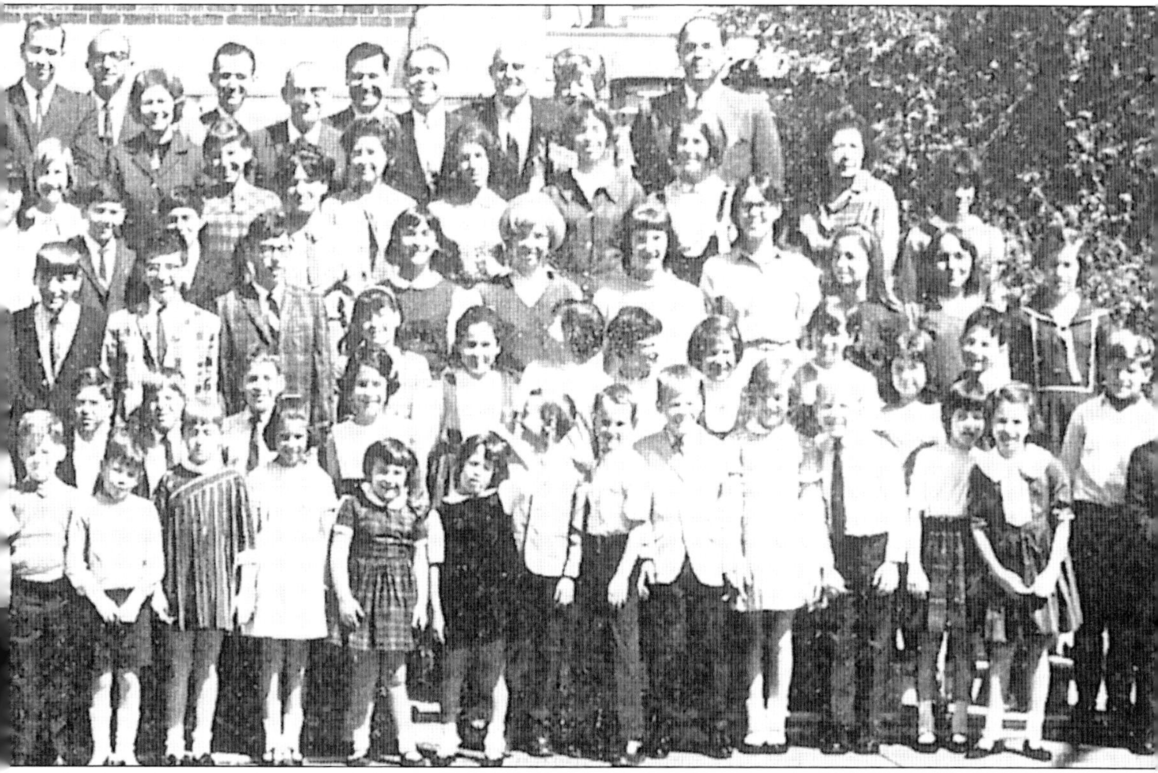

Coplon, Moore, Geismar, Silverstein, Olins, Tepper, Rubenstein, Long, Gordon, Maisel, Solomon, Sobel, Jaffrey, Tasman, Levine, Spector, Zuckerman, Hodes, Leventhal, Weill, Brody, Blumberg, Cohen, Kass, Weber, Schwartz, Levitt, Adler, Henning, Wolensky, Speer, Shavin, Kalis, Morris, Kornfeld, Marx, Patz, Kaset, Mendel, and Wygoda families.

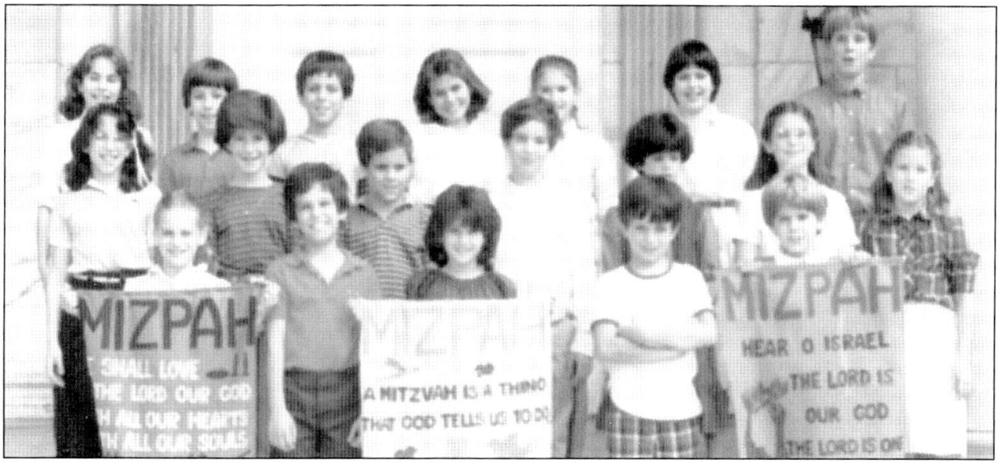

In 1977, each of Mizpah's classes had banners with mottoes dating their confirmation year. Here are three classes with their banners. Pictured from left to right are as follows: (front row) Teri Richard, Skip Schwartz, Vanessa Ettkin, Eric Kleiman, and Edward Shalett; (middle row) Michael Monen, Austin Center, Jennifer Ulin, Dana Stoller, and Kasey Reisman; (back row) Wensdy Lindsey, Josh Chrusciel, Mathew Kleiman, Kelly Reisman, Jamie Siskin, Andrea Brener, and Trent Center.

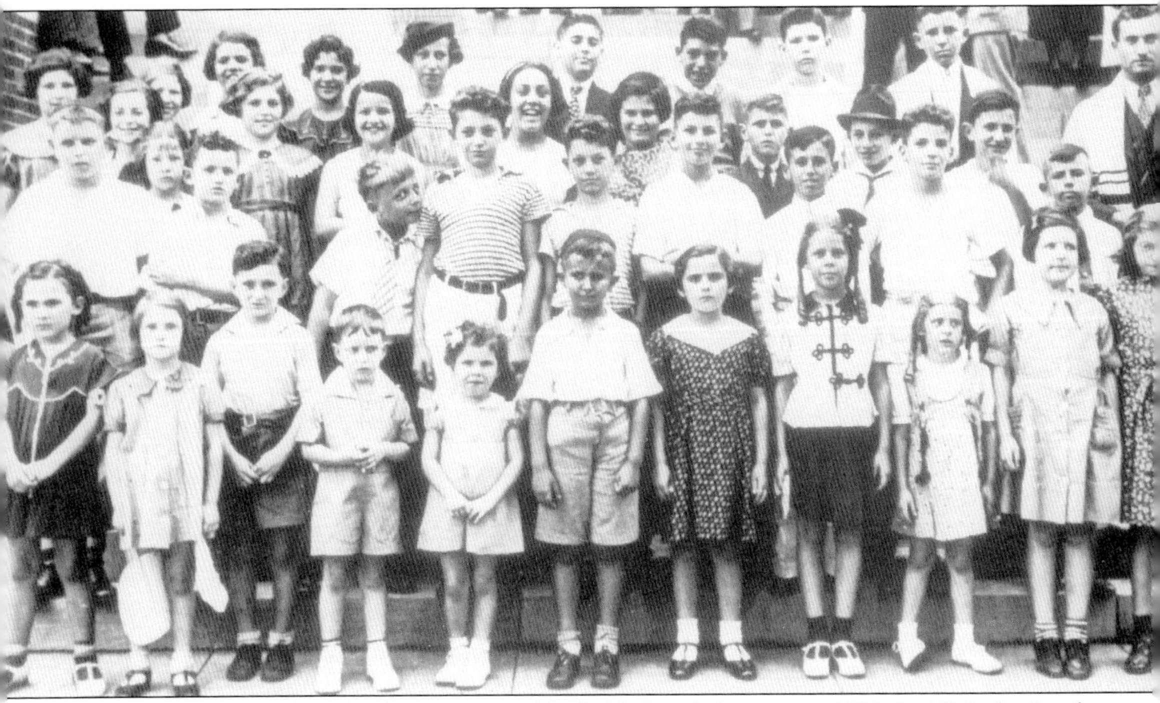

B'nai Zion's Sunday school was organized by Rabbi Israel Gerstein in 1934. In 1936, the Sunday school assembled in front of the Vine Street Synagogue. From left to right are as follows: (front row) Rose Fox, Claire Rudolph, Philip Bush, Robert Prigoff, Claire Siskin, Wolf Lebovitz, Esther Tandetta, Helen Siskin, Anita Siskin, Harriet Prigoff, and Reba Cassell; (second row) Earl Prigoff, Farol Fay Finkelstein, Julius Spector, Myron Kushner, Art Montrose, Jack Montrose, Joe Spector, David Freeman, Ben Alper, and Leon Lebovitz; (third row) Bella Shavin, Gitta Sulman, Geraldine Daneman, Carolyn Kolodkin, Marilyn Goldstein, Miriam Fanburg, Alvin Shoenig, Marvin Kolodkin, Arthur Saloshin, and teacher Martin Deutsch; (back row) Marjorie Brener, Mildred Schwartz, Leatrice Elson, Ann Wise, Julius Brandman, Marty Fanburg, Milton Kolodkin, and Herman Lebovitz.

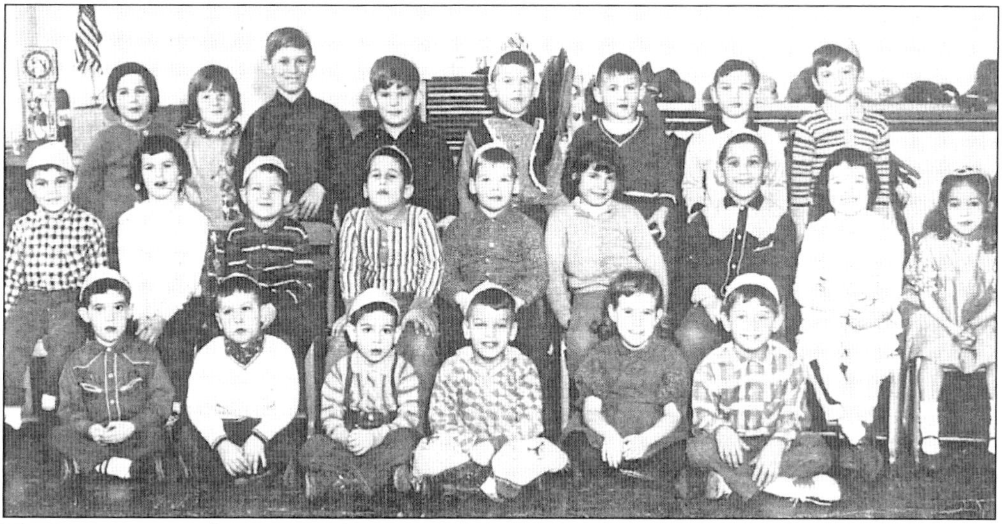

The B'nai Zion Kindergarten and Nursery Class in 1963, under the direction of Miriam Rhodes, consisted of the following children, from left to right: (front row) Eric Trotz, Barry Brouner, Leon Shavin, Jonathan Speal, Melanie Young, and Bobby Klein; (middle row) Daniel Tepper, Susie Spector, Richard Epstein, David Benowitz, Scott Seretean, Ellen Binder, Gary Bell, Ronni Trotz, and Wendy Deitch; (back row) Marilyn Yagoda, Janis Creim, John Pregulman, Jeffrey Zurret, Eric Richelson, Michael Hanan, Keith Dressler, and David Schwartz.

A much beloved teacher of the nursery and kindergarten classes, Mrs. Albert (Miriam) Rhodes had a different theory of classroom management. The important thing was that the young children were doing something in the classroom and not just sitting passively in quiet decorum. She taught in the Jewish Day School, the Chattanooga Public School System, and in the B'nai Zion and Beth Sholom Religious Schools. She was married to Dr. Al Rhodes, an optometrist, and they had four children: Alicia (Nelson), Clayton (married to Janice Wright), Selena (Katz), and Harvey (married to Terri Pollack).

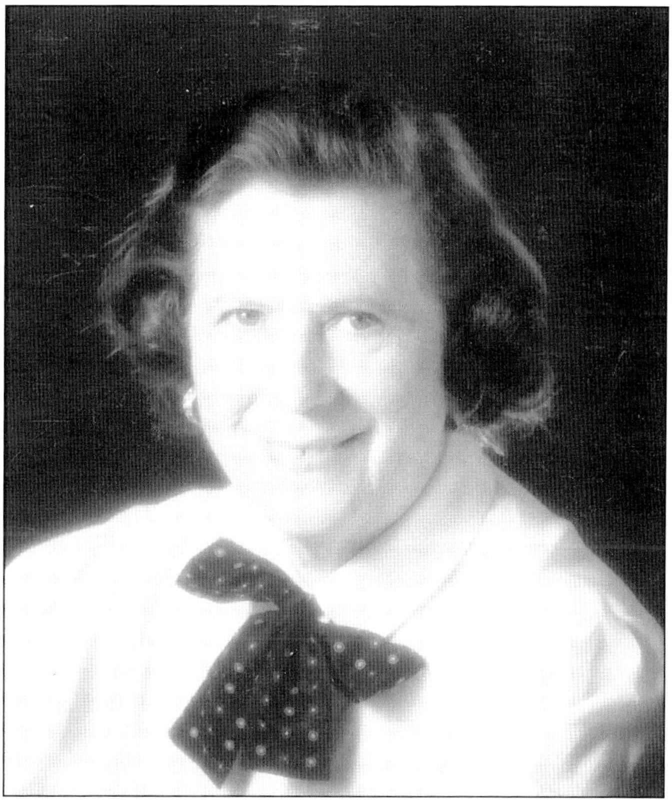

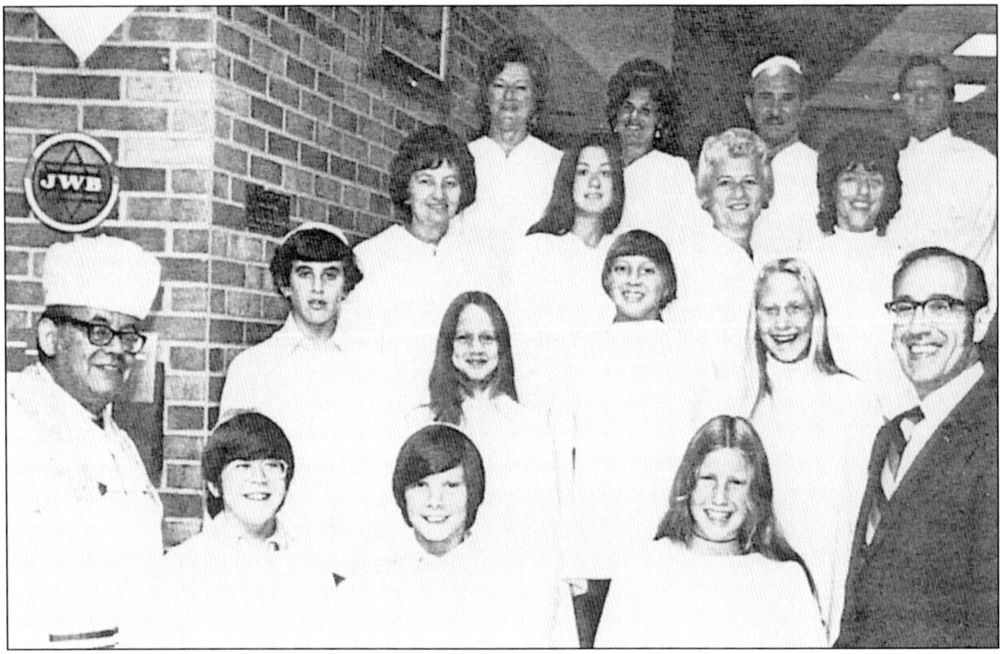

The B'nai Zion's Choir in 1972 included the following people, from left to right: (front row) much beloved Cantor Louis Rothman, Brian Lander, Dean Backer, Zelda Menuskin, and Rabbi Harold Markman; (second row) Joe Prebul, Beth Nusbaum, Evan Collins, and Sharon Berman; (third row) Esther Feigenbaum, Mimi Rothman, Ray Hasden, and Lucile Speal; (back row) Gladys Pressman, Lil Reingold, Ben Kellman, and Max Wolfe.

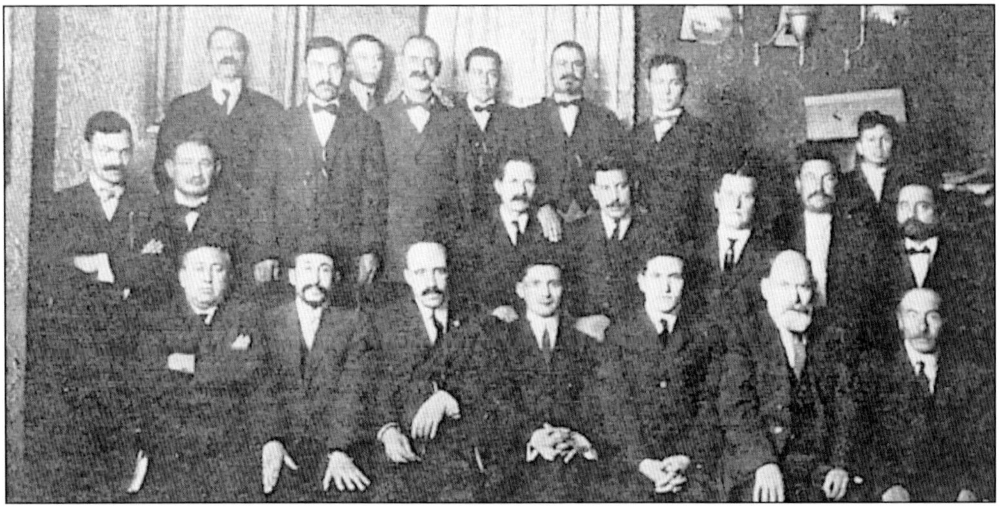

The teaching of Hebrew to children was begun as early as 1880 by Leib and Mendel Silverman, Abraham Einstein, Lipman Mirkin, and Simon J. Rausen. In 1910, the first officers and directors of the Chattanooga Hebrew School included the following, from left to right: (front row) Max Brener, Reverend Block, M.H. Silverman, Mr. Bardin, S.J. Rausen, and I. Perlman; (middle row) J.M. Fine, B. Shapiro, Mr. Jacobs, L. Lulove, Sam Shweidelson, M. Brandman, and Reverend Max Contor; (back row) S. Sacks, L. Koblentz, H. Koblentz, S. Soloff, E. Mennen, and I. Berman. By 1923, a charter of incorporation, with perpetual existence, was applied for and received for the school.

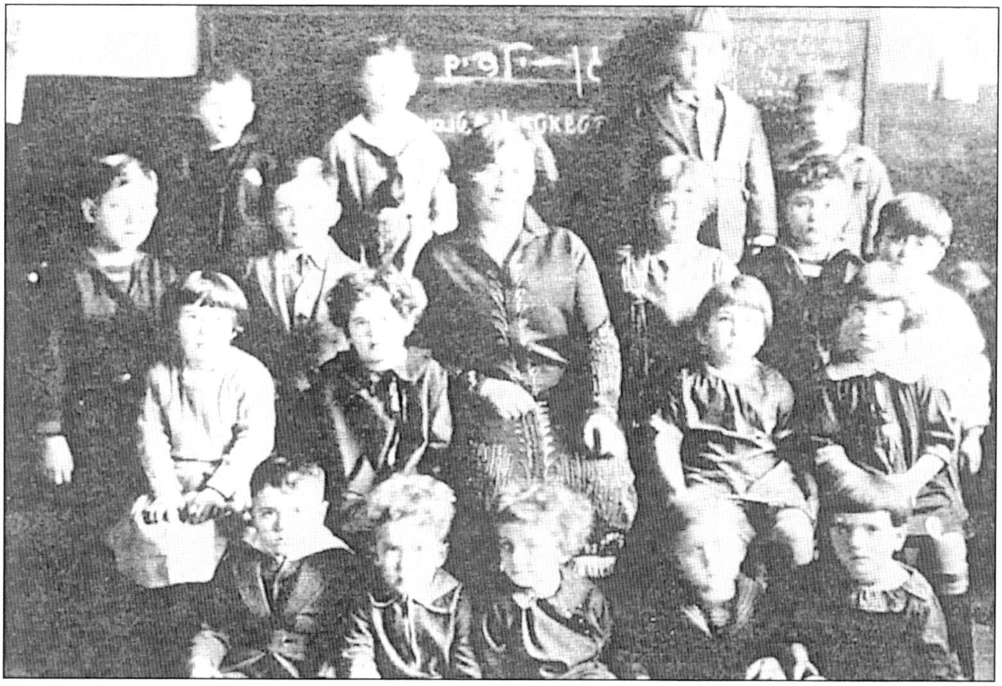

The kindergarten class of the Chattanooga Hebrew School in 1922 was taught by Mrs. Max Sadikoff. Shown here are the following, from left to right: (front row) Morris Tandeta, Marvin Cassell, Rosalyn Edelstein, Mark Spector, and Bluma Tandeta; (second row) Anna Gordon, Jean Weber, Eleanor Winer, and Lillian Alper; (third row) Harold Alper, Alex Alper, Mary Press, Herbert Abelson, and Billy Raider; (back row) Edward Goldstein, Harold Goldstein, Joe Press, and Meyer Hasden.

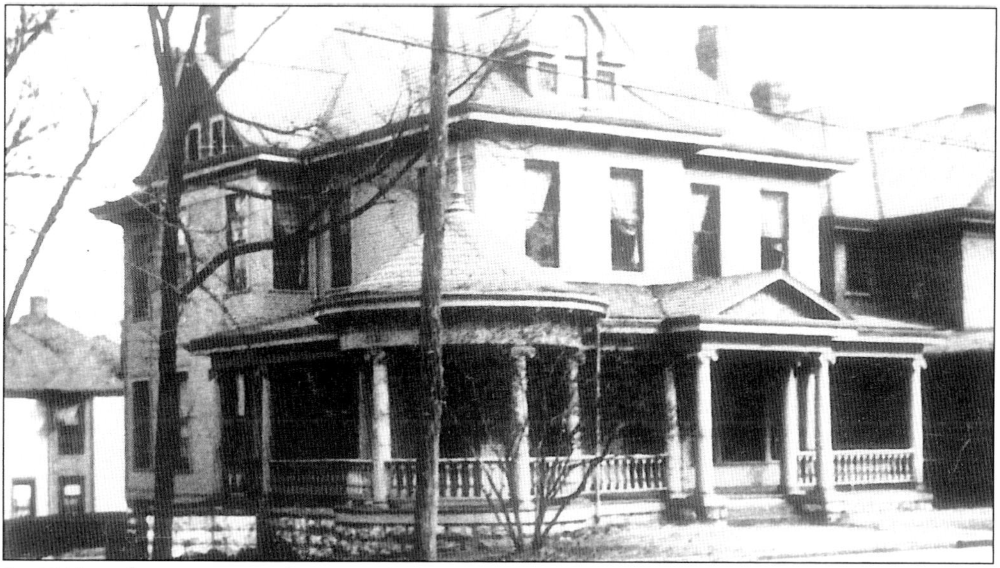

In 1937, a former private home with five classrooms on the first floor and a large assembly room on the second floor was purchased on Vine Street and became the Hebrew Institute, where the Hebrew school was held. Classes continued in the afternoons after public school secular classes ended.

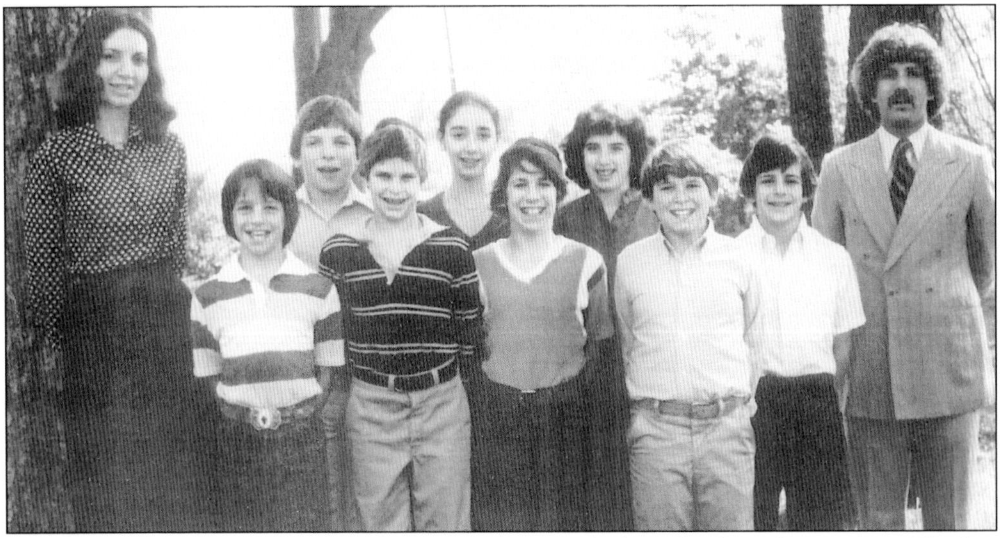

There have been two failed attempts to establish a Jewish day school in Chattanooga. The first school was started in 1949, but dissolved for lack of support. The second Jewish day school started in 1973 and reflected membership from all three of the Chattanooga congregations. Its location was the Chattanooga Jewish Community Center and it was partly funded by the Chattanooga Jewish Federation. Pictured is the first graduating class in 1980, which had completed six years of study at the school from the time the school first opened. They are, from left to right, as follows: (front row) Keith Pearlman, Greg Wiston, Steve Stern, and Chuck Kaplan; (back row) Beverly Millner (teacher of secular studies) Russell Castagnero, Irene Brodsky, Julie Smith, Art Winer, and Chaim Charyn (Hebrew studies teacher).

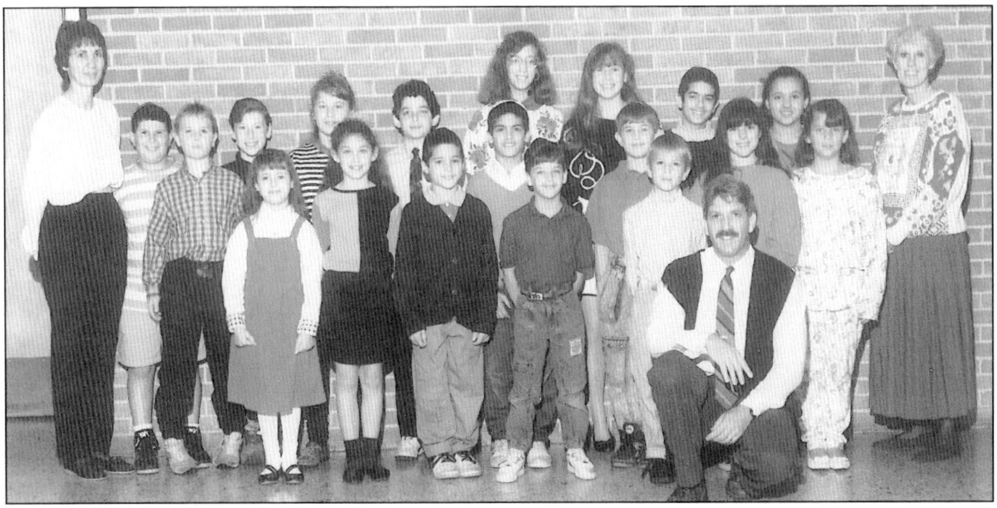

The children in grades one through six in the Jewish Day School during the 1991–1992 school year are, from left to right, as follows: (front row) Chaya Annavi, Stephanie Spector, Guy Zachmy, Shai Zachmy, Daniel Speal, Andy Susman, Jesse Charyn, Julie Teer, and Jana Manaker; (back row) Geoffrey Stahl, Micah Charyn, Jason Hillner, Beth Susman, Gabe Hankin, Jennifer Richelson, Deborah Spector, Adam Zachmy, and Marrissa Shrum. The teachers are Beverly Millner, Chaim Charyn, and Judith Gribben.

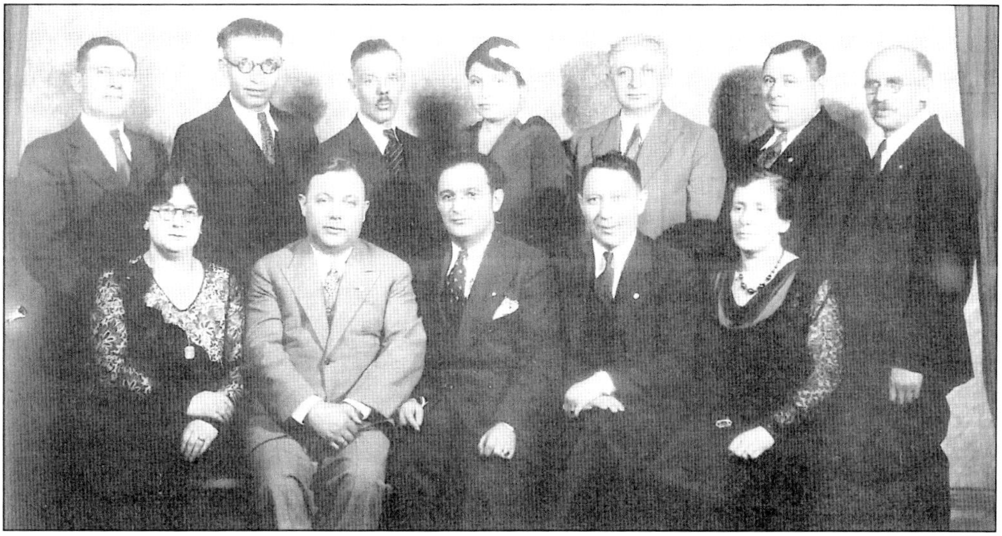

The 1931–1932 school board of the Workman's Circle Yiddish School consisted of the following people, from left to right: (front row) Ethel Parker, Izzy Berman, teacher Louis Silver, Louis Shavin, and Annie Kaset; (back row) Ben Margolin, Sam Page, Max Pressman, Eva Shapiro, Nathan Page, Jake Kaset, and Barney Kaplan. These residents had backgrounds in Soviet Russia, where religion was forbidden. Thus they emphasized the teaching of the Yiddish language rather than Hebrew in their school.

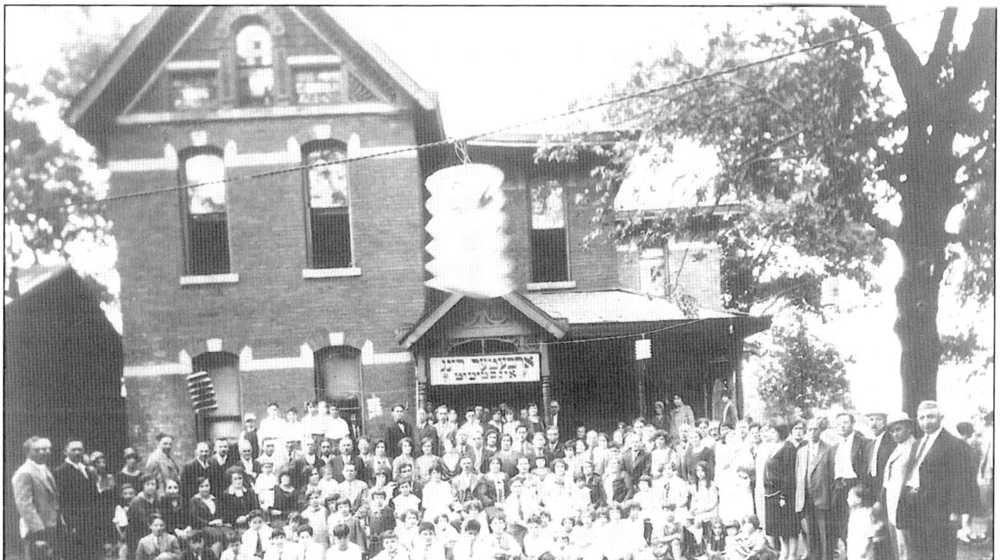

The Chattanooga Workman's Circle Yiddish School, called the Shuli by the children but better known as the Lyceum, was located on College Hill in 1924. This picture shows the building and the congregation. Classes were held every weekday after secular school ended.

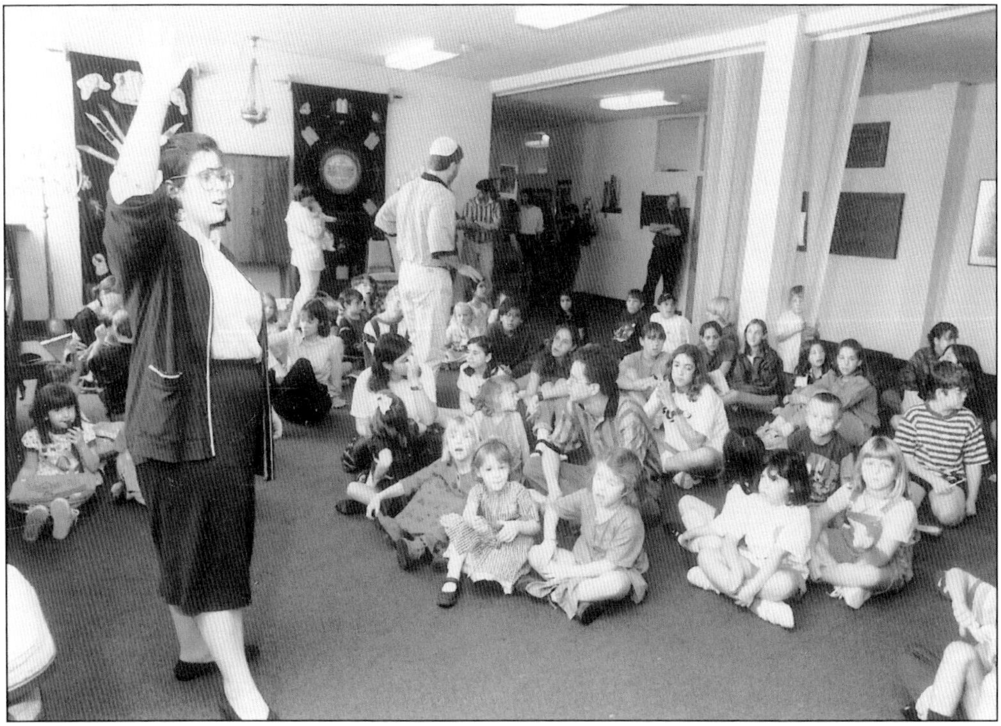

In 1994, because of dwindling enrollment in both the Mizpah and B'nai Zion Religious Schools, a merger was brought about to combine the two schools. The classes were larger, and a professional religious educator was hired to run the school in 1995, using funds provided by the Jewish Federation. The Beth Sholom Congregation joined the merger and also sent its students to the school. Ziporah Altman-Shafer was the first director; Amy Cohen, a fourth generation Chattanoogan, is the second director.

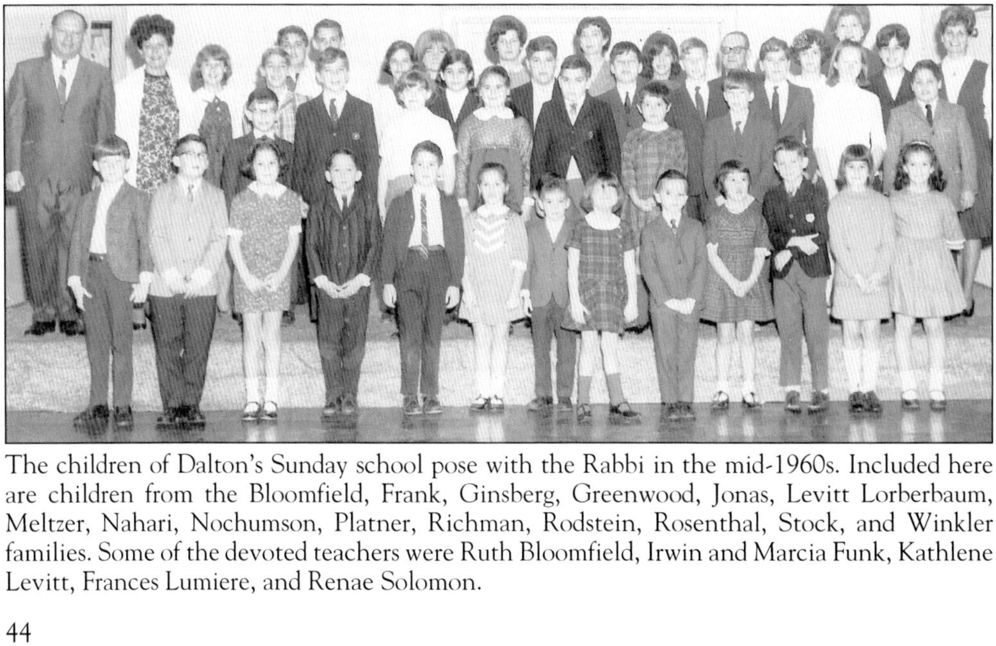

The children of Dalton's Sunday school pose with the Rabbi in the mid-1960s. Included here are children from the Bloomfield, Frank, Ginsberg, Greenwood, Jonas, Levitt Lorberbaum, Meltzer, Nahari, Nochumson, Platner, Richman, Rodstein, Rosenthal, Stock, and Winkler families. Some of the devoted teachers were Ruth Bloomfield, Irwin and Marcia Funk, Kathlene Levitt, Frances Lumiere, and Renae Solomon.

Three

Celebrating Families:

Family Portraits

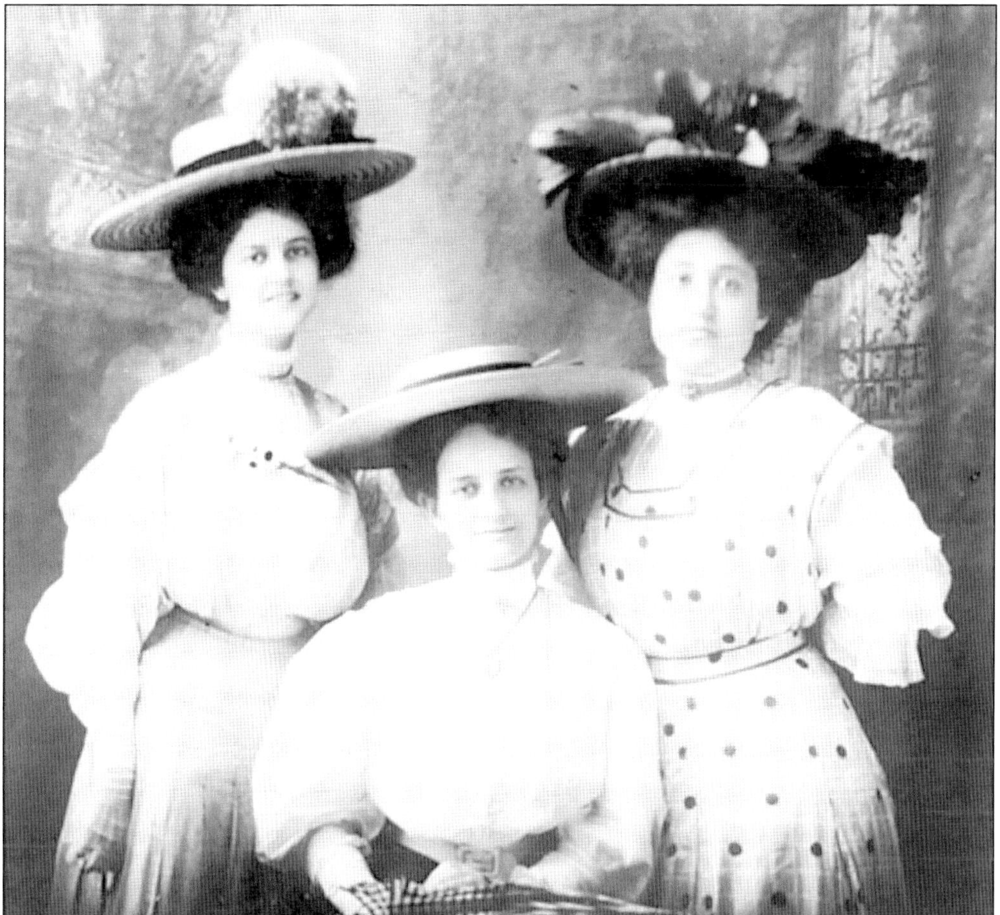

Isabelle Schwartz, Cecile Schwartz (Friedman), and Fannie Geismar are dressed for a big outing in 1907. Isabelle married Dr. Leopold Shumacker. Their two children were Leo Shumacker Jr., who had a military career in the USAF, and Jane (Seidman).

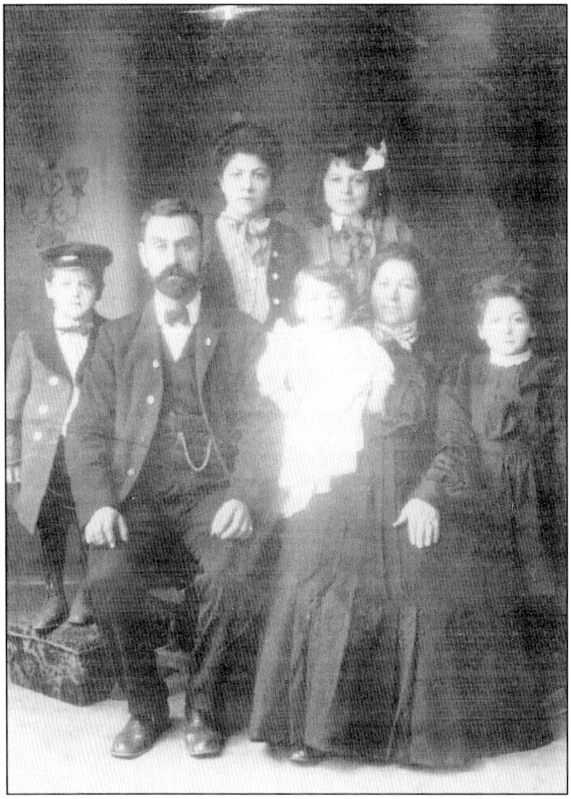

The Louis and Hannah Koblentz family posed for a photograph in 1898. They are, from left to right, as follows: (front row) Abe, Louis, Hannah, baby Ben, and Mina (Plottler); (back row) Kate (Robbins) and Rose (Michelson). The Koblentz family members were merchants and had stores in East Chattanooga and downtown on Market Street. Abe Koblentz had a second successful career selling life insurance. He also founded SCORE (Service Corps of Retired Executives), which taught would-be entrepreneurs how to run businesses. Kate Robbins had one daughter, Erma, who married Louis Lebovitz. They had two sons: Larry and Bruce.

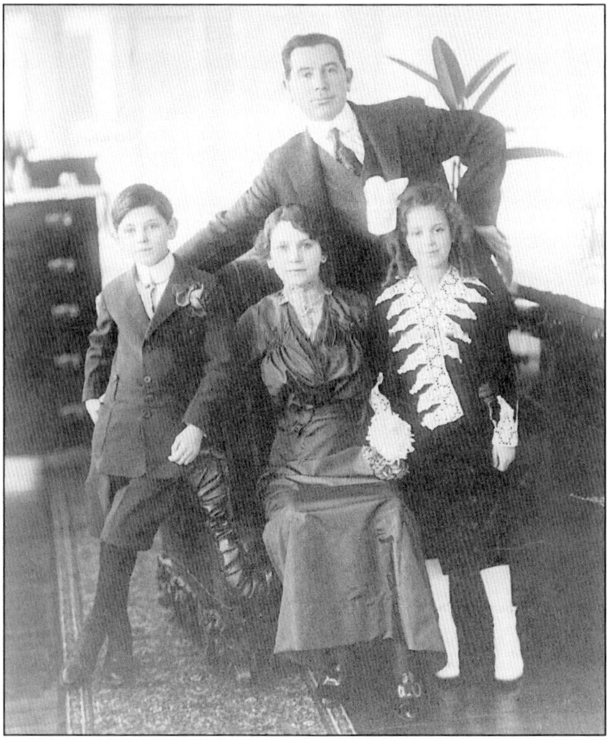

David and Sara Effron are pictured here with their children, Raymond and Bertha, in 1916. Raymond married Fanny (Kahn) of Columbus, Ohio, and they had two children, Sheryl (Rose) of St. Louis and Rosann of Mt. Vernon, Kentucky. Bertha married Abe Borisky, and they had two children, Sara Jo (Kobacker) of Columbus, Ohio, and Joel, of Boca Raton, Florida.

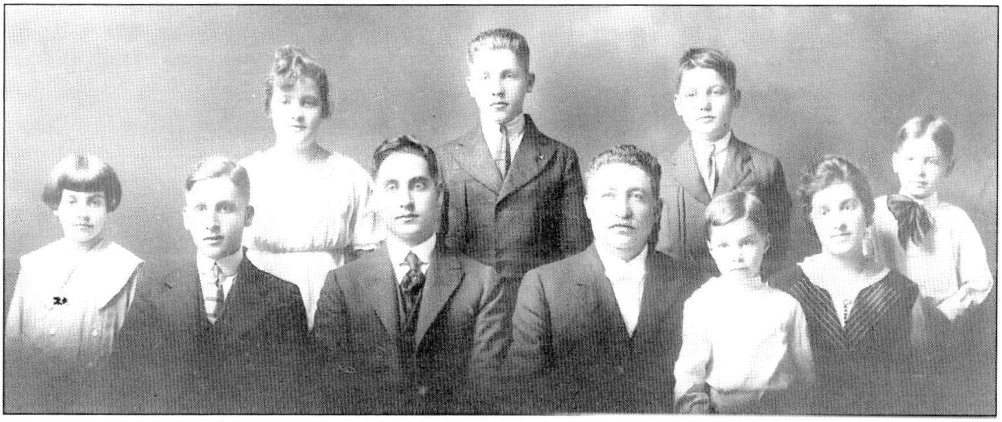

David Max Diamond and his nine children are pictured here in 1913. From left to right are as follows: (front row) Josephine (Russ), Sam, Louis, David, Aaron, Lena, and Joseph; (back row) Esther (Brockman), Abe, and Felix. David's wife, Rebecca (Slabosky) Diamond, died giving birth to her ninth child, Aaron. Aaron went to New York as a young man and became wealthy as a developer. He started his road to success when he began building houses for veterans on Roosevelt Island, next to Manhattan, after World War II. Before his death, he set up the Aaron Diamond Foundation, worth $200 million, which has been providing funds for the battle against AIDS through the Aaron Diamond Research Center. He and his wife, Irene, wanted to help the less fortunate and desired to give all of his money away to worthy causes within ten years after his death.

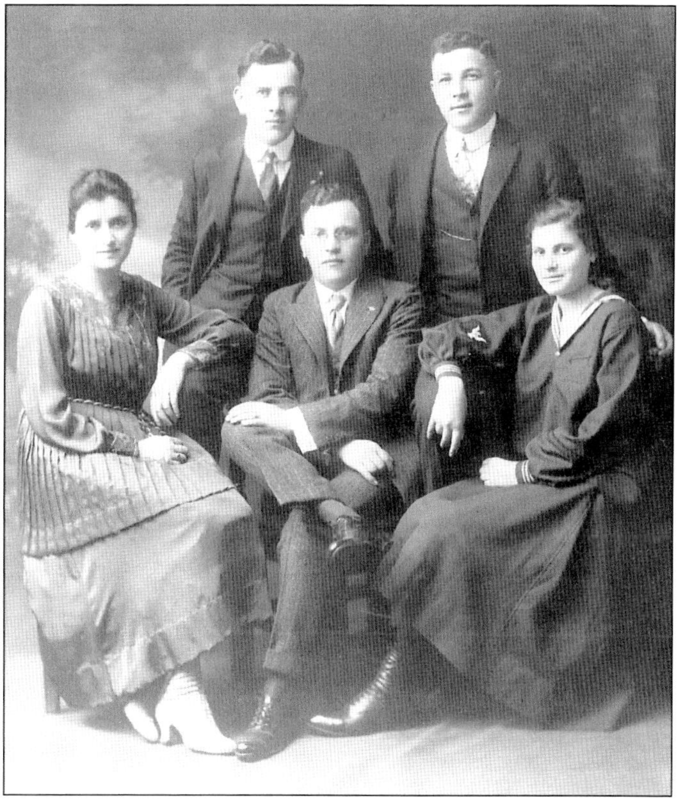

The Levine siblings and spouses are pictured here in 1917. They are, from left to right, as follows: (front row) Clara (Max Steinberg), Jake, and Celia (Manny Harris); (back row) Oscar and Morris. Morris had a son, Lawrence, who married Anita Siskin. Jake had two sons, Jay and Howard.

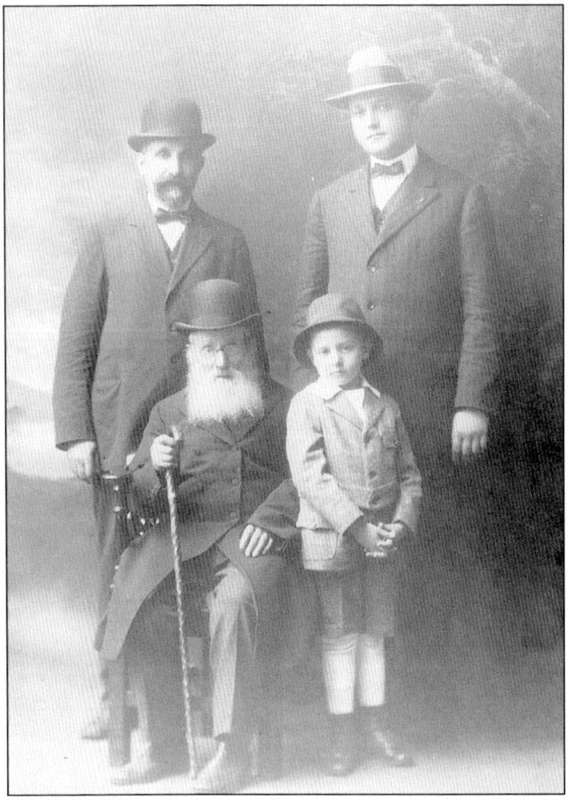

There were many unrelated Winer families in Chattanooga. Complicating matters, there were several Meyer Winers and Hyman Winers. One family, who arrived in 1893 from Latvia, included Father Hyman Winer and Mother Minnie Reevel Yankelevits. Their children were Rose (Stock), Harry, Annie, Fannie (Center), Myer H., and Ada (Abelman). Four generations of Winers are pictured here in the 1930s: grandfather Isaac (Yitchok) Winer, father Hillel Aaron, son Harry (former president of the YMHA), and grandson Stanley. George Winer had a daughter, Bryna (Yellin), whose son married Ellen Schwartz. Louis (Labe) Winer came to Chattanooga from Nyra, Latvia, in 1900. Elihu Winer, a graduate of Vanderbilt and Yale (1931–1933), was a freelance writer contributing to the *New York Herald Tribune*, *Opinion* magazine, and Universal Pictures in the story department.

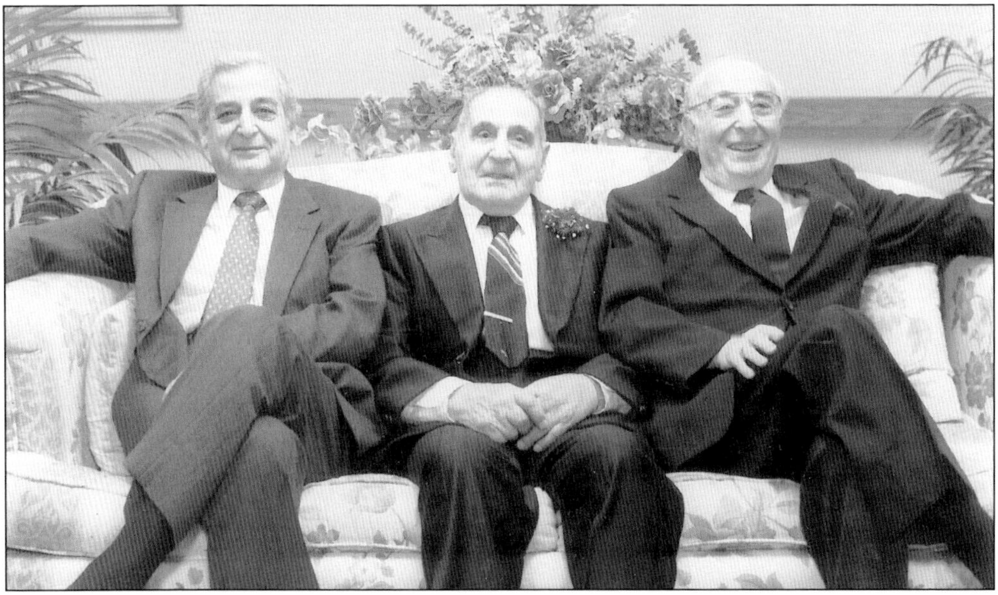

Nathan and Jenny Jaffe had four children: Irvin (Izzy), Sam and Rebecca (Malsh) of Chattanooga, and Bertha (Shub) of Baltimore. Nathan was a cobbler by trade, and the family owned shoe stores and shoe repair shops. Nathan is pictured in the center, with Sam on the left and Izzy on the right, at his 100th birthday celebration. He passed away in 1998 at the age of 108. (Contributed by Dennis Wilkes, *News Free Press*.)

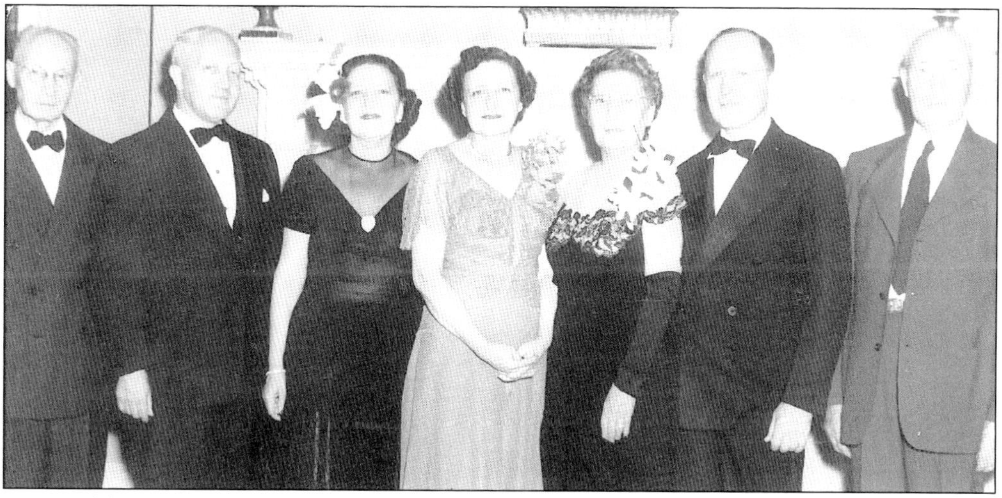

Seven of the children of Israel Abelson and his wife, Sophia, are pictured at the 1948 wedding of Carolyn Eplan, in Atlanta: Harry, Sam, Lena (Levy), Bess (Eplan), Annie (Levin), Jake, and Morris. Sam, Lena, Annie, and Morris lived in Chattanooga. Harry, Bess, and Jake lived in Atlanta. Sam had two children, Robert and Charlyne (Epstein). Lena had one son, Ronald. Bess was the mother of the bride, Carolyn, and had a son, Leon. Annie had three children: Frances (Greenberg), Harry, and Carl. Morris had two sons, Bernard and Herbert. Jake had two children, Sonya (Rabinowitz) and Hershel.

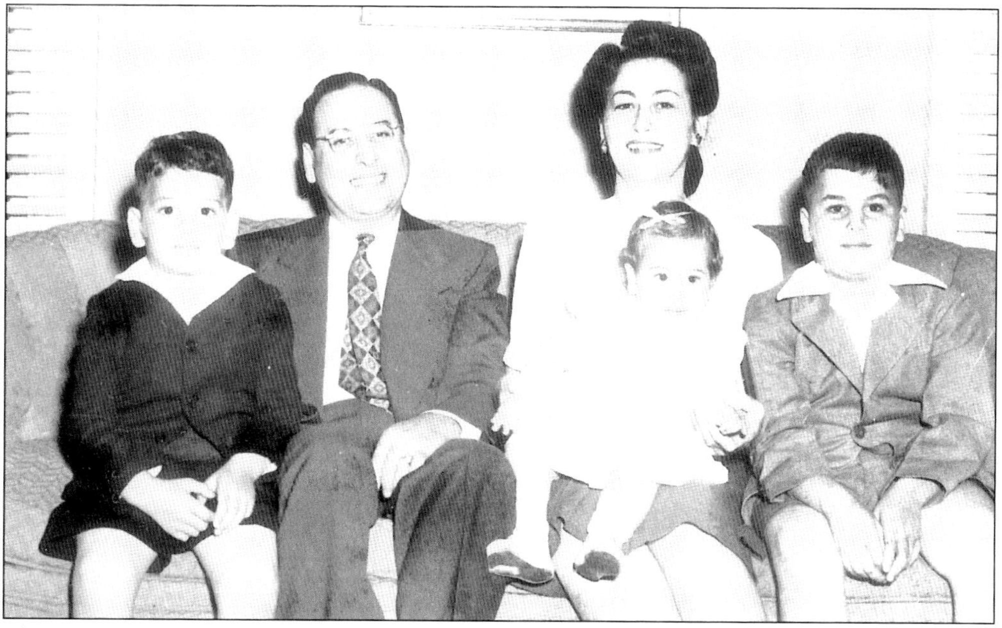

Theodore Berz came to Chattanooga in 1923 and helped organize the Orkin Exterminating Company. His family is pictured here in 1945. They are, from left to right, Paul, father Ted, mother Hannah (holding baby Diane), and Robert (Bob). Paul lives in Memphis, and Bob and Diane (Stoller) live in Chattanooga. Bob's children include Kerren of Atlanta, Jennifer and Kate of Chattanooga, Robert Samuel Berz Jr. of Savannah, and Eliot of Chattanooga. Paul's children are Jonathan and Caroline, of Boston, Massachusetts. Diane's children are Seth of Charlotte, North Carolina, and Dana of Nashville, Tennessee.

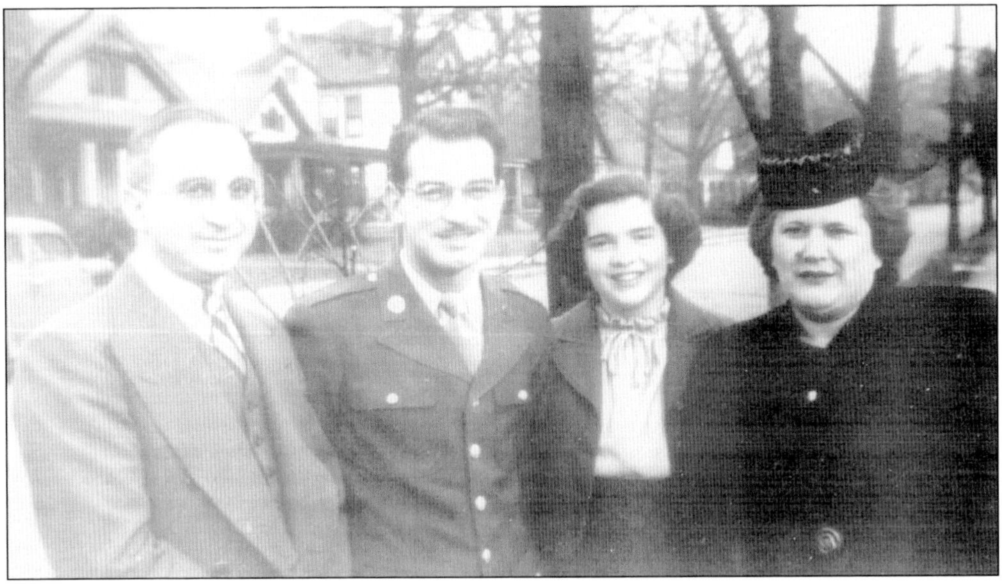

Fred and Sara Ann, of the Henry and Elizabeth (Angel) Morris family, are pictured here in 1943. Fred married Charlotte and lived in Nashville. Sara Ann (Stoloff) lived in Chattanooga and had two children: Henry (married to Bonnie) of Chattanooga and Buffy (Vehse) of Morgantown, West Virginia.

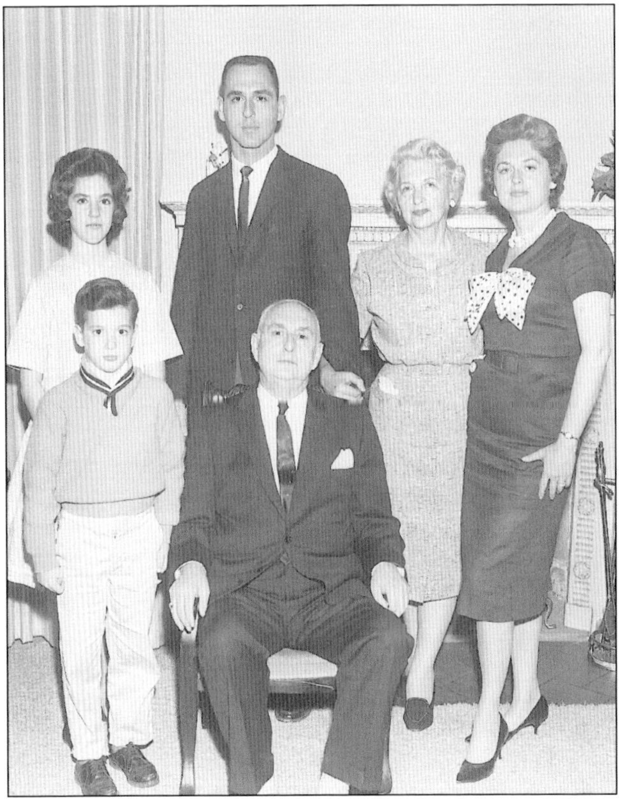

The Jacob Daneman family has been in Chattanooga since 1903. He had eight children: Ben, Ida, Issy, Harry, Dave, Bertie, Max, and Joe. Pictured here are three generations of the Harry and Rae (Lebovitz) Daneman family: Gerri (Haber/Sadow) and Jay of Nashville (children), and Dan Haber of Franklin, Tennessee, and Lynn Haber of Nashville (grandchildren). Harry was in the mercantile business with Ben Block, whose parents had settled in Chattanooga in 1908. Ben married Florence (Korn) of New York, and they had three children: Maxine (Alper), (Zudie) Lorraine (Leventhal), and Roy.

The Samuel (Shimmy) and Martha Berman family suffered a tragic event in 1973 when Shimmy was gunned down and killed in an attempted robbery in his liquor store. Shimmy had been a great advocate of sports in Chattanooga and was inducted into the Chattanooga Jewish Sports Hall of Fame. His picture is on the wall behind his family. They are, from left to right, Sharon (Bass), Martha (his wife), Edith (Floyd), and Abbie (Bailey). Likewise, a similar fate took the life of Herman Geismar Jr. in 1979, while he was working in his liquor store. Herman's wife was Marion Seigel, and they had two sons, Neil and Frank.

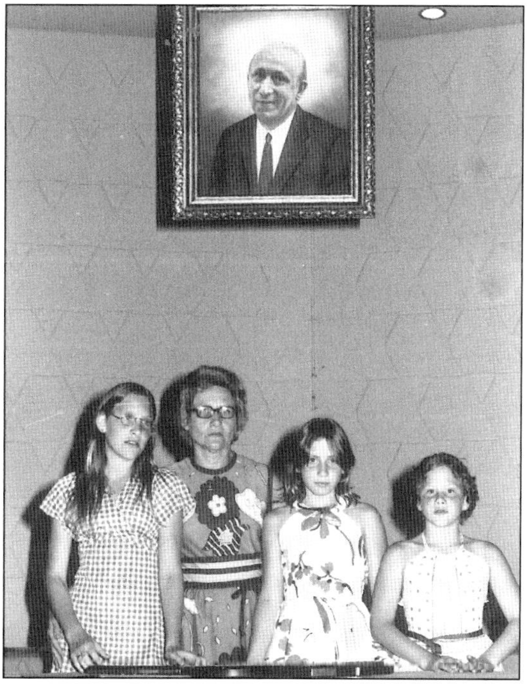

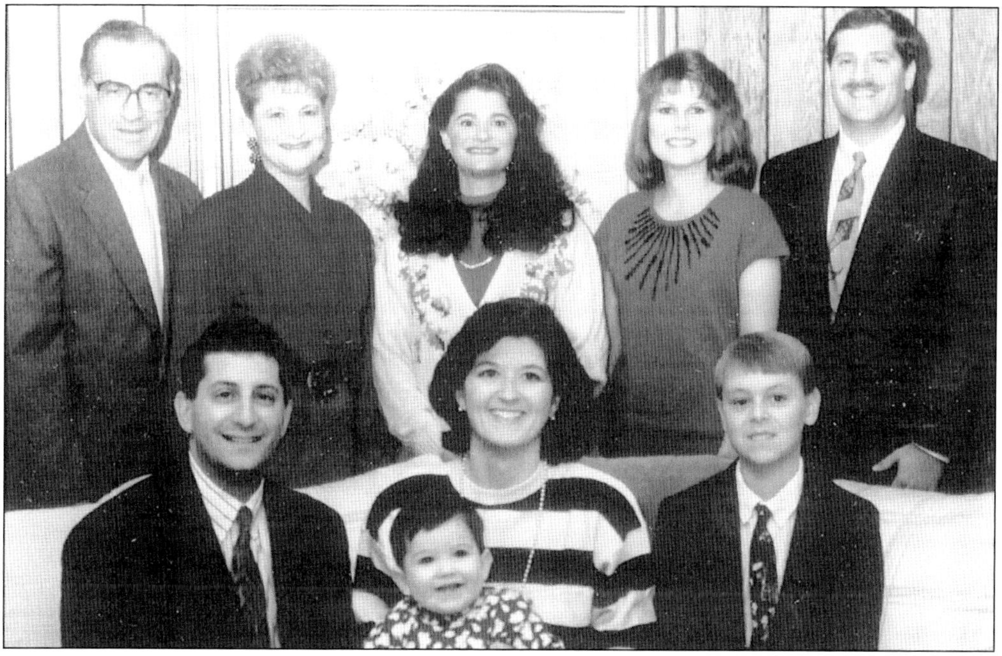

Several people who escaped the Nazi Holocaust, including Arno Goldstein, Herbert St. Goar, Fela and Isadore Green, and Ethel Berger, to name only a few, chose to make Chattanooga their home. Bill Klein is a survivor from the Dachau and Auschwitz death camps during the Nazi Holocaust. He is pictured here with his wife, Shirley (Tyber), and their three children: Bobby (married to Susie), Joel (married to Rhonda), daughter Felicee, and grandsons, Ethan and Chris Harvey. David and Jenny Brodsky and their two children, Irina and Edward, arrived in Chattanooga in 1976 from communist Russia.

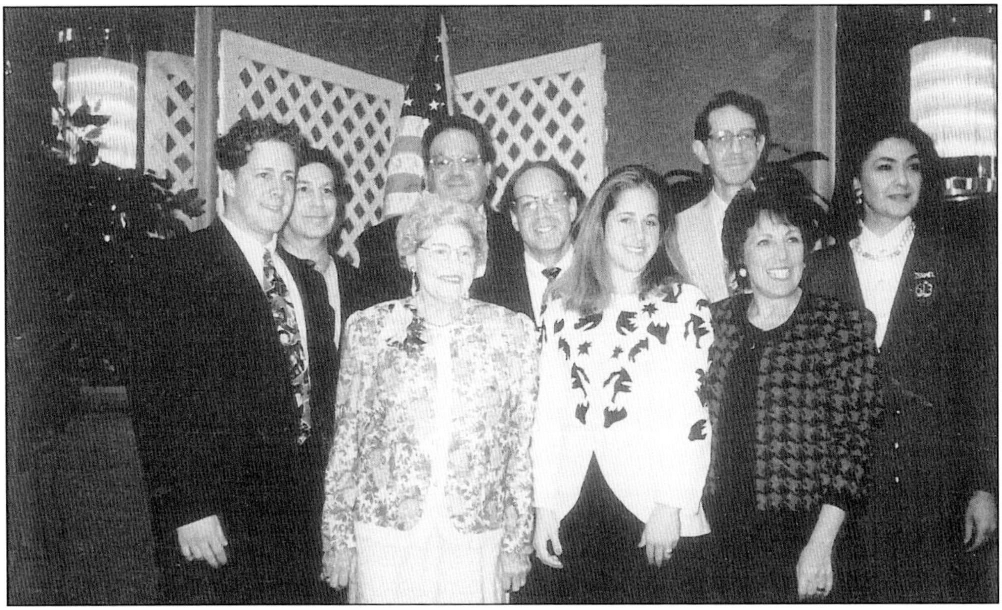

Sylvia Frumin is pictured with her sons and their families when she was honored by Hadassah in 1995. They are, from left to right, as follows: (front row) Sylvia, Beth, and Susan; (back row) Steven, Marshall, Jerry Jacobs, Butch, Harvey, and Rita. Sylvia's husband was Abe, who operated a scrap iron and metal company.

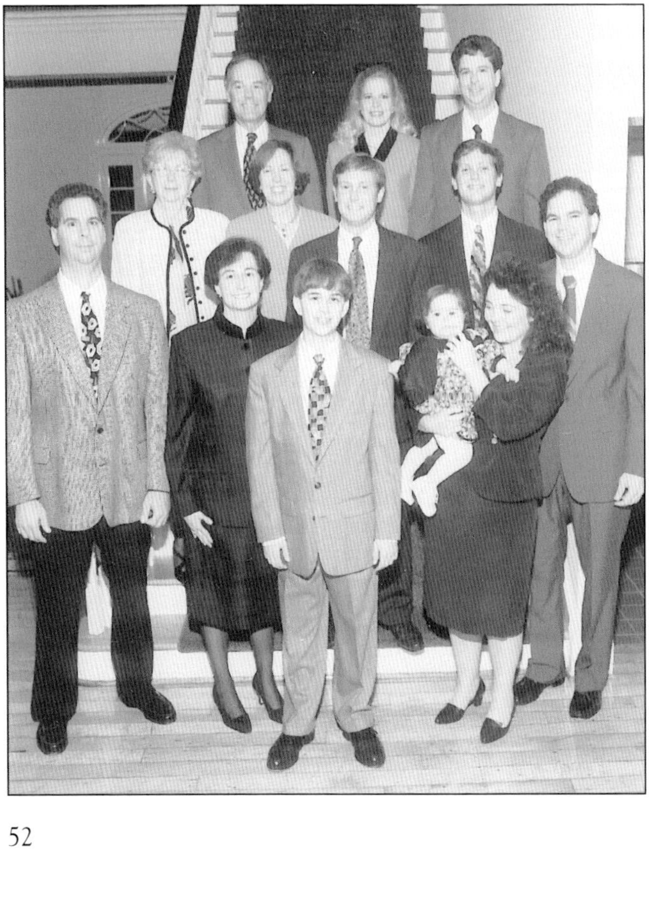

The Hi and Liz Raisin family poses for a photograph in Dalton, Georgia, in 1996. Shown here are their daughter Linda (with her husband, Rob Robison, and their sons, Michael and Frank, of Sanibel, Florida), their son Jimmy (with his wife, Yvonne, and their son Saul); their son John (with his wife, Kathy, and their baby, Nicole); and their son Phil (with his wife, Teresa). All three sons live in Dalton. Jim and John founded the Raisin Textile Company, and Phil has his own plastics finishing plant, DALTEC, Inc. (Courtesy of Finley's Studio, Dalton, Georgia.)

Four

REJOICING IN FREEDOM:

The Holidays and Life Cycle Events

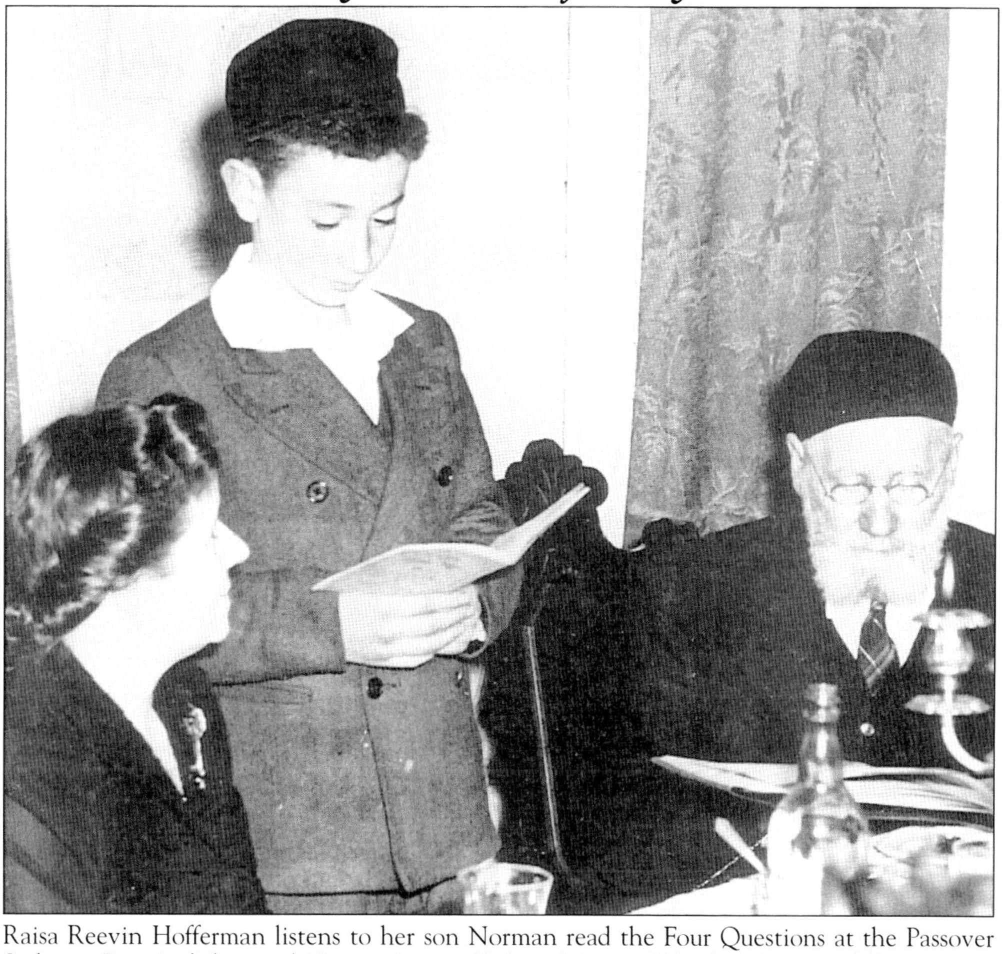

Raisa Reevin Hofferman listens to her son Norman read the Four Questions at the Passover Seder as Raisa's father and Norman's grandfather, Honon (Charles) Reevin, follows in his prayer book in 1941. Norman's sister Gitta was married to Herb Stein, and they had four sons: Charles, Alan, Stuart, and Ira.

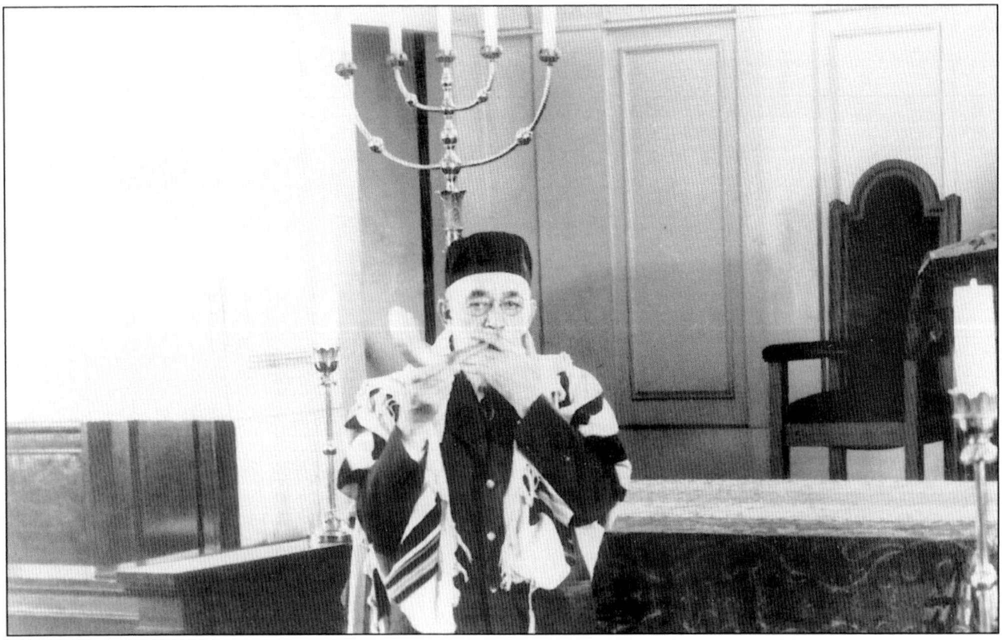

On Rosh Hashanah, the Shofar is blown to welcome the new year. Here, Reverend Isaac Maisel is welcoming the new year in 1935.

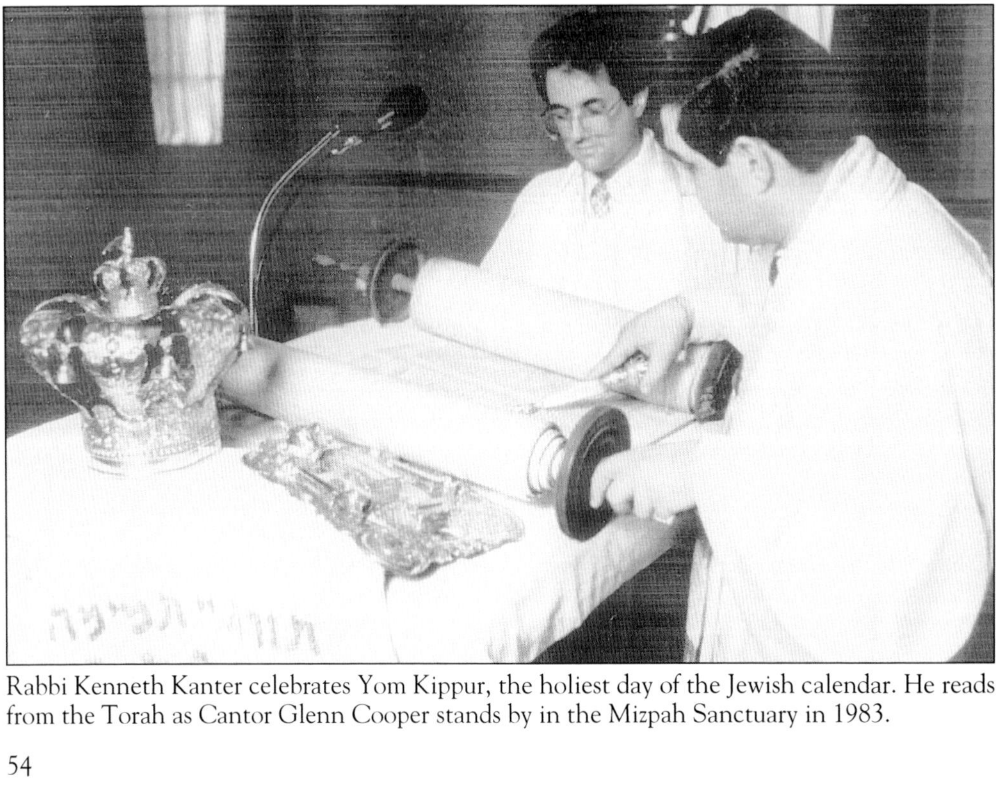

Rabbi Kenneth Kanter celebrates Yom Kippur, the holiest day of the Jewish calendar. He reads from the Torah as Cantor Glenn Cooper stands by in the Mizpah Sanctuary in 1983.

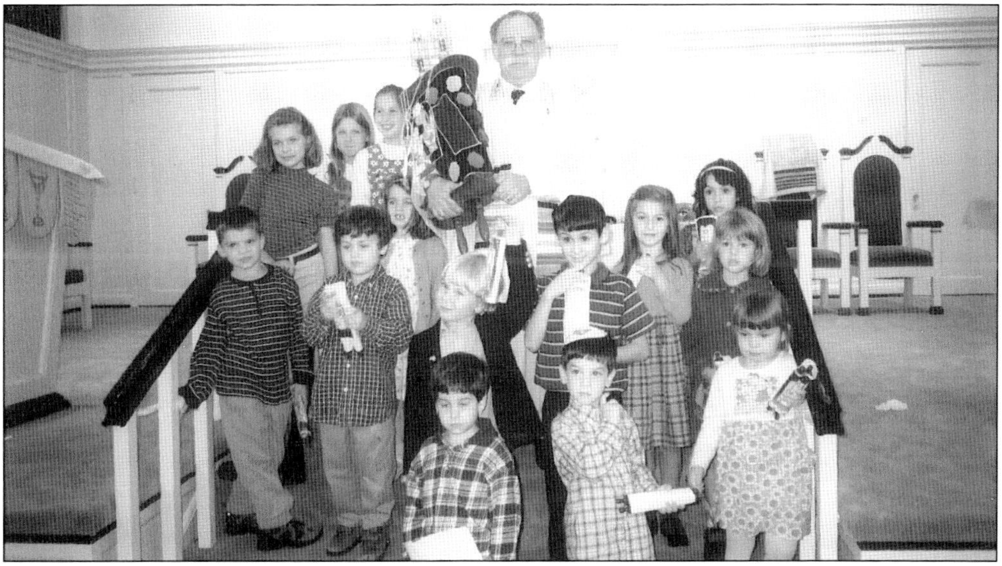

Consecration is a ceremony created by Reform Congregations in which parents bring their pre-school children to the temple to be blessed and entered into the religious school. This is similar to the Bible account of Hannah bringing her son, Samuel, to Eli, the priest, to be taught to serve God. The children recite the *Shema* during the ceremony. From left to right are as follows: (front row) Bobby Brouner, Jared Rosenberg, and Molly Minnen; (middle row) David Brody, Eliot Berz, Ariel Resnick, Aaron Steinberg, Michael Schulson, Courtney Rosenberg, Leah Schulson, and Rachel Felton; (back row) Elizabeth Brody, Hannah Steinberg, Jennifer Brounner, and Rabbi Philip Posner.

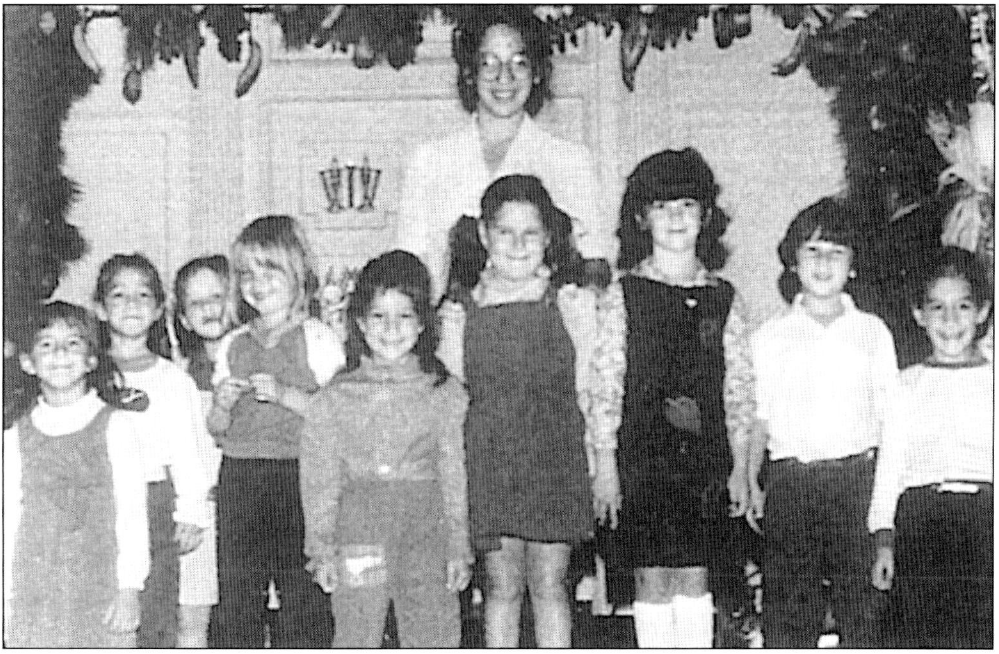

Succot, the Feast of Booths, is one of the joyous harvest festivals. Here is Karren Berz, whose students are standing under the bountifully laden Succah in the 1970s. Among those pictured here are Paige Ginsberg, Jennifer Ulin, Brian Ettkin, and Jenny Berz.

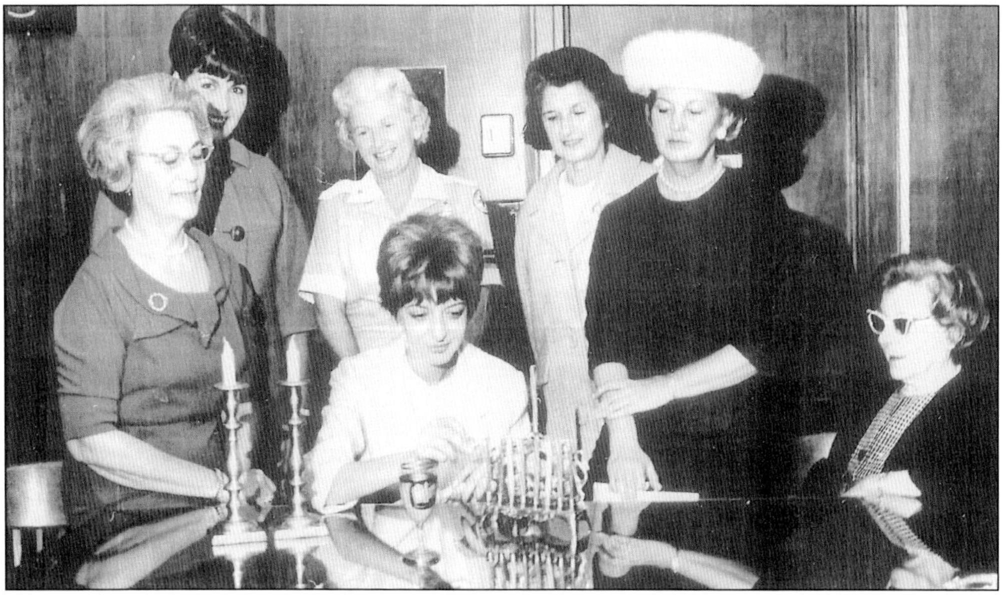

The next holiday on the Jewish calendar is Chanukah. In 1969, some of the Mizpah Sisterhood watch Gail (Greenberg) Kirk, president, as she lights the Chanukah Menorah. Pictured, from left to right, are Hannah Berz, Miriam Levine, Klari Koblentz, Helen Cohn, Edna Wolensky, and Florabelle Geismar.

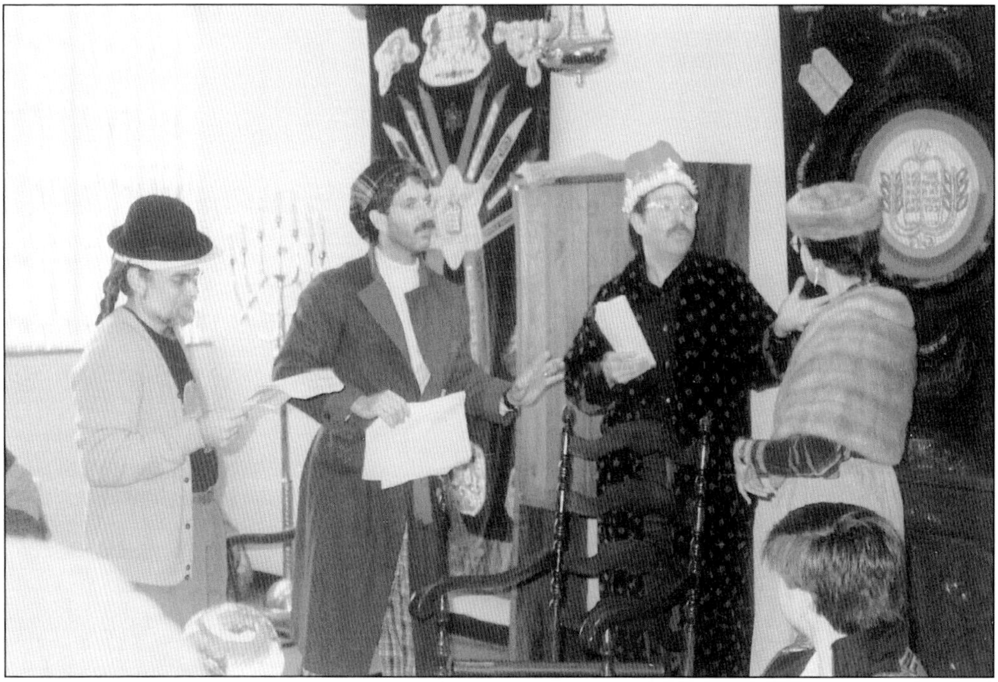

Purim finds the children dressed as Queen Esther, King Ahasuerus, Haman, and Mordecai at the Purim Carnival at the religious school. In 1995, the faculty of the religious school gave a play. Bill Lefton, Chaim Charyn, Dr. Jeff Gefter, and Judy Bloom-Minnen are shown here.

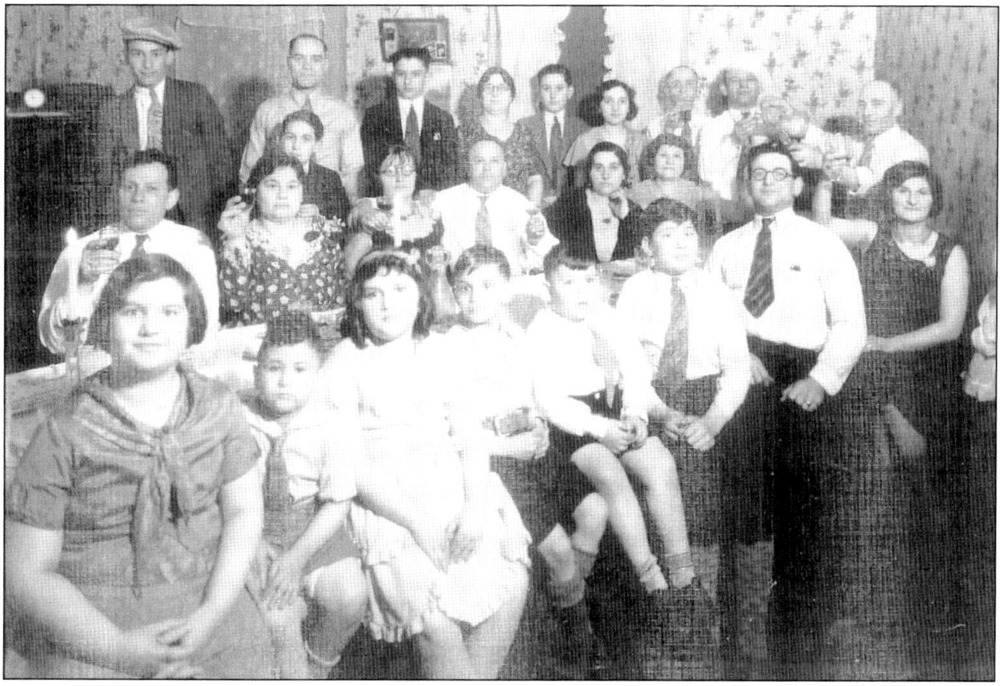

Passover is celebrated with the Seder. In 1930, the Parker family, the Elsons, the Stahls, the Hymans, and the Chernics gathered around the Seder table.

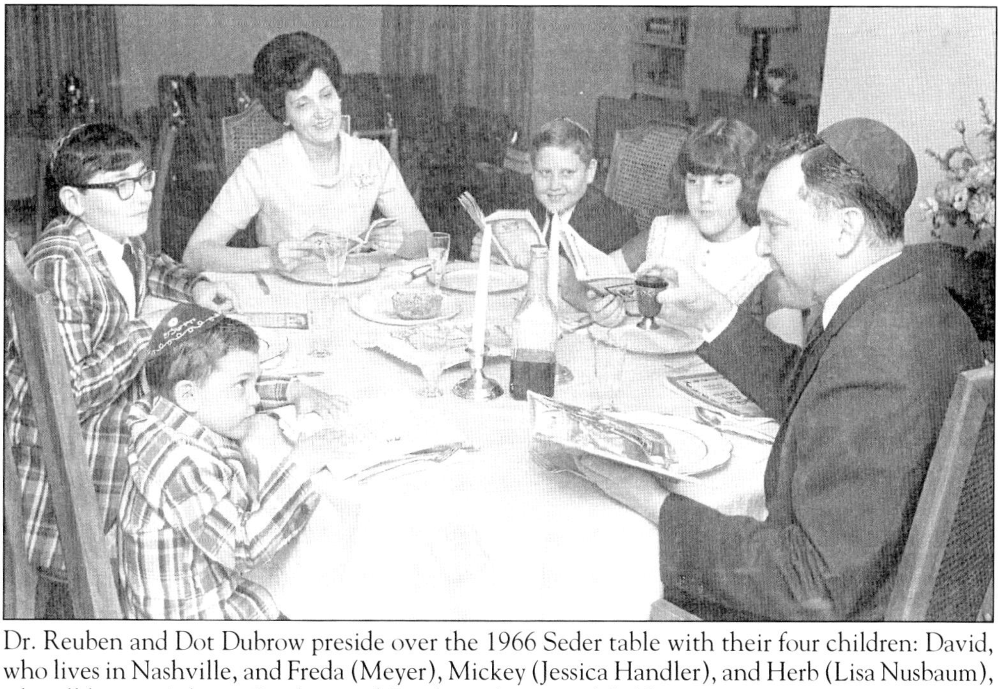

Dr. Reuben and Dot Dubrow preside over the 1966 Seder table with their four children: David, who lives in Nashville, and Freda (Meyer), Mickey (Jessica Handler), and Herb (Lisa Nusbaum), who all live in Atlanta. Reuben and Dot have four grandchildren.

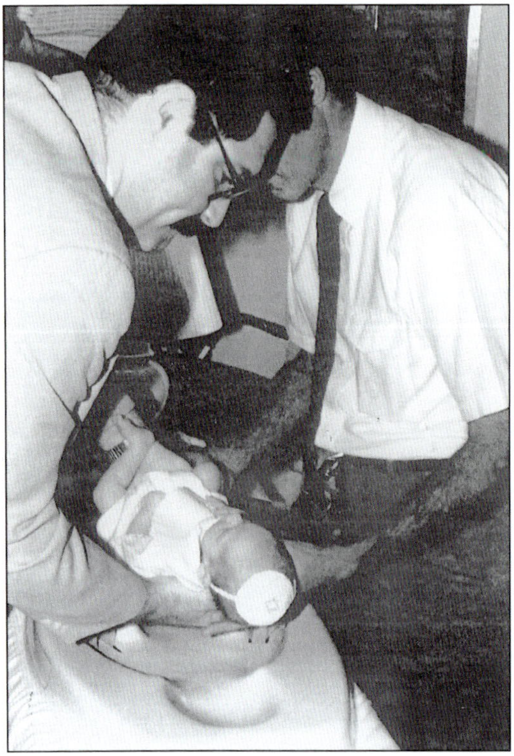

Life Cycle celebrations mark the milestones in a Jewish person's life, starting with the Bris (circumcision). Barnetta (Rosenberg) Allen attended the Bris of her grandson, baby Adam Barnet Sack of Mobile, Alabama, in 1985.

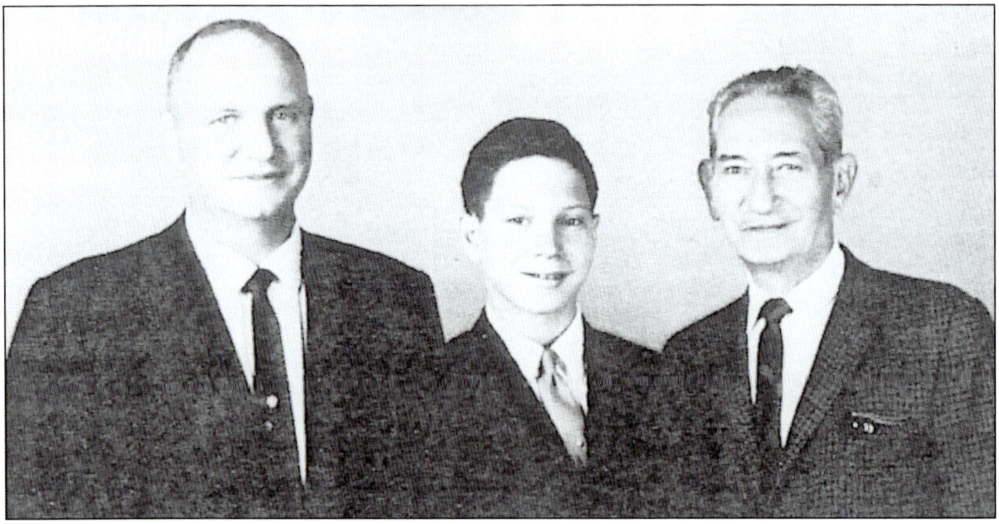

Nowadays both boys and girls can have a bar/bat mitzvah. In 1956, Trudy Gault (Trivers) was the first girl to have a bat mitzvah in Chattanooga, having been taught by Rabbi Swift. In 1974, Beth Ann Nusbaum had the first bat mitzvah performed at the McBrien Road B'nai Zion on a Saturday morning. The Edelstein family has three generations celebrating bar mitzvah at B'nai Zion. Mike was born in Chattanooga in 1892 and had his bar mitzvah in 1905 in the Carter Street Shul. His son Milton (Buster), also born in Chattanooga, had his bar mitzvah in 1933 in the Vine Street Synagogue. The third generation bar mitzvah took place in 1963, when Mike's grandson, Jay Goldblatt (the son of Mike's daughter Genevieve and her husband, Sam), was called to the Torah. Another grandson who celebrated his bar mitzvah was Shelton Goldblatt.

In 1925, Irving Polsky was a bar mitzvah boy in New York City, before he moved to Chattanooga. His wife is Fannie Dubrov, and their children are Reah (Friedman) of Nashville and Sybil (Carey) of New Hampshire.

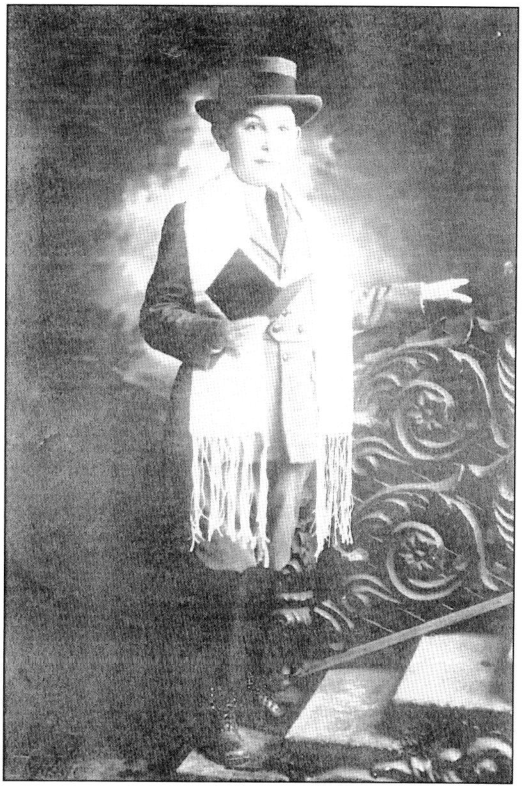

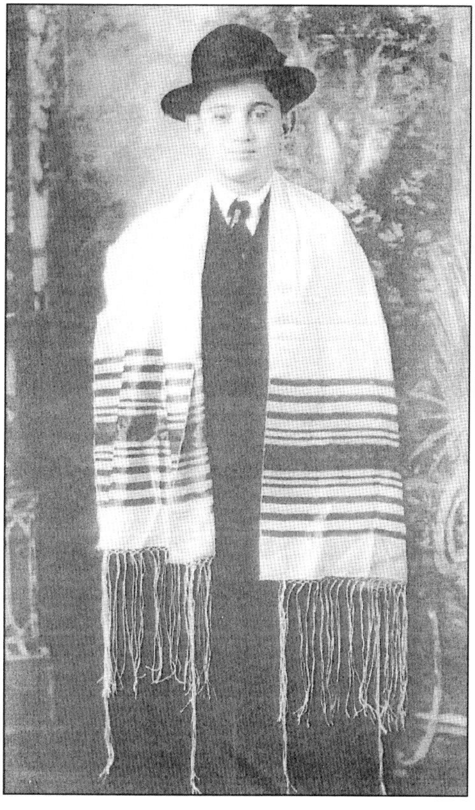

Harold Shavin, a Chattanooga native, had his bar mitzvah in 1940 at B'nai Zion. He is married to Yuppie (Sir), and they have three children: Alan in Tempe, Arizona, Rita (Brook), and Gayle (Johnson) of Chattanooga. Harold and Yuppie have four grandchildren.

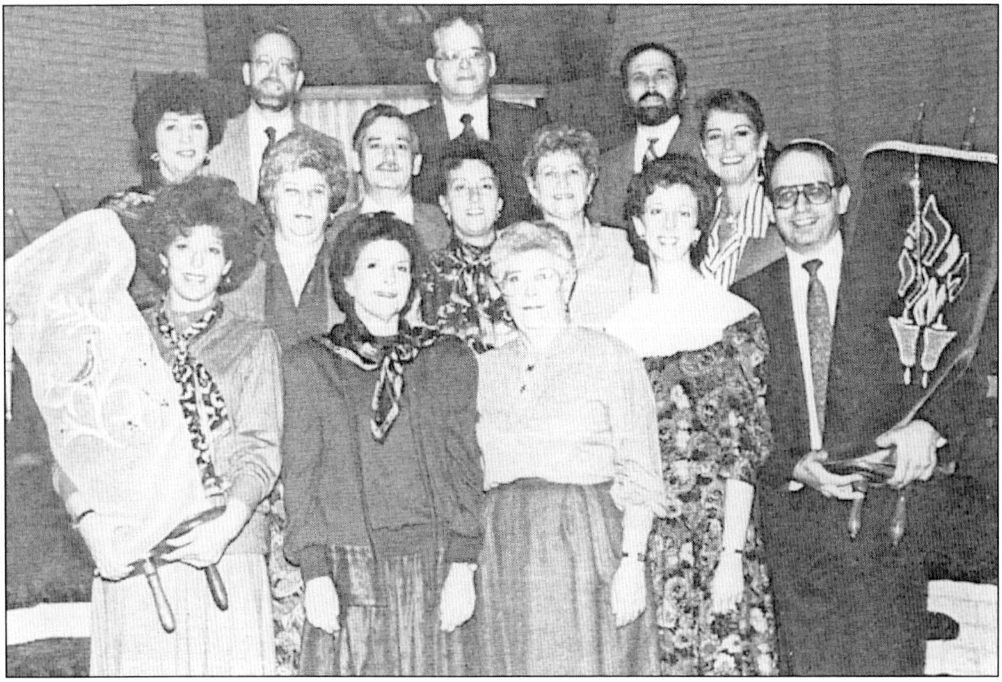

Adult B'nai Mitzvah classes have been held at B'nai Zion in 1984, 1986, and 1988. At the Mizpah Congregation there was a B'nai Mitzvah class in 1991. Pictured here is the 1988 B'nai Mitzvah Class of B'nai Zion. From left to right are as follows: (front row) Joy Greenberg, Claire Binder, Mary Spector, Sandy Zuckerman, and Larry Zuckerman; (middle row) Amelia Lebovitz, Sheila Cohen, Lester Cohen, Elinor Cohen, Martha Berman, and Pris Siskin; (back row) Barry Parker, Lester Votava, and Rabbi Richard Sherwin.

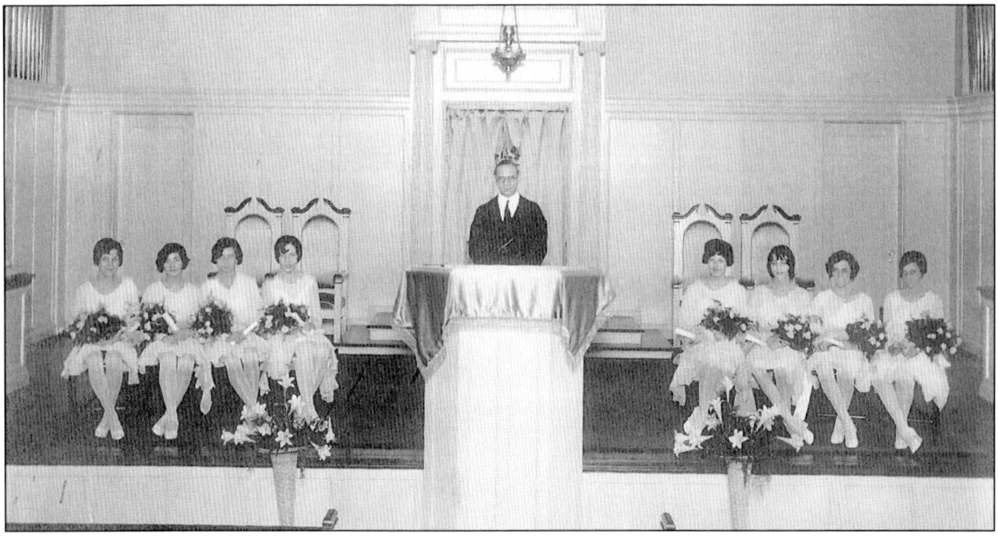

The Mizpah Congregation was the first in Chattanooga to hold confirmations. This Reform ceremony was held to mark the child's graduation from religious school. Pictured is the 1929 Confirmation Class of Rabbi Samuel Shillman. They are, from left to right, Eleanor Miller (Schwartz), Irma Robbins (Lebovitz), Rose Pearlman, Marjorie Block, Martha Josephs, Nadolyn Yalowitz, and Rosalind Feld (Baron).

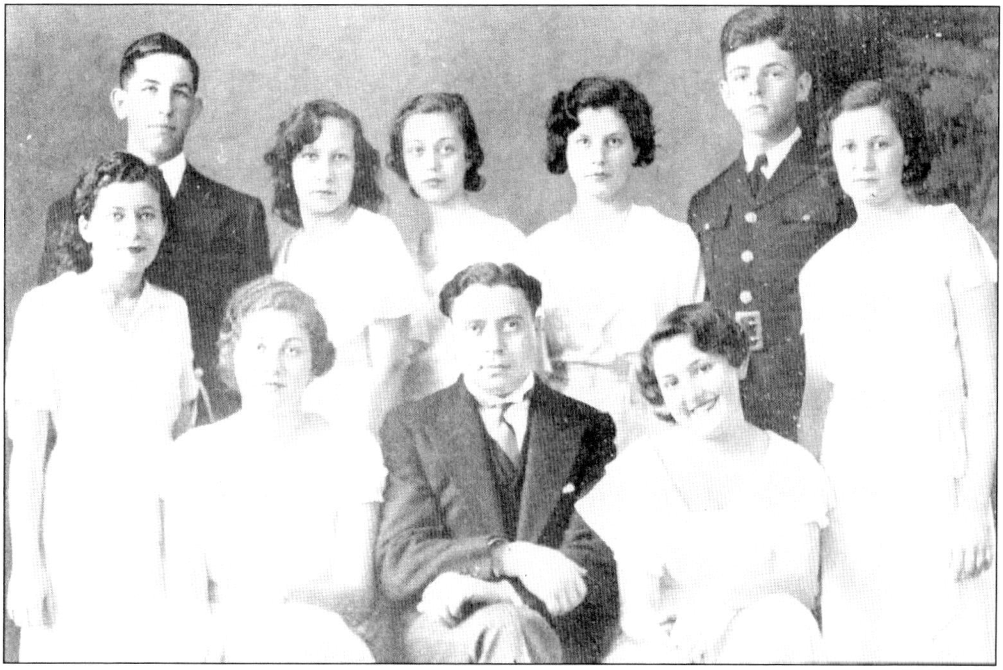

Rabbi Benjamin Parker's Confirmation Class of 1931 consisted of the following, from left to right: (front row) Goldie Raider, Frances Josephs, Rabbi Parker, Libby Winer, and Miriam Edelstein; (back row) Harry Weill, Josephine Davis, Marian Goldstein, Rebecca Winzimer, and Leo Rosenblum (Rose).

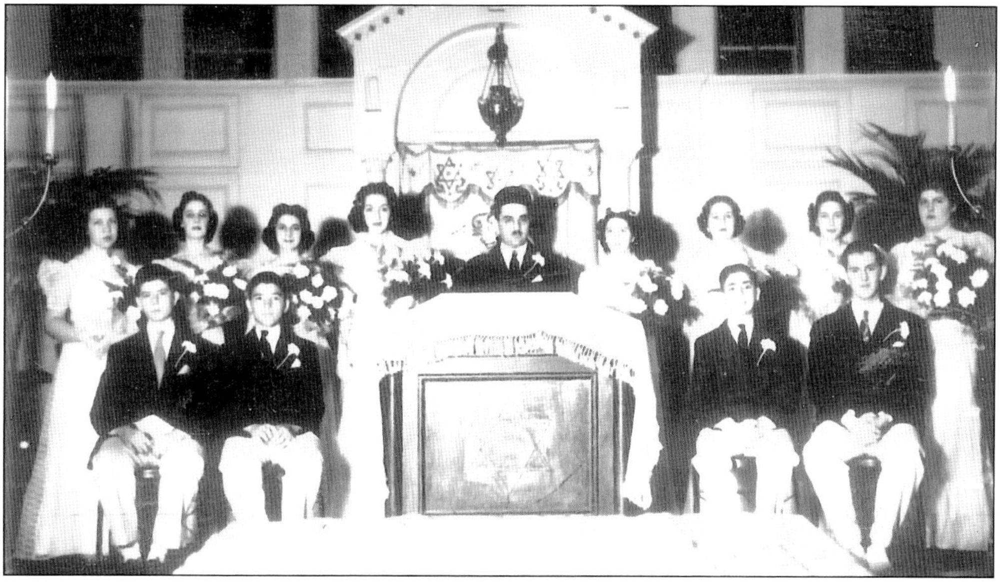

Rabbi Israel Gerstein started the religious Sunday school at B'nai Zion in 1934. The second graduating class at B'nai Zion (Confirmation) was in 1938 and included the following, from left to right: (front row) Milton Kolodkin, Marvin Finkelstein, Julius Brandman, and Herman Fine; (back row) Henrietta Rosenthal, Berneice Siskin (Wolkin), Beady Fanburg (Lieb), Sadele Prosterman (Gottler), Rabbi Gerstein, Mollie Kress (Norman), Frances Shoenig (Lander), Maxine Block (Alper), and Hannah Sayers.

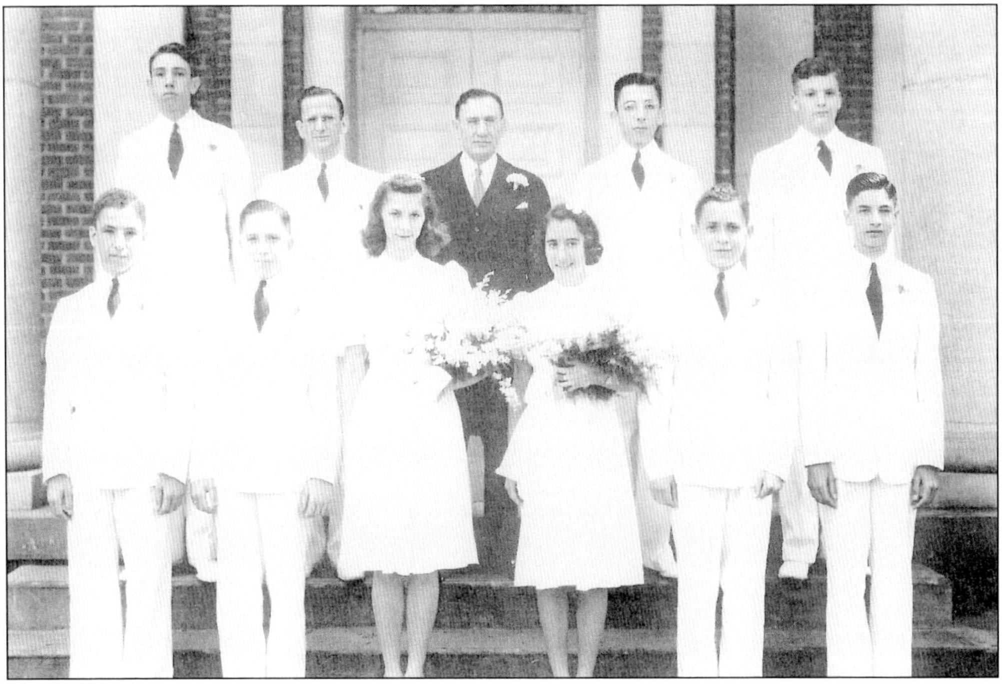

Rabbi Feinstein's Confirmation Class of 1940 included the following, from left to right: (front row) Jack Cassell, Saul Klaus, Elizabeth Effron, Barbara Schwartzman, Hershel Copelan, and David Schwartz; (back row) Henry Goodman, Ervin Newman (teacher), Rabbi Feinstein, Harris Gould, and Ira Long.

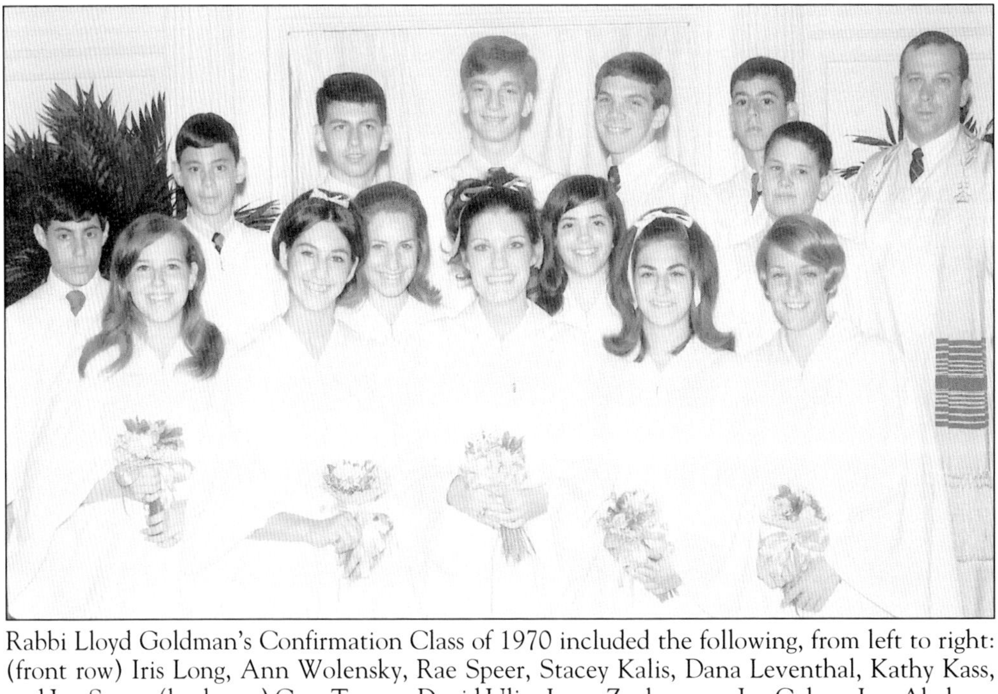

Rabbi Lloyd Goldman's Confirmation Class of 1970 included the following, from left to right: (front row) Iris Long, Ann Wolensky, Rae Speer, Stacey Kalis, Dana Leventhal, Kathy Kass, and Jan Speer; (back row) Gary Tepper, David Ulin, Larry Zuckerman, Joe Cohen, Lee Abelson, Steve Rubenstein, Elliott Shavin, and Rabbi Goldman.

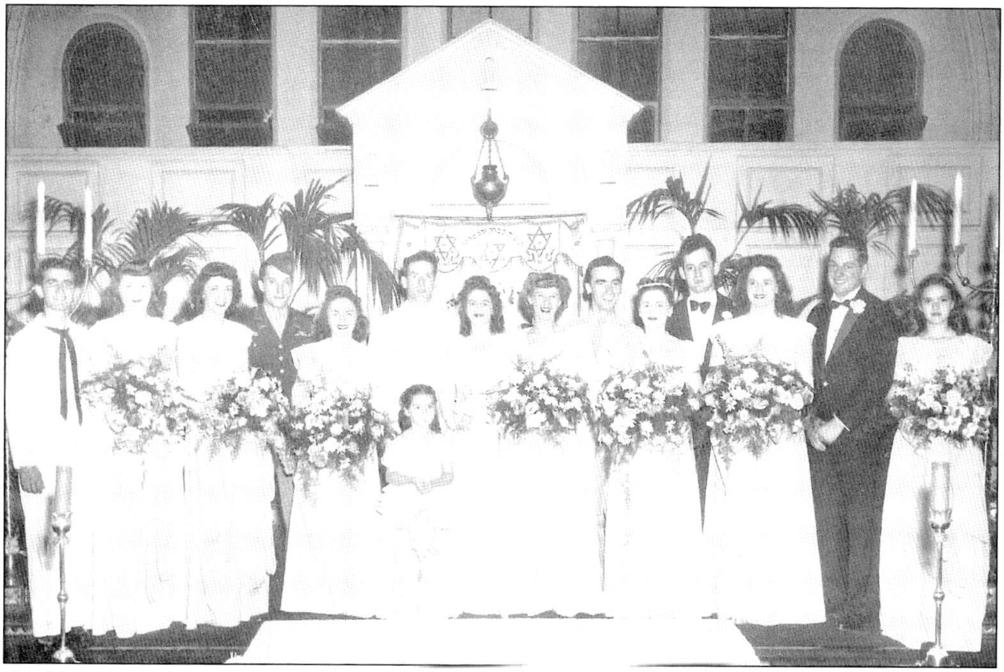

Weddings are always a joyous occasion and Jewish weddings are especially joyous! Katie Trotz and Hy Kweller were married in 1946. From left to right are Max Trotz, Dorothy Sir (Kaset), Sylvia Margolin, Syd Kweller, Esther Tandetta, groom Hy and bride Katie, flower girl Reah Polsky (Friedman), Mae Greenberg (Kaset), Herman Trotz, Helen Tandetta (Vine), Joe Sir, Rose Sir (Levine), Nat Kweller, and Shirley Trotz (Posner).

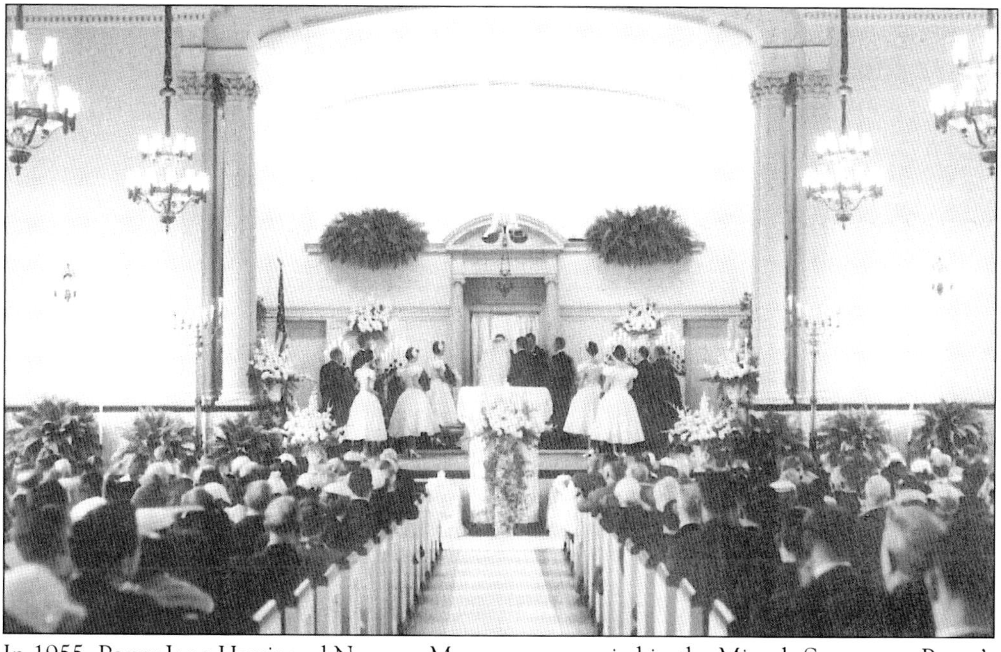

In 1955, Peggy Jane Harris and Norman Moore were married in the Mizpah Sanctuary. Peggy's parents were Celia (Levine) and Manny Harris. Peggy and Norman have two daughters, Julie and Debi.

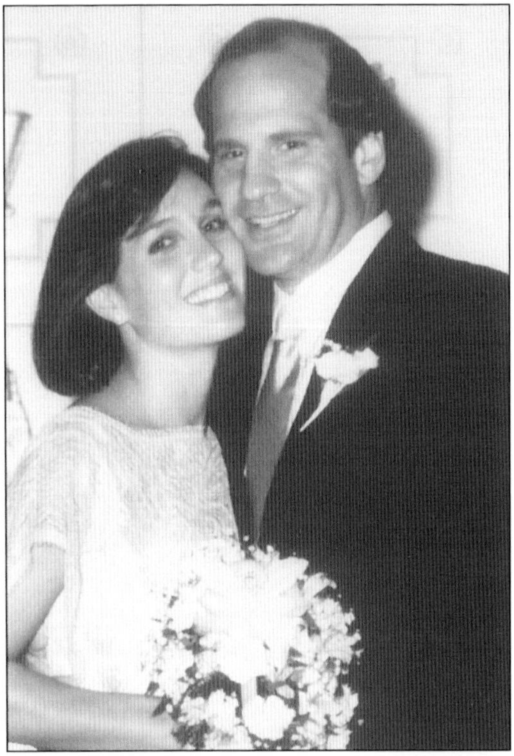

Peter and Jane Mallen are pictured on the bima of Mizpah immediately following their marriage in 1985, with Rabbis Ken Kanter and Abraham Feinstein officiating. It was the last marriage ceremony Rabbi Feinstein performed. Peter's company, Mallen Industries, Inc., is a leader in the textile industry and is designated as an IESO-9000 corporation, a coveted International certification assuring reliance on its representations. As a leader in the Atlanta Jewish community, Peter has received a letter of recognition from the Israeli Knesset signed by Eli Dayan, the Knesset majority leader.

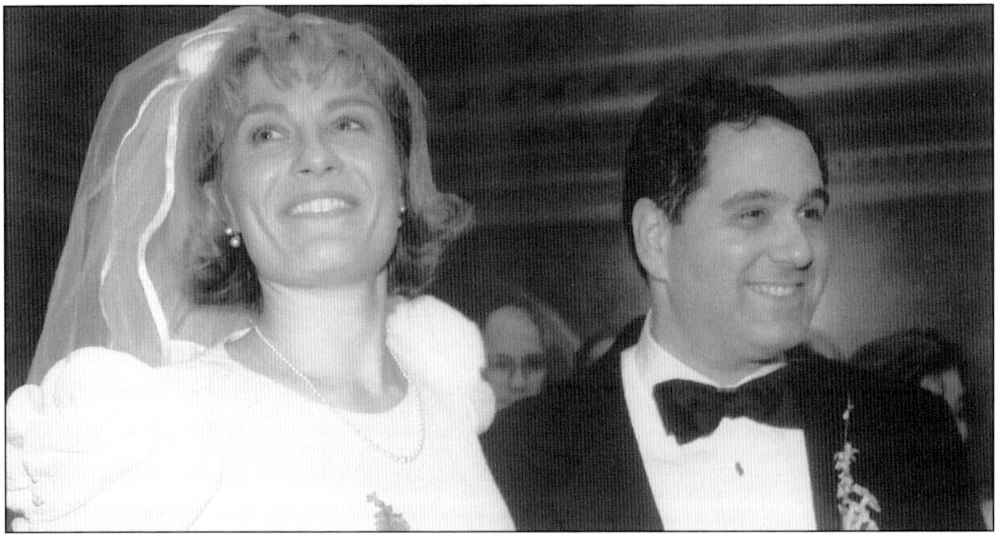

Rabbi Kenneth Kanter and Wendy Koplow were married in the Mizpah Sanctuary on February 29, 1992, with a host of friends in attendance. During his stay in Chattanooga, Rabbi Kanter served as president of the Chattanooga Clergy Association for two terms and also served for six years as chairman of the Chattanooga Human Rights and Human Relations Commission. He was honored by the Chattanooga Bar Association in May of 1992 with the Liberty Bell Award, which is presented to "a person who has given outstanding service in the promotion of better understanding of the U.S. Constitution, of the Bill of Rights, and of the rule of law." After serving the Mizpah Congregation for ten years, he moved to Nashville, Tennessee, to lead the newly established Congregation Micah.

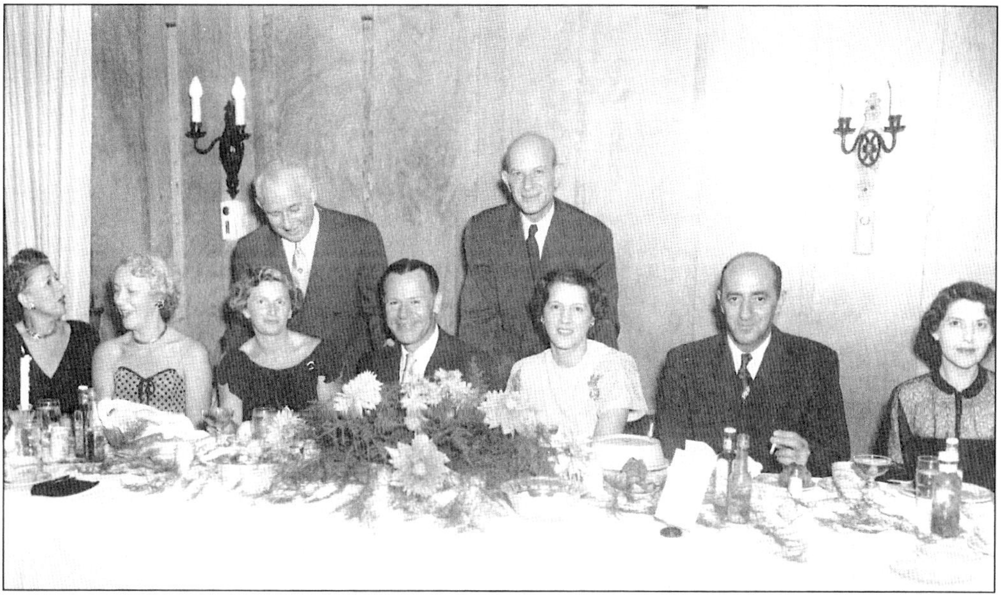

Birthday parties are fun to have! Abe Koblentz regularly celebrated his birthdays. This is his 50th birthday party at the Jewish Edgewood Country Club in 1949. Attending were Ethel Miller, Florence Block, Klari Koblentz (Abe's wife), Jo Russ, Manny Russ, Lillian Feinstein, Harry Miller, and Ben Block, among others.

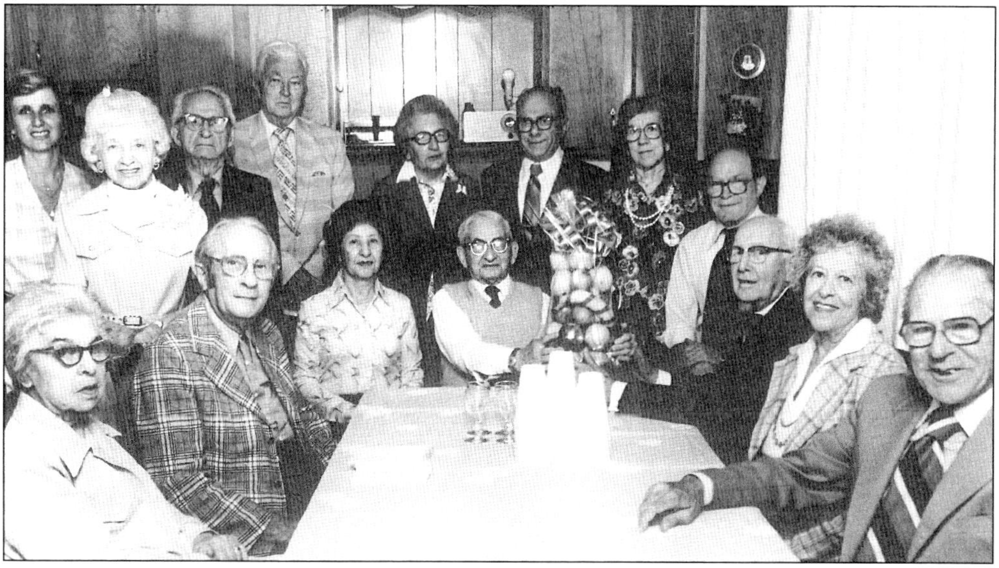

Sol Kopkin celebrated his birthday at home with a party given by the Half-Century Club in 1982. Among those present were Dora Frumin, Jack Jamieson, Lena Mott, Natalie Jamieson, Abe Koblentz, Marsha Menuskin, Mr. & Mrs. Hyman Stein, Mr. and Mrs. Alfred Ratowe, Ida Parrish, and Louis Chawkin.

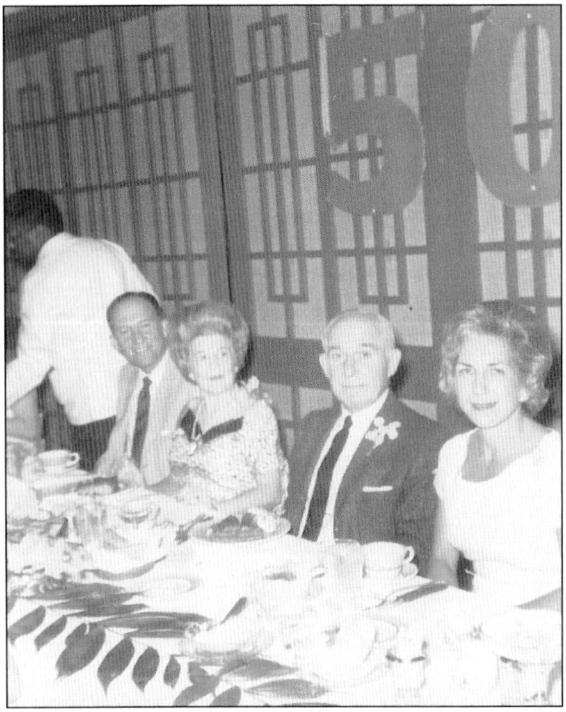

Ethel and Harry Miller celebrated their 50th (golden) wedding anniversary in 1961 at the Edgewood Country Club. With them are Dr. Harold and Eleanor Miller Schwartz, their daughter, and her husband.

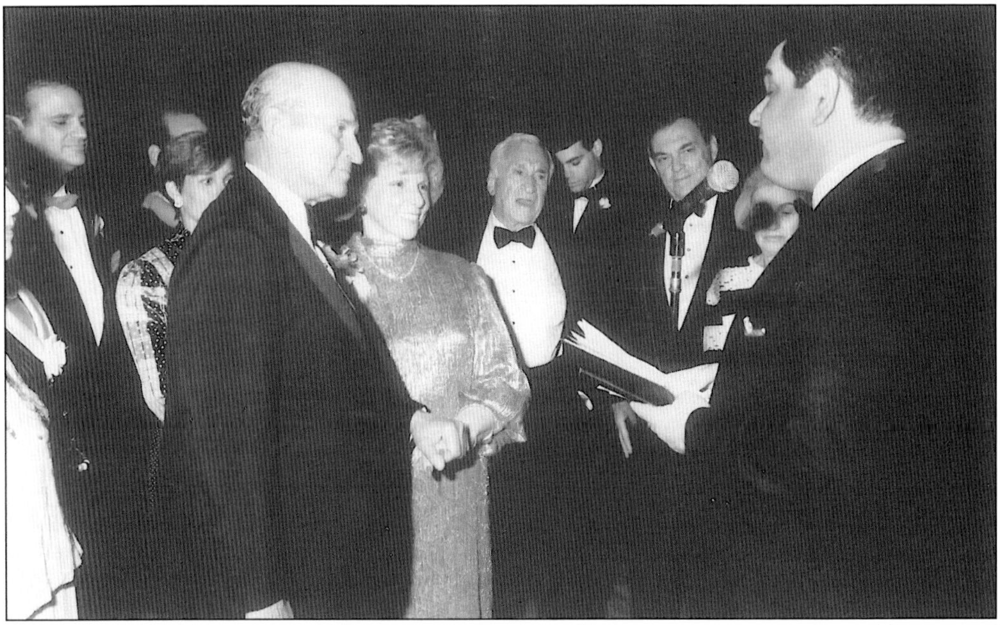

Saul (Twom) and Muriel (Goldberg) Mallen renewed their marriage vows in celebration of their 50th wedding anniversary in 1989 with Rabbi Ken Kanter officiating. Saul, an attorney, spent his career as a businessman in the textile industry. He developed a unique method of manufacturing insert pieces for women's panty hose and pioneered the use of cotton fabric in their manufacture. At one time, he was producing 100% of all panty hose crotch pieces used in the United States and abroad. Saul and his wife had three sons: Steven (who was killed in a plane crash), Ted, and Peter.

Five

Surviving with Free Enterprise:

Businesses and Commerce

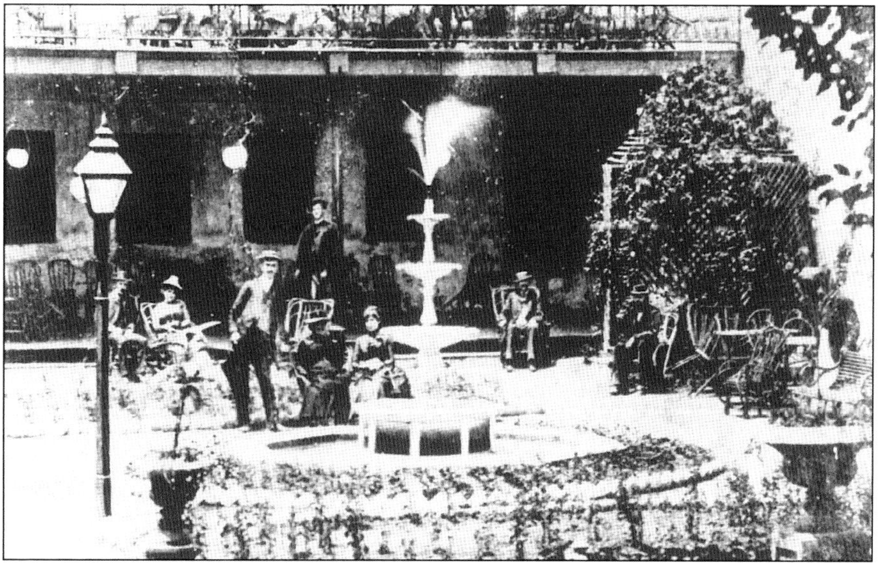

Some of the early settlers to Chattanooga opened shops of their own on Market Street. Other Jewish newcomers became peddlers and walked with their backpacks to rural districts of the South to sell their wares. Soon Halman and Reuben Blumberg opened a peddlers' supply business in Chattanooga. They not only sold supplies to the peddlers, but also went to New York to find new arrivals and to pay railroad fares from the point where the ship docked to Chattanooga. Adolph Tschopik came to Chattanooga in 1866 when he was 27 years old. He owned Tschopik's Confectionary and Fancy Grocery Store on Market Street. In 1869, he created behind his store a "sunken garden," called Tschopik's Garden, which became the real center of society in those days. This was where amateur shows, social hops, and evening parties took place. The garden had four large ornamental gaslights, which provided the illumination for these evening events. Besides his business, he was a leader in Mizpah's Hebrew Benevolent Society. (Chattanooga/Hamilton County Bicentennial Library.)

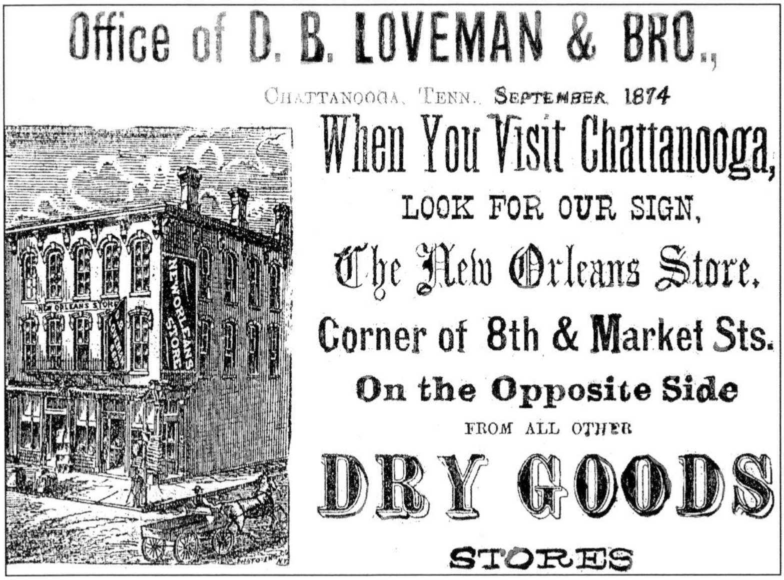

D.B. Loveman opened the earliest department store in Chattanooga on Market Street, named the New Orleans Store, in 1875. The name was soon changed to Lovemans. It operated into the 1980s in several bigger and more handsome buildings that Loveman built. An earlier businessman was Simon Geismar, who came to town in 1869 and opened Geismars' Store on Market Street with his brother Samuel.

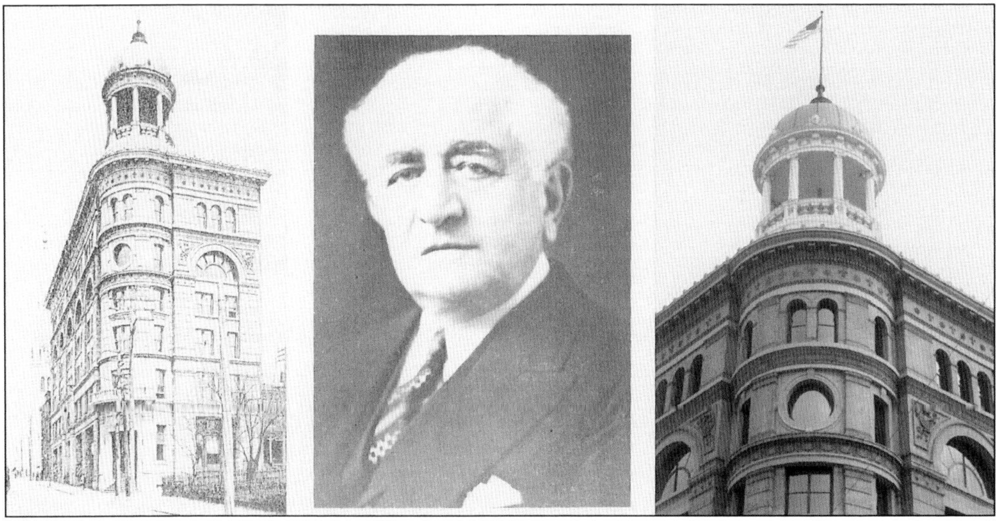

In 1878, Adolph S. Ochs, at age 20, purchased *The Chattanooga Times* for $250 and started operating his newspaper empire with $37.50 in capital. In 1896, Ochs purchased the *New York Times*, but continued to publish his Chattanooga paper as well. Adolph was a great philanthropist in early Chattanooga. He helped to build the public library, roads, hospitals, synagogues, public parks, and an opera house for stage productions, vaudeville acts, orchestra presentations, and silent films. The newspapers are still owned and operated by his descendants. The Times Building is located at Georgia and Eighth Streets and was completed in 1892. In 1942, the newspaper moved to larger quarters. With its golden dome, it is sometimes called the Dome Building, and is a prominent Chattanooga landmark. (Times Building photo courtesy of the *Atlanta Jewish Times*.)

The Schwartz family came from Hungary. Henry settled first in Nashville, then Murfreesboro, then Atlanta, and finally in Chattanooga in 1875. He opened the Schwartz Brothers Shoe Store at 812 Market Street with his three brothers. Sam is shown here in front; in the back are Bob, Leo, and Henry.

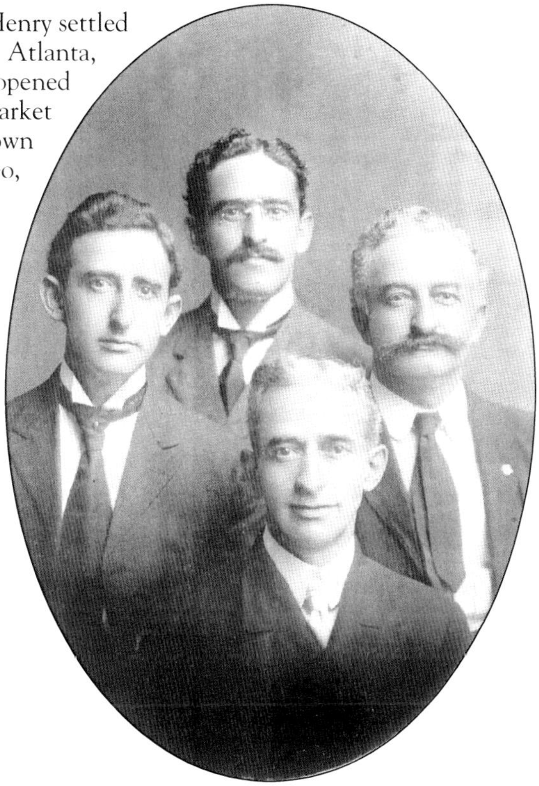

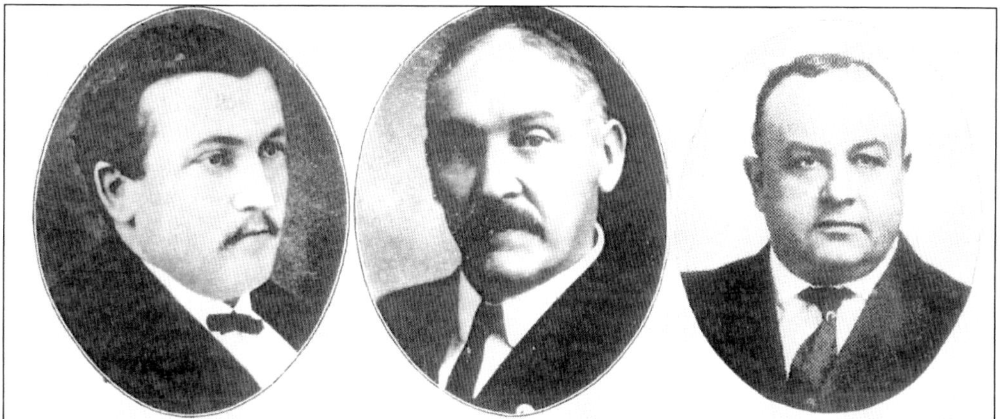

The Gottschalk Furniture Company operated at 732 Market Street from 1878 until 1920, having been started by James Gottschalk. Henry Rose entered the business in 1883, and L.B. Wertheimer entered in 1894 (he was the great-granduncle of Iris Long Abelson and Flossie Weill). The company was the largest exclusive furniture house south of the Ohio River.

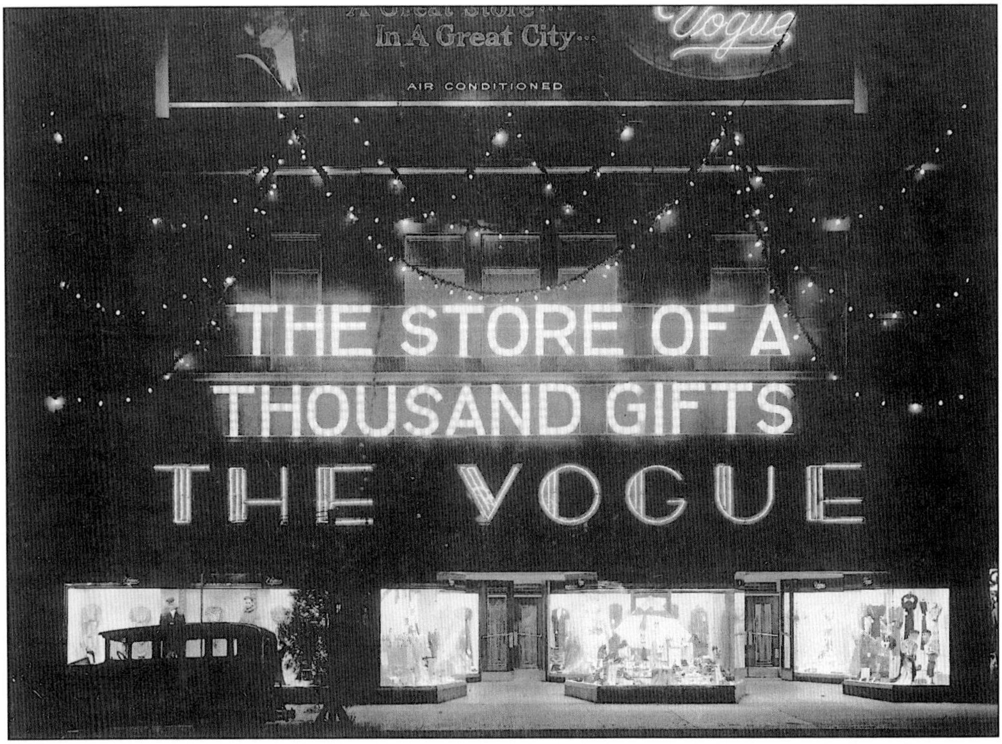

The Vogue, founded by Harry Miller in 1921, operated on Market Street until 1955. It was a high-class, ladies, ready-to-wear store for over 50 years. Here is the store, decorated for Christmas business in 1938.

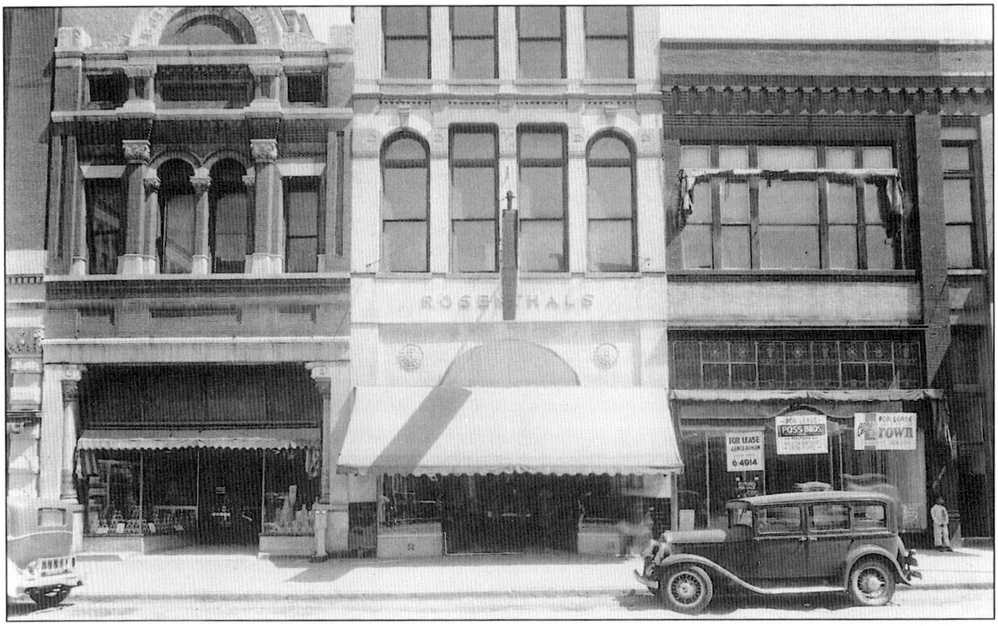

Rosenthals' clothing firm was located at 812 Market, the old site of Morris Friedman Clothiers and before that the Schwartz Bros. Shoe Store. Charles M. Rosenthal began conducting business in Chattanooga in 1904.

In 1920, Abe and Lou Effron opened a clothing store on the corner of Sixth and Market Streets. In 1928, the business had grown so much that a new three-story Effrons' Department Store was built at Sixth and Market Streets (where the new Municipal Courts Building is today). The store was known as "The Home of Low Prices." Abe's children were Sidney of Chattanooga and Anita (Shalett) of Washington, D.C. Lou's children were Joy (Adams), Jo Ann (Richelson), and Louise (Spector), all of Chattanooga, and Elizabeth (Raisin) of Dalton, Georgia.

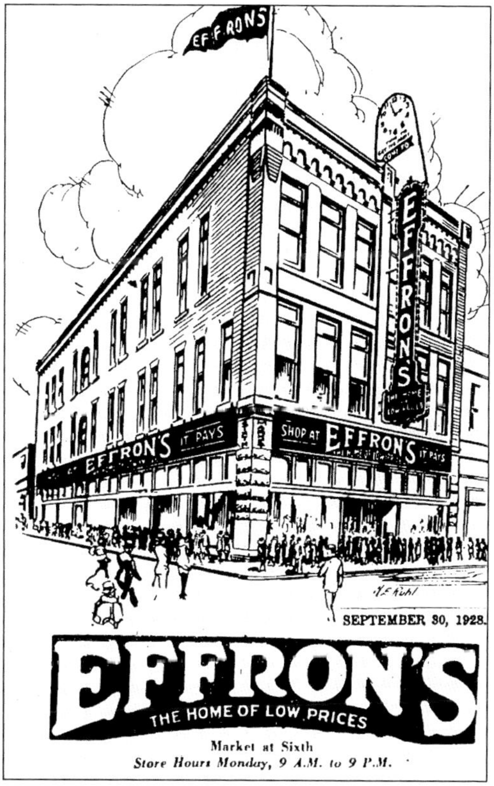

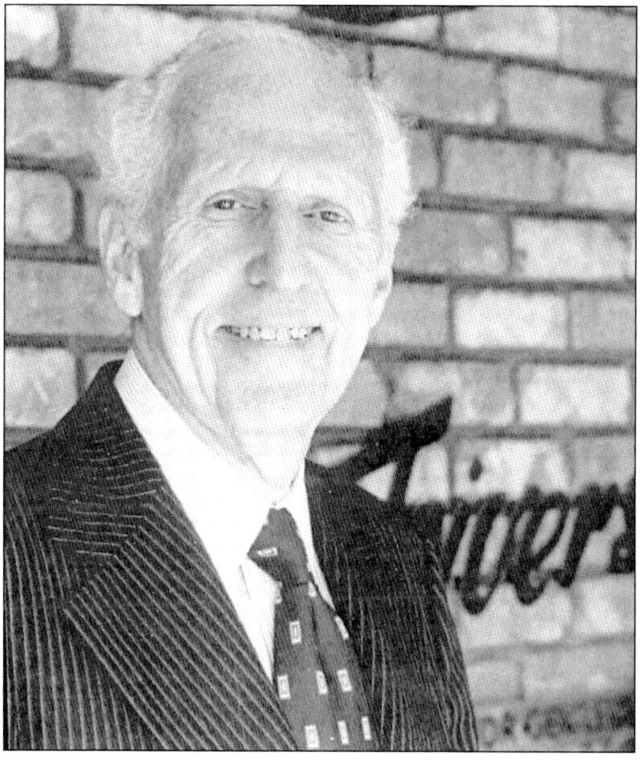

Ira Trivers opened an exclusive men's store in the early 1940s. He and his son Tom operated the shop until 1990. Arno Goldstein, Abe Koblentz, and the Abe Goldstein family also operated clothing stores in downtown Chattanooga.

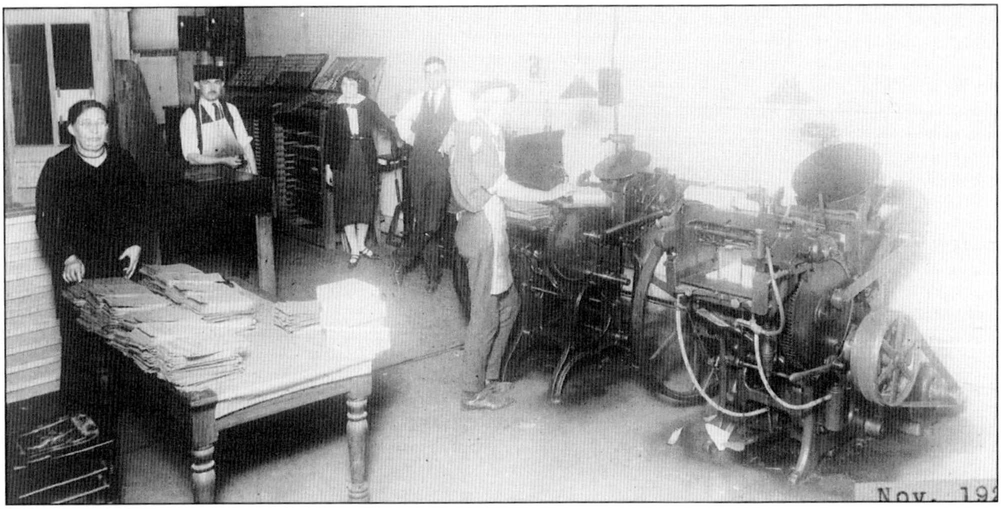

Jewish printers Phil Angel and Henry Morris opened the Angel Printing Company in 1919. It operated for over 72 years. Phil was married to Sadie and their children are Elinor (Breman) of Atlanta and Jeanne (Weil) and Celia (Helman.) of Columbus, Georgia. Henry's family is noted in Chapter 3. Both founders were very active in every phase of Jewish life in Chattanooga.

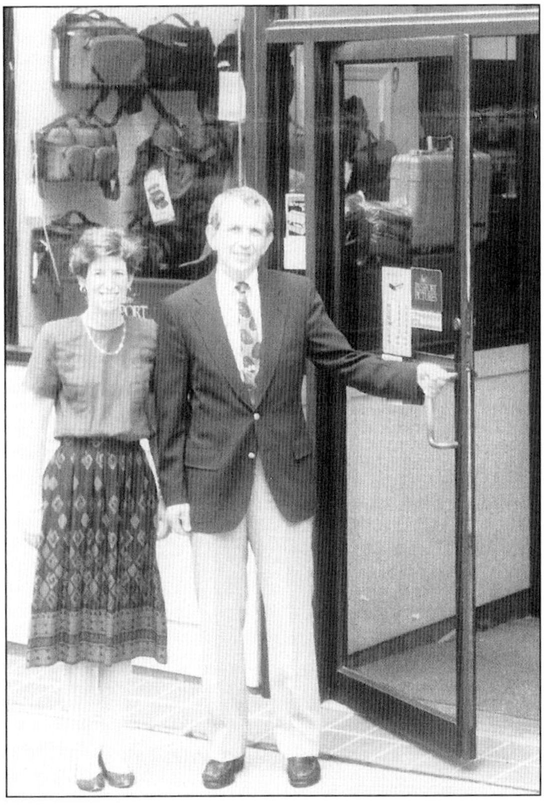

In 1915, the Violet Studio Shop was founded by Herman Cohn. His son Lester continued the operation, and by 1996, the third and fourth generation of Cohns were still operating the Violet Camera Shop on Seventh Street. Pictured here are Herb Cohn and his daughter Amy (Cohen). The Boys' Shop operated on Market Street for over 40 years and was founded by Henry Silverstein. Henry was married to Lena, and they had one son, Jay, who joined his father in the business. Jay was married to Pearl Ann, and they had two daughters, Jan and Mathilde.

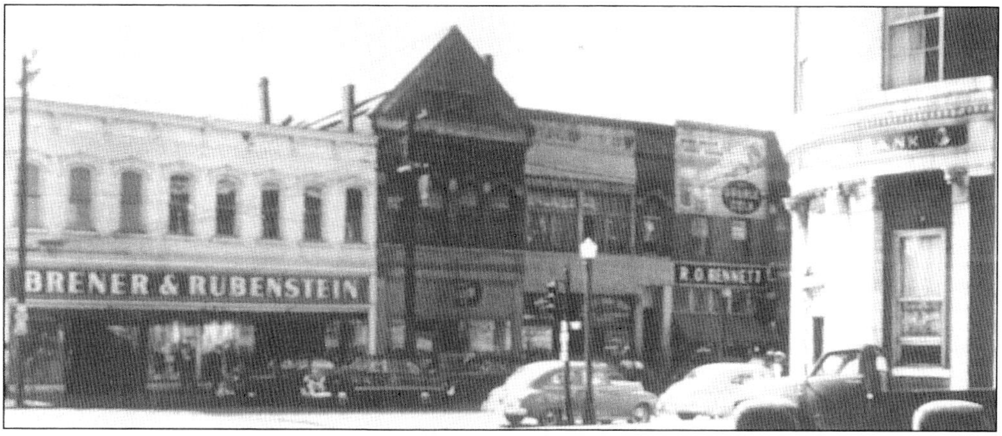

Main Street was another location for the stores of Jewish merchants. Patriarch Max Brener came to Chattanooga in 1889 from Lithuania and became a pack peddler. He was naturalized in 1894 and opened Breners' Department Store in 1896. His son Robert, along with Max's son-in-law, Lawrence Rubenstein, and Lawrence's son Henry, continued to run the store until the late 1970s. Other Main Street merchants were Center's, Levin's, Eidex's, and Winer's. Max Brener's first wife was Gussie Dora Long (the daughter of I. Long), and his second wife was Tillye Schas of Asheville, North Carolina. He had six children: Jeannette (Orkin), Annabelle (Rubenstein), Gussie (Abel), Marjorie (Seigel of Livington Manor, New York), Herman, and Robert. Herman Brener operated Uncle Herman's Shoe Store on Market Street.

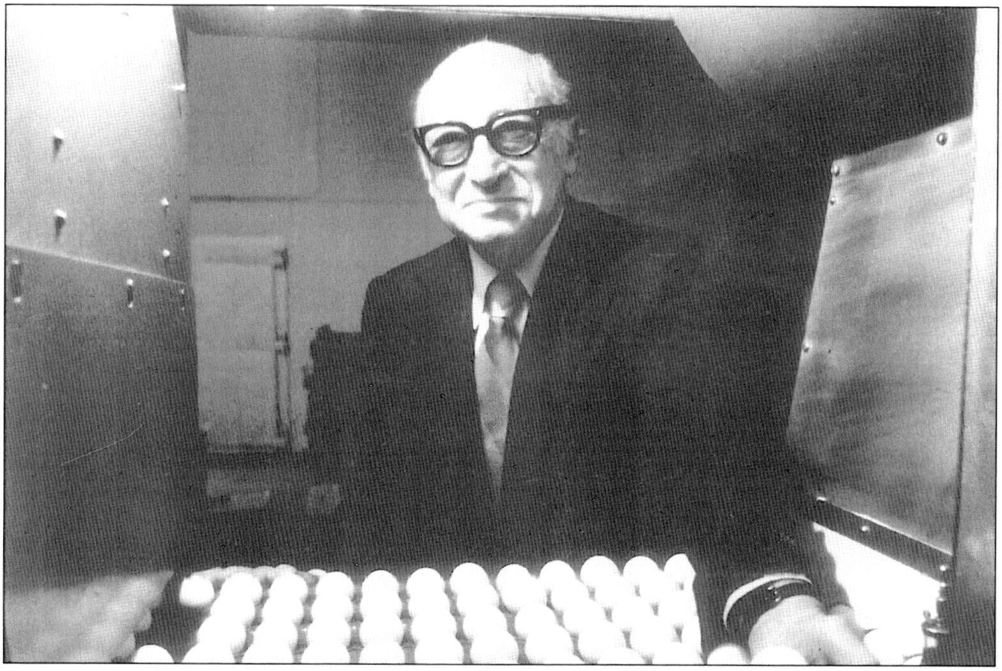

Harry Levin was perhaps Tennessee's most adept businessman. He started his business empire during the Depression in 1932 and became the president and owner of the Seed Feed Supply Company, Loret Mills, Farms of Loret, the Loret Chick Hatchery, the Loret Resort Villas, and the Loret Marina on Chickamauga Lake. Levin was known throughout the South for his egg and broiler business. He named his companies Loret by combining the nickname of his wife, Ette (Edelstein), with that of his daughter Lori.

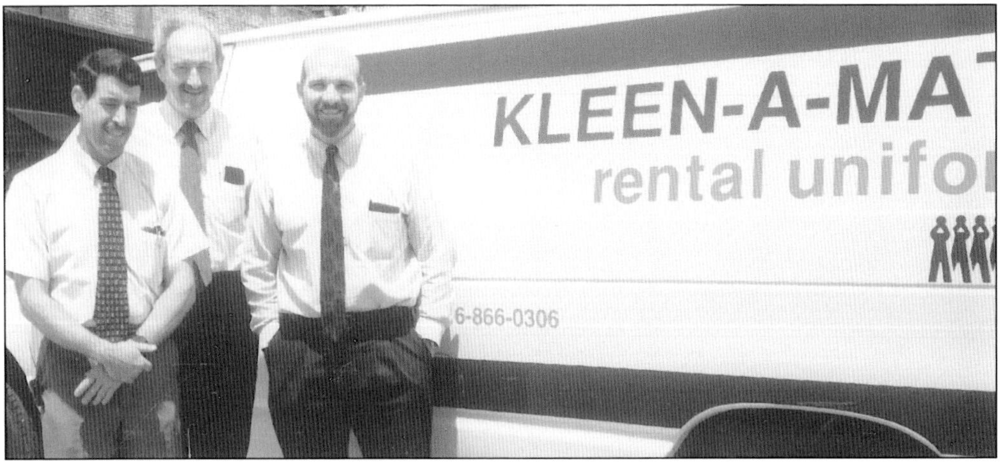

The Kleen-A-Matic Enterprises were started in the late 1930s by Sam, Marvin, and later, Mark Spector. Today, besides the rental uniform plant in Rossville, there are seven retail dry cleaning branches. The greatly expanded business includes divisions of dry cleaning, rental uniforms, dust control rental, and service to the health care industry. Partner Susan Spector (Harker) is at the Highway 58 plant, and partners Michael (the son of Mark), Julius Spector (a brother of the founders), and Lee Abelson (a nephew of Julius) are at the McFarland Avenue rental uniform plant. Julius (Juby) is married to Louise (Fuz) (Effron), and they have three daughters: Cheryl (Bethune) of Los Angeles, California, Barbara (Siegelman) of Atlanta, Georgia, and Susan (Harker) of Chattanooga.

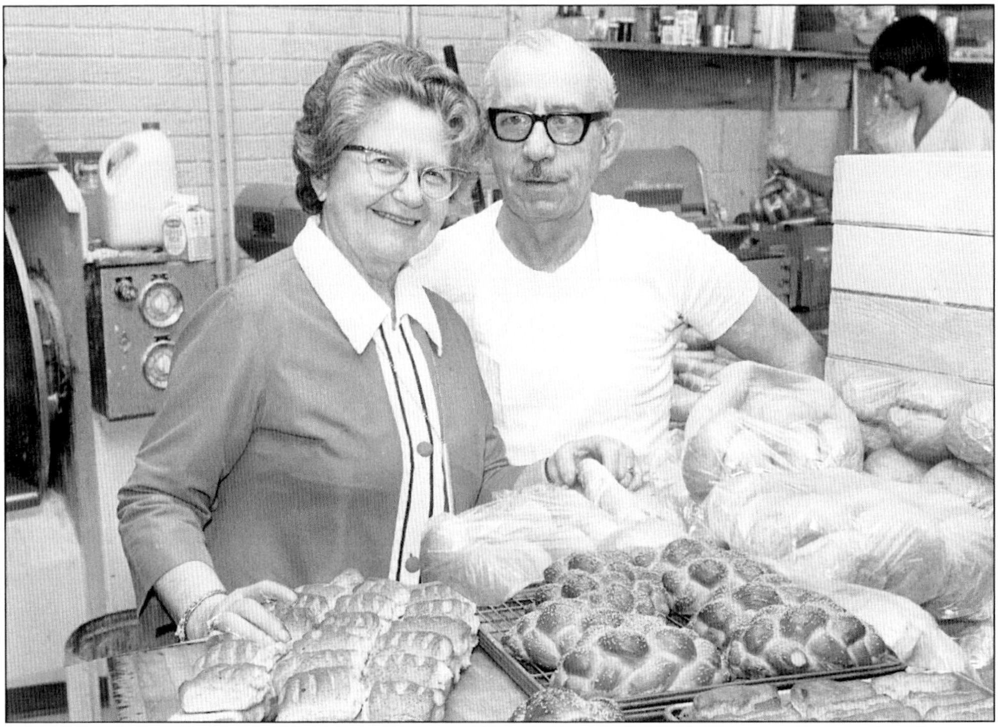

The Greens' Bakery and Grocery was owned by Isadore and Fela Green, who came to Chattanooga in the 1950s, having survived the Holocaust. They owned the city's official Jewish bakery until the 1980s. The couple had two children, Henry and Mitzi.

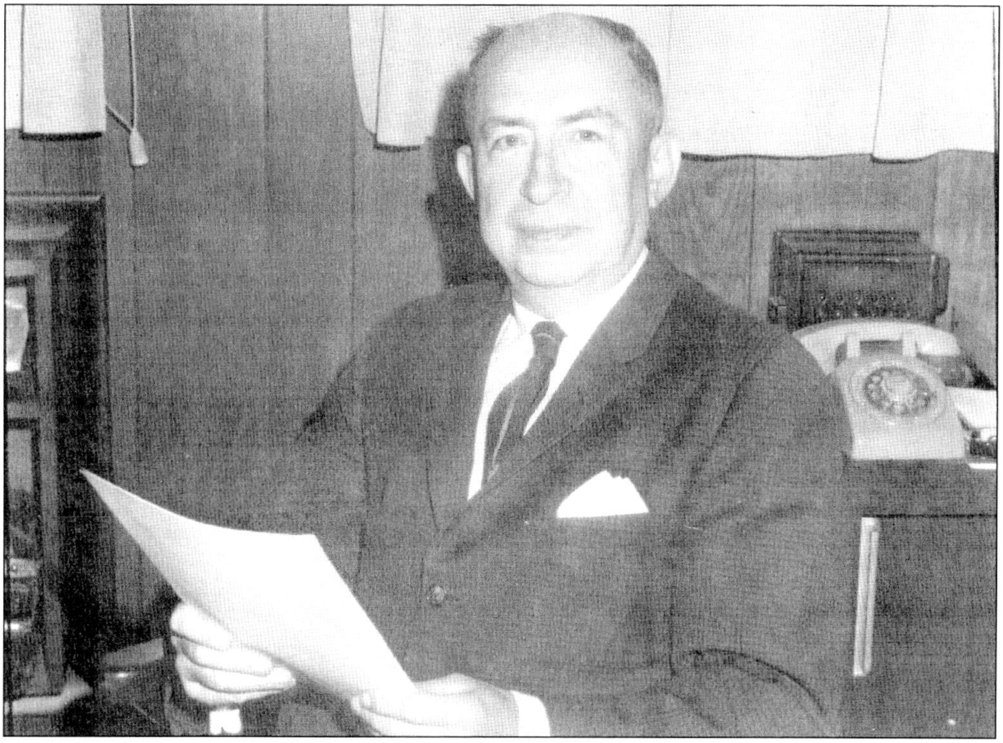

George Berke was the president, manager, and one of the organizers of the Dixie Savings Stores Grocery Cooperative, beginning in the early 1930s. Many newcomers to Chattanooga in the 1930s went into the grocery business by opening small "Mom and Pop" grocery stores in neighborhoods all over town. They bought their stock from the Dixie Cooperative. Herbert St. Goar was associated in the business, too, and by the 1990s, his son Edward was helping manage the company.

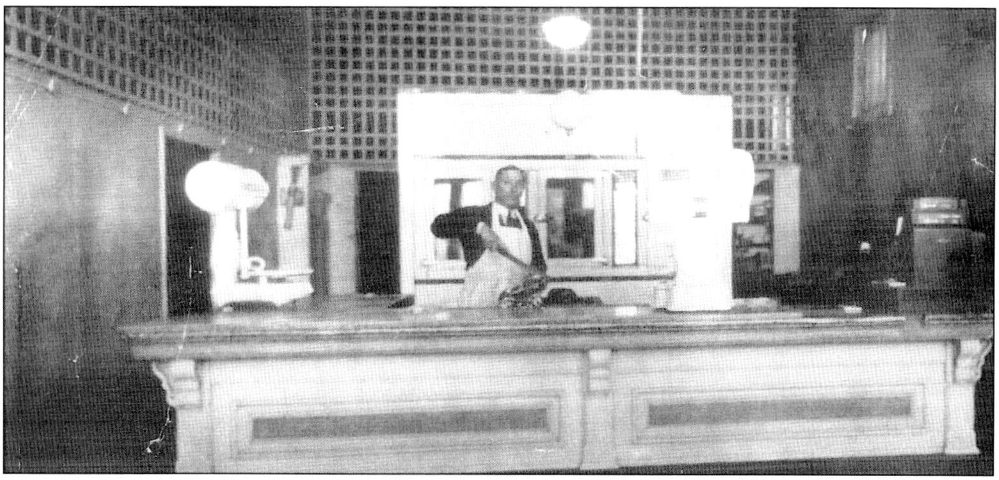

A Kosher butcher shop was owned by the Isadore Saluk family from 1919 until the 1980s. It was known as the New York Meat Market and was located at 401 West Eighth Street.

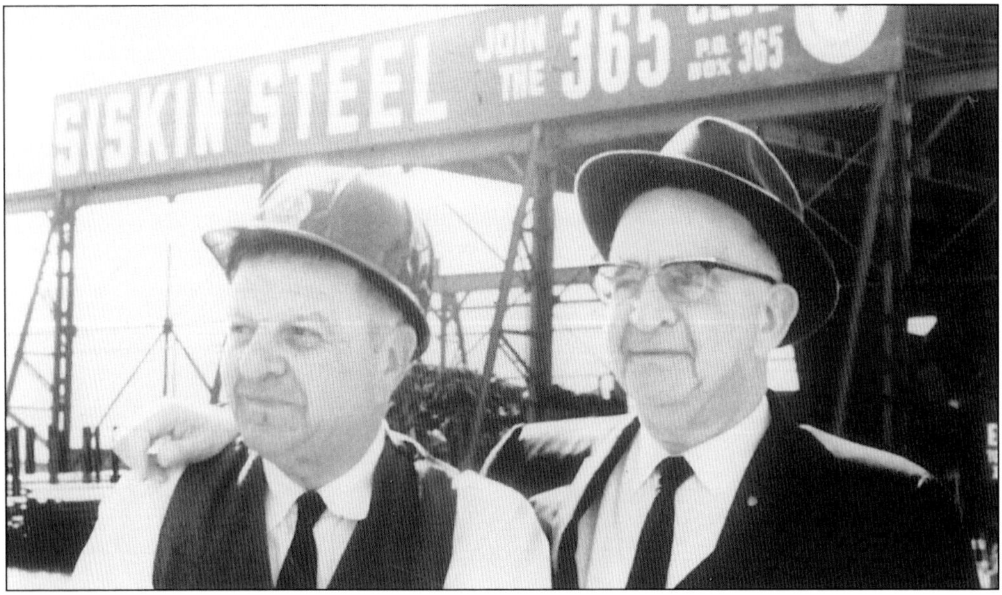

Siskin Steel was a family business from the earliest of days when Robert Siskin and his wife Hannah, immigrated to the United States from Lithuania in 1895. Robert and Hannah lived on the West Side and had three children: Sarah (Prigoff) , Mose, and Garrison. By 1917, Mose and Garrison joined their father in the business, and they became sole owners. In 1932, Mose married Eva Witt of Columbus, Georgia, and they had two children, Claire Ethel and Robert Hyman. Garrison married Goldie Temmerson of Birmingham, Alabama, and they had two daughters, Helen and Anita. Mose's son Robert and Garrison's son-in-law, Merv Pregulman (married to Helen), came into the business. The business continues to grow in 1996 with the fourth generation of the family in the operation. The 365 Club was started in the early days by Mose and Garrison to help raise funds for the rehabilitation of the handicapped. The slogan was "Give a penny a day for each day of the year." Eventually, the Siskin brothers established the Foundation and poured thousands of dollars into the hospital and their other endeavors.

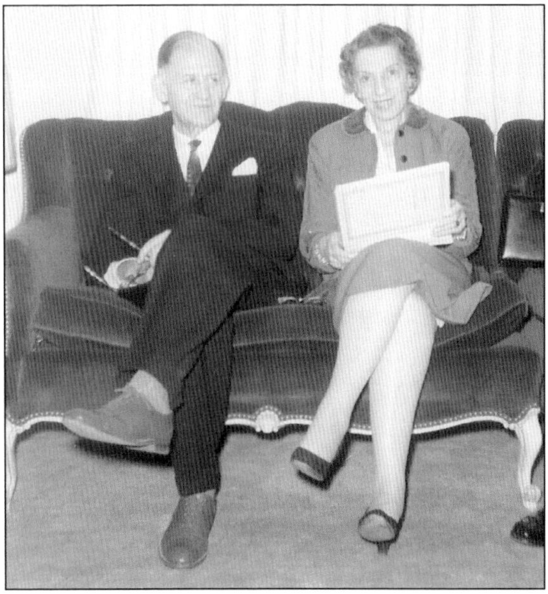

The Brody Jewelry Store in Rossville was founded by Louis and Lil Brody in the mid-1930s. Louis' father, Philip, married Annie in Chattanooga in 1890. They had eight children: Lena, Louis, Hymie, Mannie, Ida, Sam, Hilda, and Harry. All but Louis' family moved to either Atlanta, Birmingham, or Rochester, New York. Louis and Lil had one son, Edward. He married Helen, and they had two children, Mike and Cindy. Others in Chattanooga in the jewelry business were Jerry Bogo, Kenneth and Steve Gordon of Matisoffs, Morris Levine of Elesay Jewelry, and Al and Bert Shulman of Hamilton Distributors.

Ray Solomon is a man of three successful careers! After serving in the Navy in World War II, he graduated from the University of Tennessee at Knoxville in engineering, with a specialty in heating and air conditioning, and went to work at the Chattanooga Dupont Plant. He and his wife, Helen, then started a wedding photography business (the outgrowth of a childhood hobby) and "covered" 500 weddings in five years! Then, in 1953, they founded the Camera and Craft Shop and ended up with a chain of five shops, which they sold to Wolf Camera in 1981. Ray then started a new enterprise in life insurance and financial planning. By 1997, he had formed the Solomon Financial Group with grandson Stuart Wood. Ray and Helen are the parents of seven children: Gail, Louise, Karen, Rose Ann, Lee, Michael, and Barton. (Robert William Copelan.)

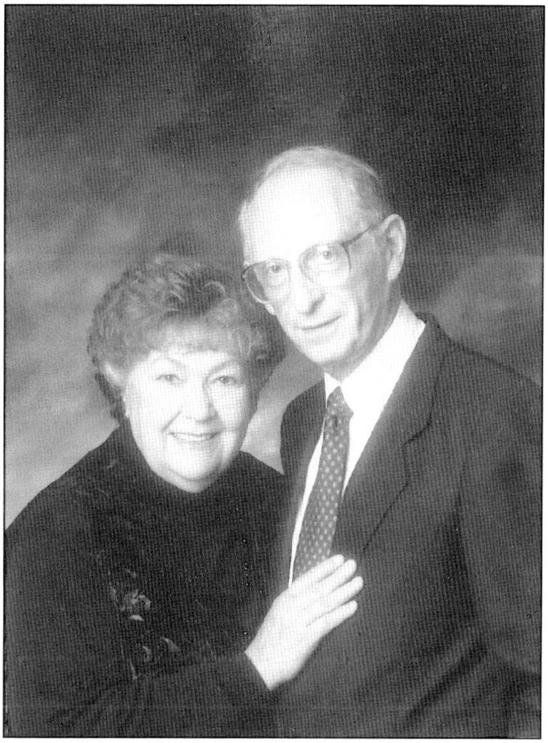

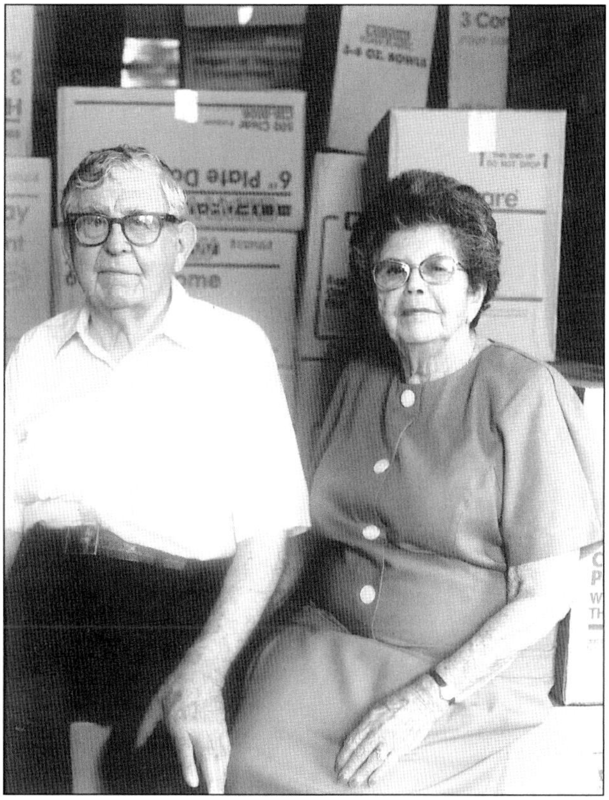

Jacobs' Wholesale Candy Company was founded in 1934 by Adolph and Dorothy (Abramson) Jacobs on Market Street. Through the years, the name has been changed to the Jacobs Wholesale Paper Company; it is now operated by their daughter Helen, her husband, Victor Hanan, and their son Michael at 1300 Chestnut Street. Adolph and Dorothy had three daughters: Helen, Audrey (Mahler) of Boston, and Rosalind (Goldberg) of Boynton Beach, Florida. (John Pregulman.)

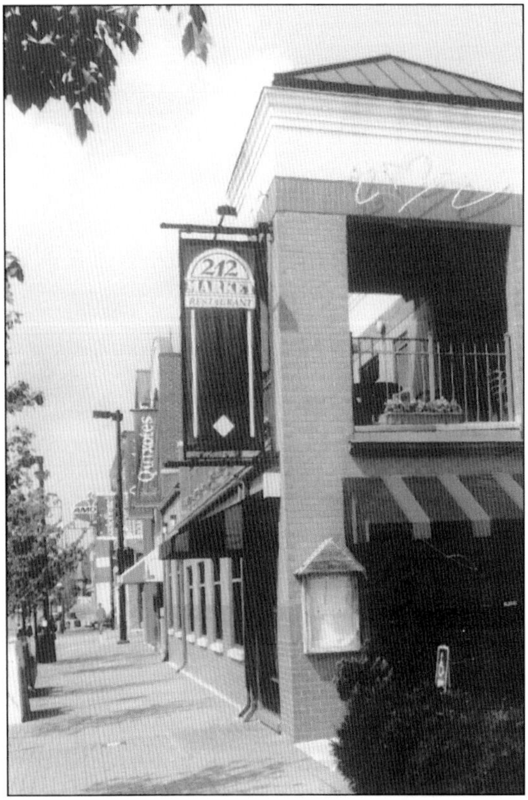

Maggie and Dr. Tibor (Ted) Moses arrived in Chattanooga in 1975 following Ted's 25-year career in the USAF as a dentist. Maggie, a registered dietitian, served for 15 years as the nutrition director for the Southeast region of the Tennessee Department of Public Health. They had four children: Frank, a physician at the Walter Reed Army Hospital; Jon, a systems programmer at the Tennessee Valley Authority for 18 years until his untimely death; Susan, who has an associates chef's degree from the Culinary Institute of America; and Sally, who manages the family restaurant. After Ted passed away, the three women decided to go into the restaurant business in 1992, and a new building was built at 212 Market Street, named the 212 Market Restaurant. In Ted's memory, the Moses family continues supporting the Mizpah Congregation's "Goldman-Moses Scholar in Residence Fund," an ongoing event that features a different world-renowned celebrity coming each year to chair an educational program.

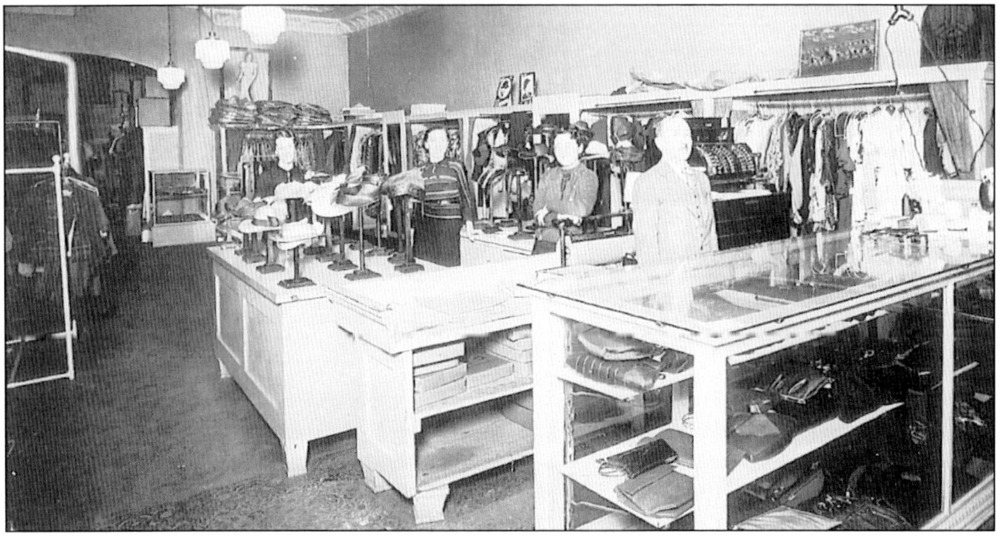

The Ard family was one of the early Jewish families in Cleveland, Tennessee. Nathan Ard opened his Ready-to-Wear Store in Cleveland in the early 1930s. His only child, Isabelle (Feintuch), is pictured with him. Her husband was Manuel, and they had two children, Theodore and Marcia Lee. Another Jewish family in Cleveland is the Sid Rubin family, who came to town in 1955 and opened Wood's Jewelers Inc. at 263 N. Ocoee Street. Sid's brother Aaron and his son Bernie are also in Cleveland. Other Jewish families who have lived in Cleveland include the Millenders, the Hecklins, and the Wenders.

Six

Creating Institutions and Organizations:

Community Centers and Clubs

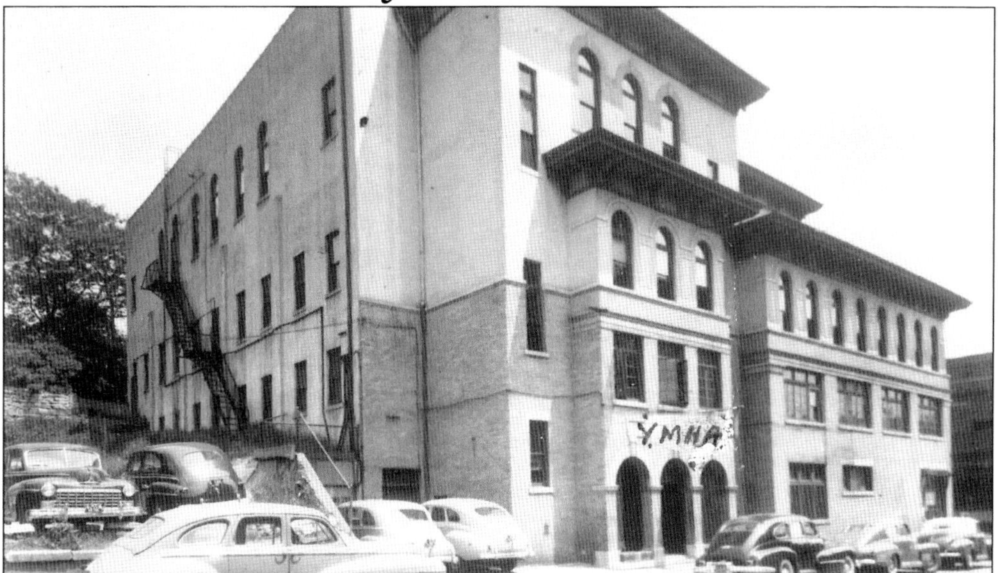

The Young Men's Hebrew Association (YMHA) was organized in 1906 by Harry Winer, Jake Levine, Stanley Lachman, Dr. S.H. Long, Dr. Edward E. Reisman Sr., Herman Goodman Jr., and Abe Solomon to promote recreation for Jewish boys of Chattanooga. A brick building at 617 Cherry Street was leased by the organization and occupied until 1920. In 1919, donations were collected that enabled the association to erect a structure at 524 Sixth Street at Cherry Street. This new building was a four-story, brick-and-stucco structure, containing a large assembly room, gymnasium, auditorium, dining room, kitchen, and five small meeting rooms. The organization became a victim of the Depression in 1935, and the building was sold to the Frye Institute. Harry Winer was the first president (1906–1916) of the YMHA, and Julius Kushner was the last (1930–1935).

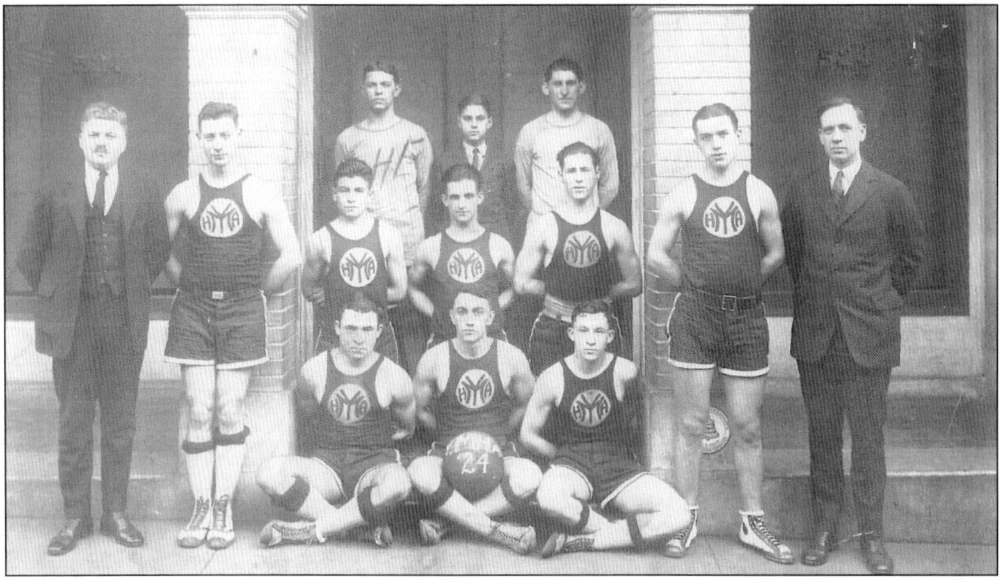

The 1924 YMHA Basketball Team poses for a photograph. Some of the young men are Myer H. Winer (in the center of the second row), Mose Siskin (at the far left in the second row), Mike Edelstein (second from the left in the second row), and Mose Lebovitz (second from the far right in the second row).

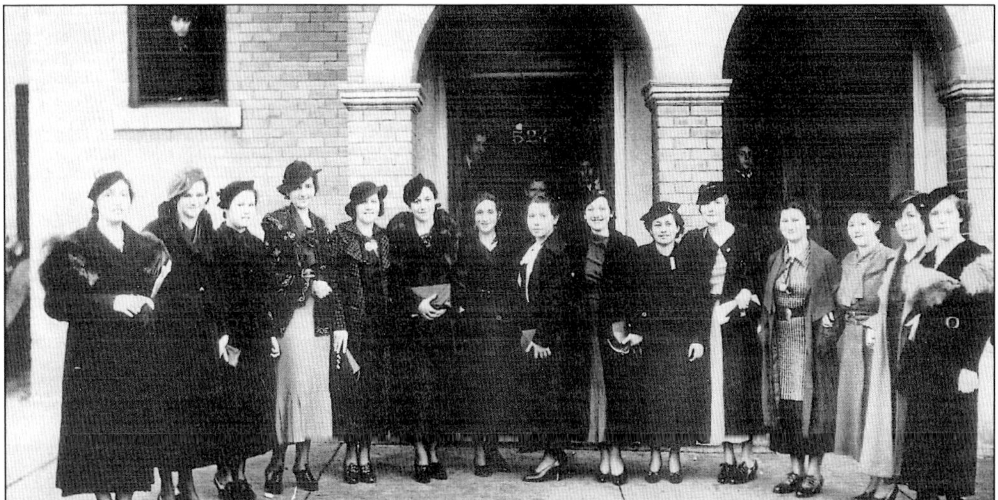

Standing in front of the YMHA Building in 1932 is the Young Judaea Club. They are, from left to right, Mary Brandman (Hecklin), Pearl Nash, Deborah Rabin (Freeman), Miriam Winer, Pauline "Pishie" Berman, Annie Freeman (Bush), Sadye Fruman, Freida Goldstein (Cohen), Mary Stahl, Goldie Raider (Velinsky), Diana Rausen, Bertha Shavin (Philips), Dinah Susman (Terkeltaub), Ruth Solomon (Liebling), and Rose Wise (Sorin). Looking through the windows are, from left to right, Annie Solomon, Teddy Morris, Joe Wise, and Danny Weintraub. The Chattanooga Young Judaea Girls' Club was organized in 1920 by Mrs. Harry Winer. Years later, a boys' group of Young Judaea, called the ZIP Society, was organized by Abe Winer. Activities of the clubs were many and varied, and included public holiday celebrations, debating contests, plays, social affairs, athletic events, and support for Zionism.

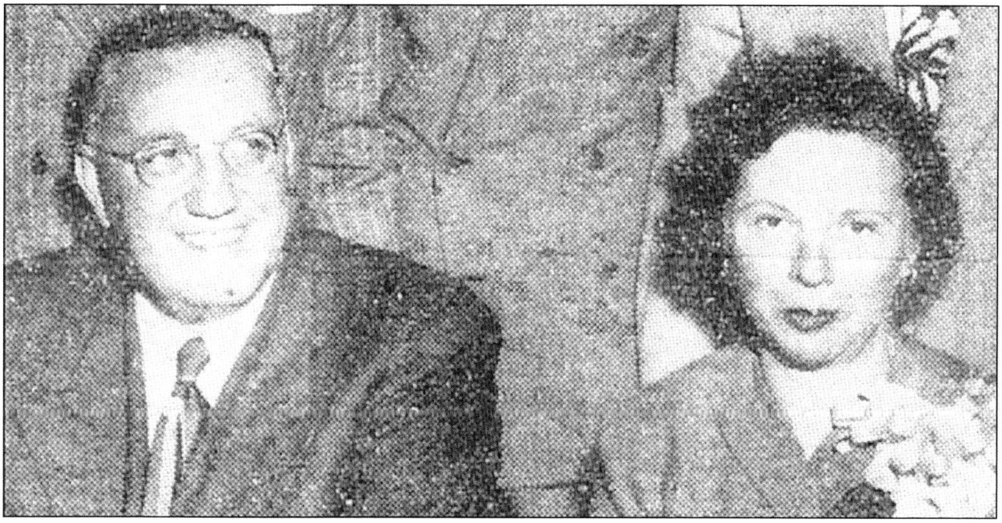

The Chattanooga Jewish Community Center (JCC) was organized in 1944 and operated until June 30, 1993, when it was merged with a federation. The combination name was the Jewish Community Federation of the Greater Chattanooga Area. Wolf K. Lefkoff and his wife, Rose, are shown at a testimonial dinner in 1950 where Wolf was honored as the first president of the JCC. Under his guidance, the building at 511 East Fourth Street was purchased, and a gym was erected. This first JCC site and old house served the community from 1953 to 1961. Rivoli Mills, on East Twenty-eighth Street, was founded in 1932 by Rose and Wolfe Lefkoff. They manufactured a variety of clothing items. In 1996, Wolfe's son Paul and his grandson David were in the 64th year of operation.

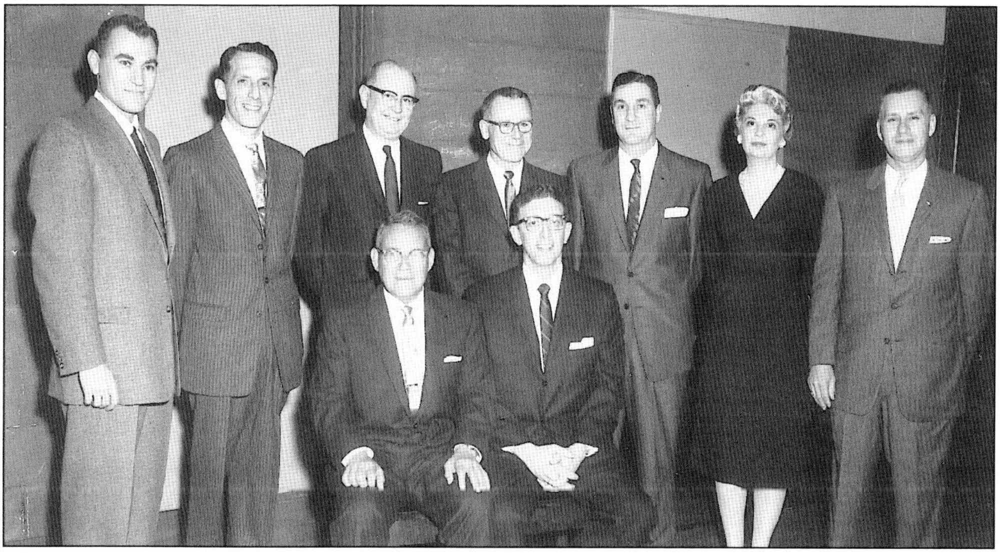

There were 20 presidents of the JCC. They were Wolf Lefkoff, Ira Trivers, Herman Lebovitz, Louis Marks, Mitchell Bush, A. Steve Ulin, Jack Tepper, Mark Spector, Harold Alper, William Raider, M.B. Seretean, Alex Alper, Paul Greenberg, Ralph Paty, Mel Young, Lynn Hochman, Hyman Kaplan, Robert Stahl, David Ulin, and Amelia Allen. Officers of the JCC in 1954 included the following, shown here from left to right: (front row) President Louis Marks and Jay Solomon; (back row) Dr. Bernard Tepper, Dr. Harold Alper, unidentified, Abe Koblentz, Mitchell Bush, Rosemary Weber, and Meyer Siskin. (Stanrich Studio.)

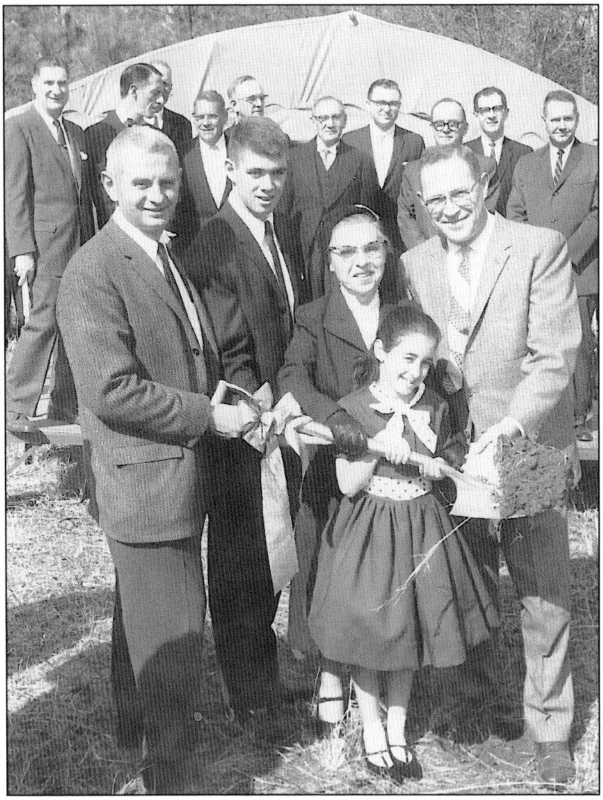

The groundbreaking ceremony for the new JCC on Lynnland Terrace in Brainerd was held in 1959. Dr. Steve Ulin and Dr. Jack Tepper were chairmen of the activities and were leaders in making the new Jewish Community Center Building happen. Some of the others present were Dora Frumin, Shirley Raider, Stuart Bush, Rabbi Abraham Feinstein, Louis Marks, Dr. Harold Alper, and Mitchel Bush.

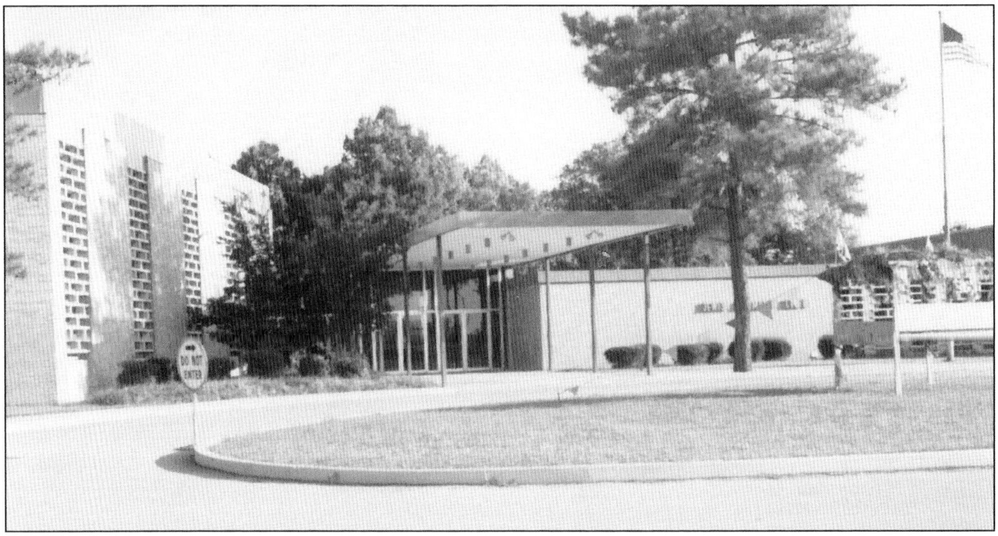

In 1961, the new JCC Building was opened and dedicated. Besides a large auditorium, the building featured an adult lounge with a fireplace, a Kosher kitchen, dressing rooms for theatrical productions, pre-school classrooms, offices, and several meeting rooms on the ground level. On the lower level was a huge gym with spectator benches, a complete health club, exercise rooms, and dressing rooms. On the upper level were more large rooms for meetings. Outside were patios and landscaped grounds, which surrounded the Olympic-sized, L-shaped swimming pool. Also outside, near the pool, were a fully equipped snack bar and tennis courts.

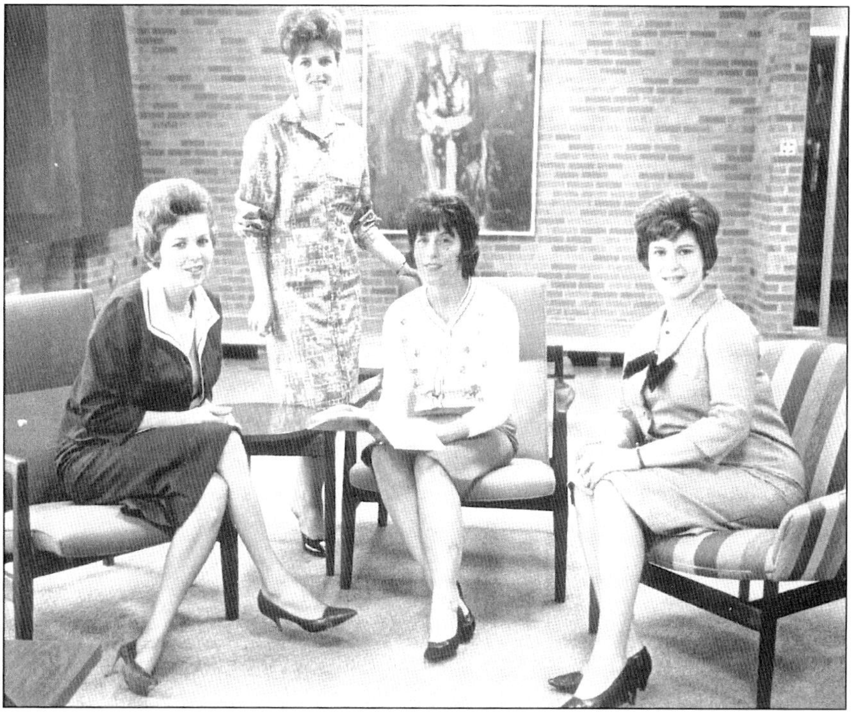

The JCC Women's Auxiliary was soon organized. Liz Hodes (far left), Marcia Menuskin (middle left), Lucile Speal (middle right), and another unidentified woman pose while planning a benefit in the mid-1960s. Marcia was married to Dr. Jay Menuskin, a professor at the University of Tennessee. They had three daughters: Jill, Zelda, and Lisa. Lucile was married to Dr. Stanley Speal, a psychologist, and they had three sons: David, Jonathan, and Kenan. Liz's family is noted in Chapter 8.

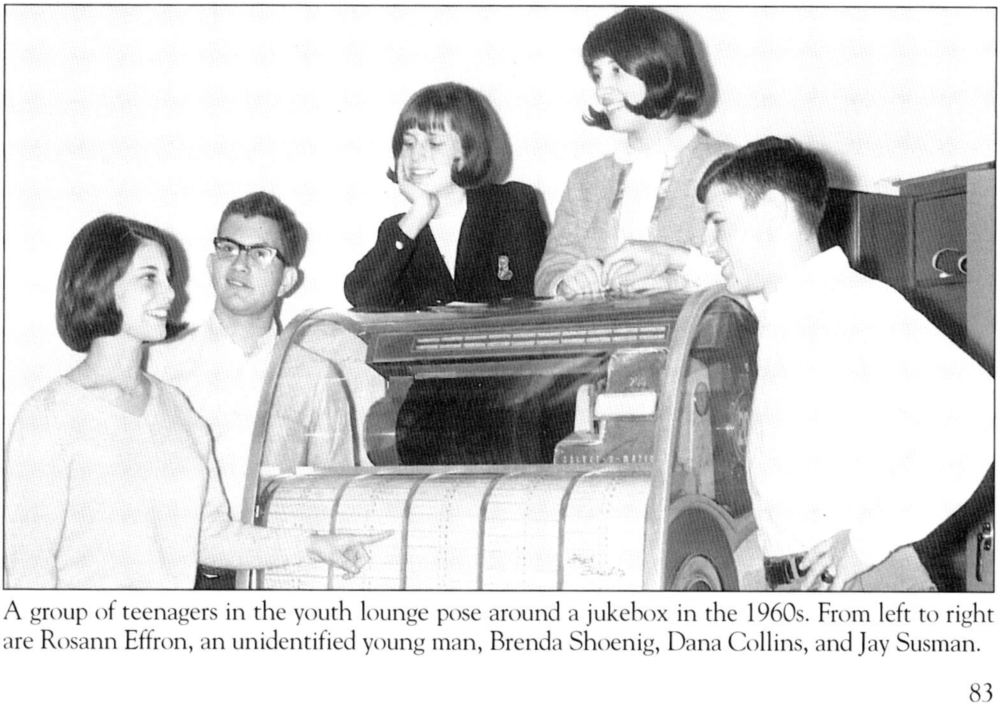

A group of teenagers in the youth lounge pose around a jukebox in the 1960s. From left to right are Rosann Effron, an unidentified young man, Brenda Shoenig, Dana Collins, and Jay Susman.

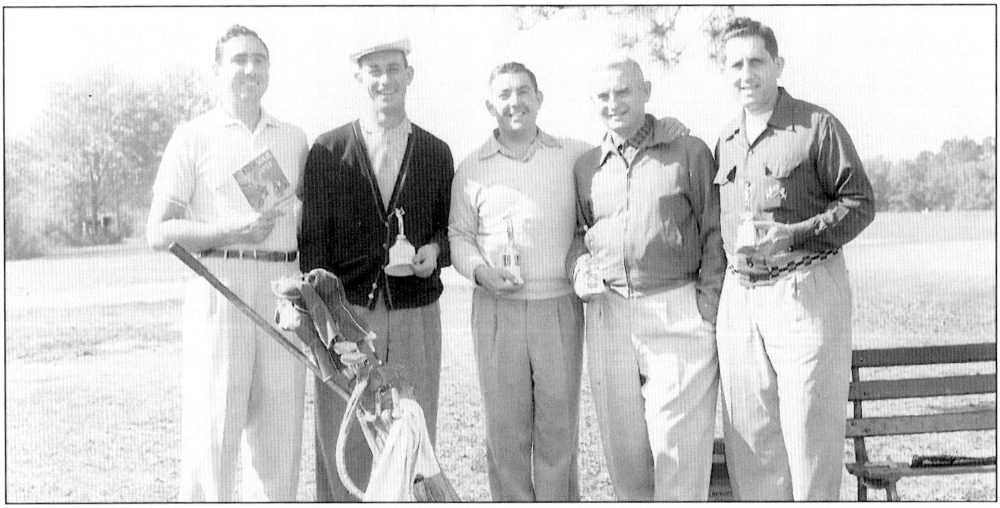

Athletic contests in all sports emerged in the 1960s, after the new JCC opened. Golf was a favorite activity. From left to right, these winners are Stanley Leventhal and Bill Springer, now of New Orleans, and Jack Baras, Steve Ulin, and Syd Gottler, now of Atlanta.

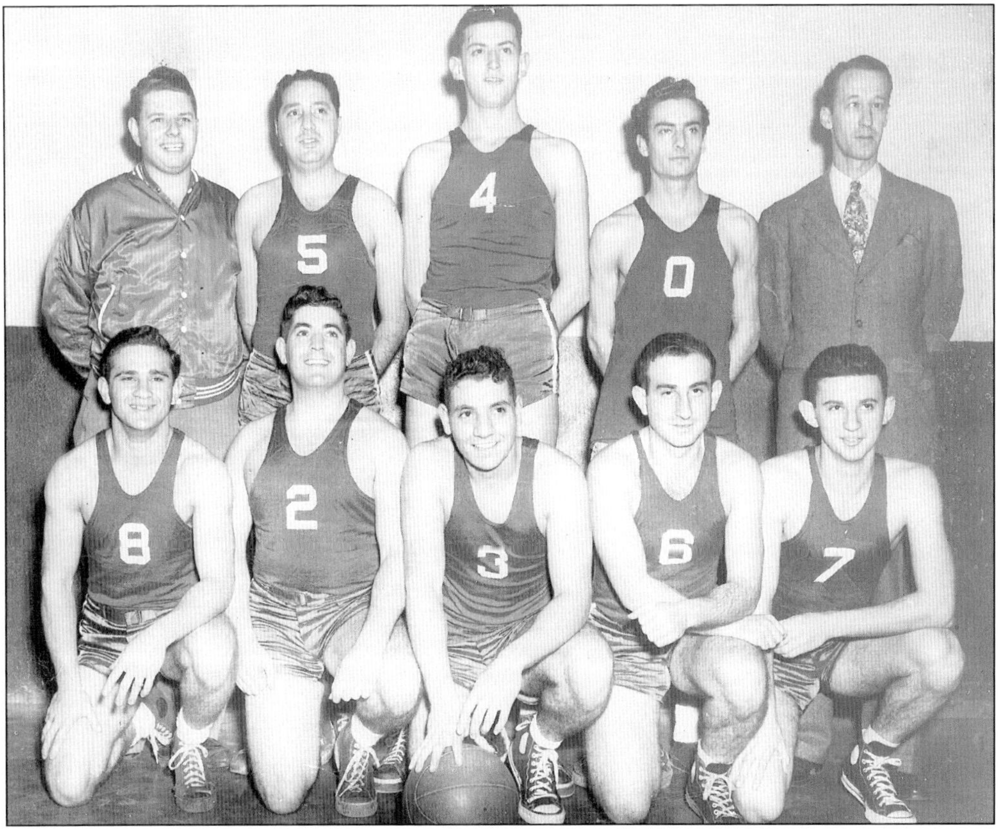

Of course, basketball was a favorite pastime. Here are some players in the 1950s. From left to right are as follows: (front row) Harold Shavin, Jack Baras, Sam Baras, Saul Rosenthal, and Izzy Frumin; (back row) Earl Prigoff, Marvin Silverman, Julius Spector, Ellis Levine, and coach "BooGoo" Biggers.

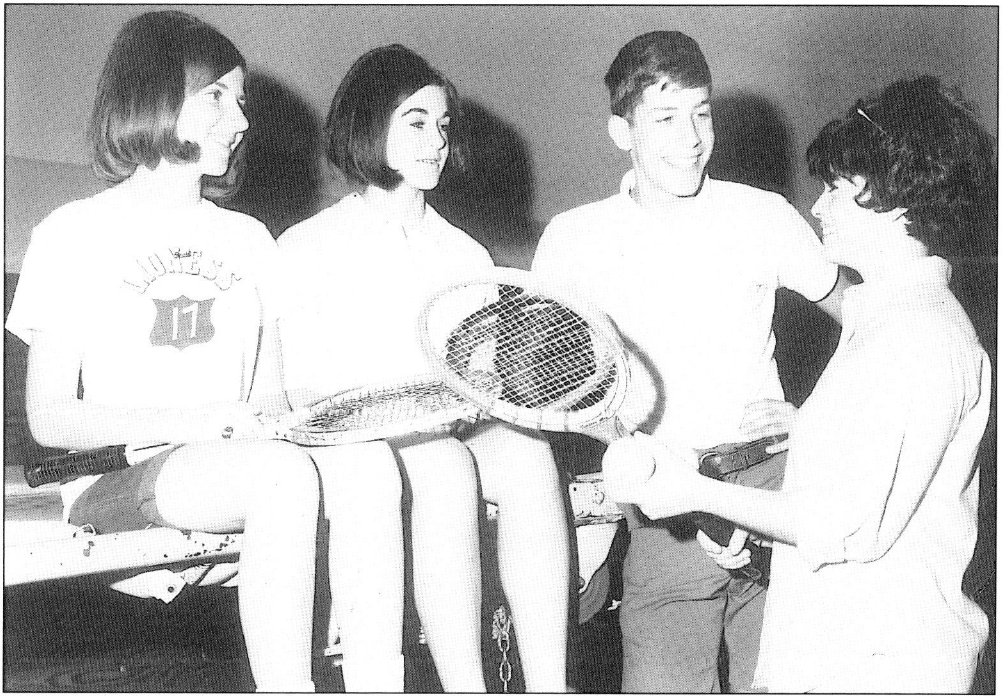

JCC tennis enthusiasts included Ches Alper, the Porter sisters, and Rosie Cherney in 1969. In the 1980s, a heated and air-conditioned tennis bubble was erected on the property for year-round tennis. Adults clamored for a time to be on the courts. (Bill Truex.)

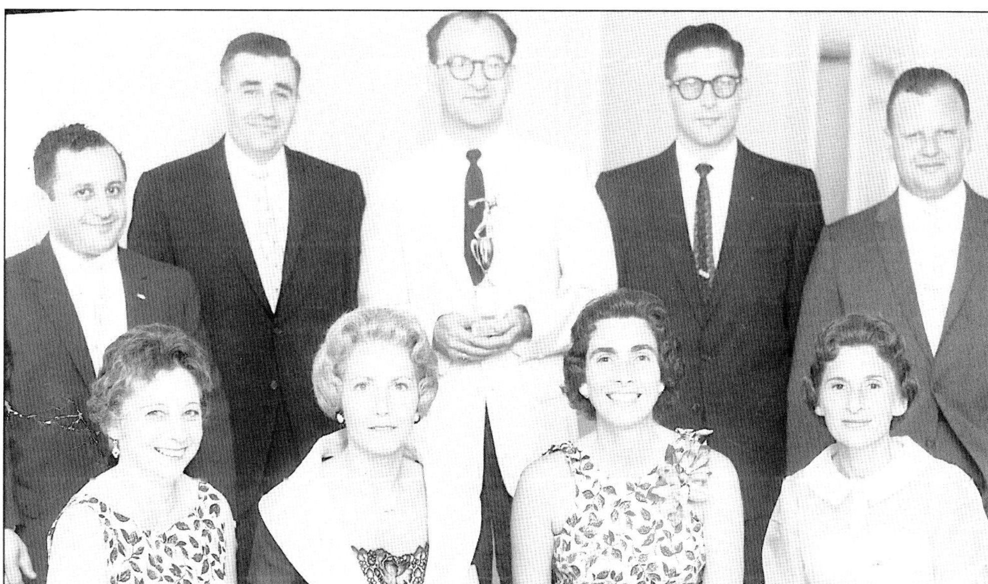

JCC bowling was another sport that was enjoyed. There were yearly tournaments and teams of all ages in the 1960s, '70s, and '80s. Some of the bowling team winners are pictured here. From left to right are as follows: (front row) Sarah Greenberg, Zudie (Block) Leventhal, Virginia (Weitzner) Raider, and Mille (Press) Wolff; (back row) JCC Activities Director Arnie Goldstein, Dr. Murray Porter, an unidentified man, Bruce Backer, and Joe Wise. (W.C. King.)

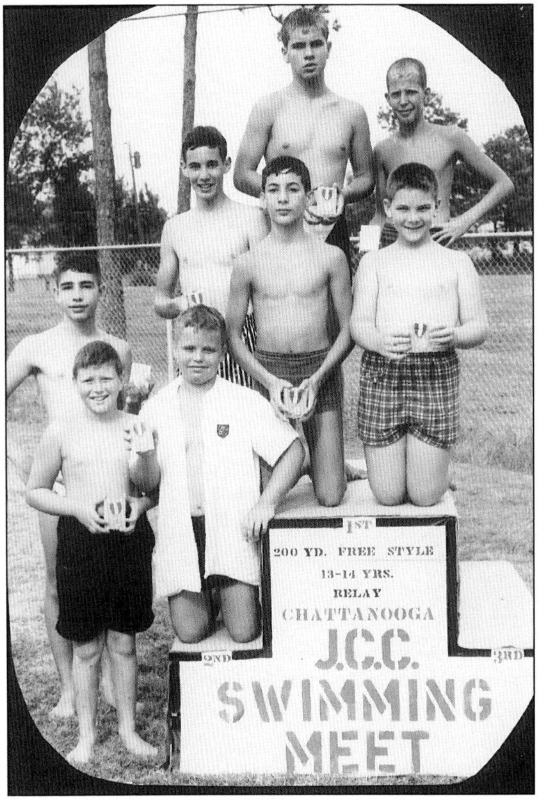

JCC swimming was the favorite summer activity with mammas and poppas and zadies and bubies. People scrambled for space to sun bathe in the 1960s and '70s. Youth swimming teams of all ages and divisions flourished. The winners of a 200-yard free-style relay included Steve Wise, Joel Kroenberg, Billy Blumberg, Steve Kaset, Lee Abelson, and Don Spiegel. A 25-yard girls' breaststroke event was won by Shirley Raider, Mindy Pregulman, and Judy Kronenberg.

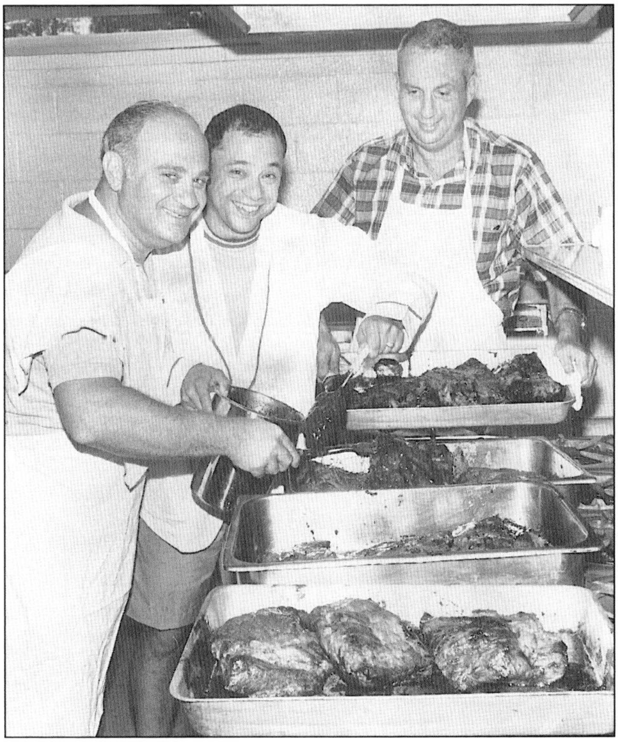

The Chattanooga JCC had many festive parties and meetings in its large auditorium and out on its tree-shaded grounds. One enjoyable event in the late 1960s was the JCC barbeque. Pictured here, from left to right, are Harold Shavin, Jerry Kleinstub, and Paul Lefkoff, posing with the beautifully cooked meats that they spent so much time preparing.

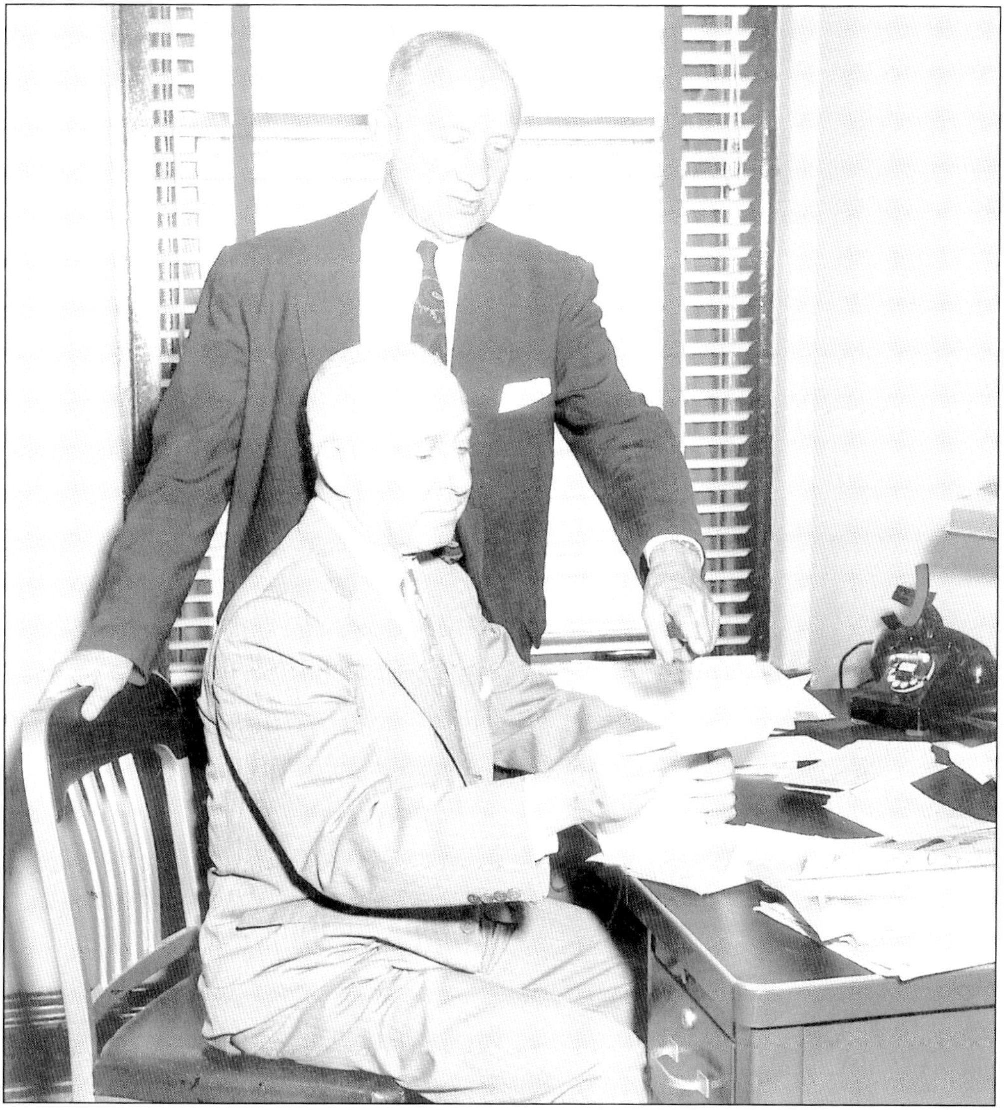

Jewish organizations and clubs abounded in Chattanooga. The Chattanooga Jewish Welfare Agency was started and organized by Harry Miller in 1931. He was president from 1931 until 1938 and took care of most of the local needs of the city. In 1938, a charter was obtained and the agency became international, under the name of the Chattanooga Jewish Federation. In 1993, the name was changed again into the Jewish Community Federation of the Greater Chattanooga Area. Pictured is Harry Miller, seated, discussing the "Big Gifts Strategy" for the 1959 Federation campaign with Julius Kushner. Harry Miller gave, most unselfishly, to many causes, organizations, and institutions. He founded the Vogue, a high-fashion ladies store, and was president of the Mizpah Congregation, the Chattanooga Chamber of Commerce, the Rotary Club, the Chattanooga Symphony Association, the Travelers' Aid Society, and the Old Ladies Home. He was a leader in fund-raising campaigns for cancer and heart drives, the memorial hospital, the YMCA., the United Way, the Red Cross, the Little Theater, the Boy Scouts, and the Siskin Memorial Foundation. He was well known by everyone in Chattanooga, and was a leader surpassed by none. Harry was married to Ethel, and they had a daughter, Eleanor. Julius Kushner was married to Jennie, and they had a son, Myron.

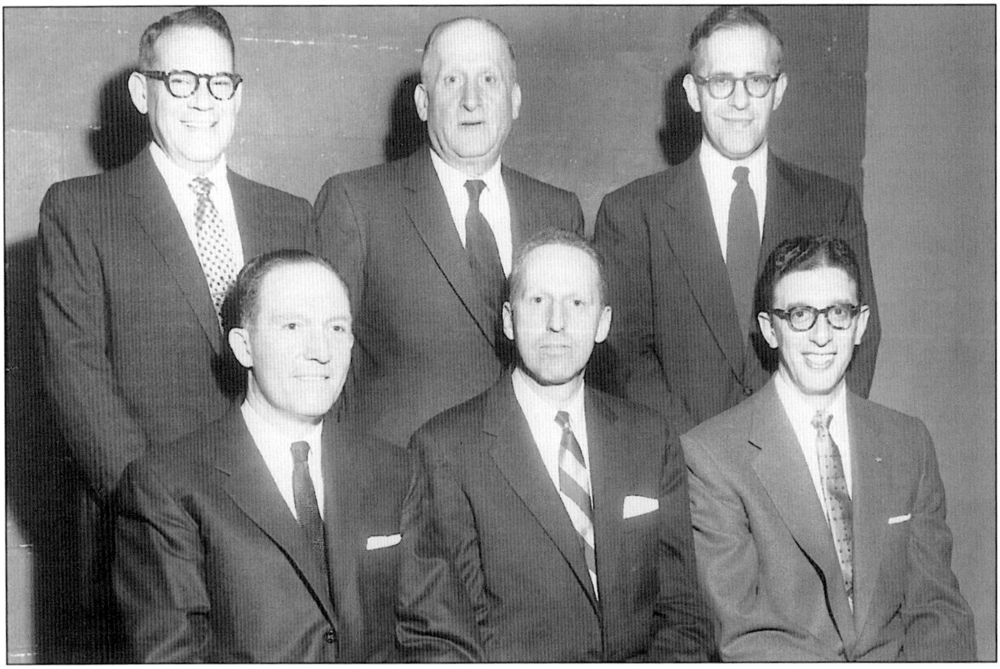

Newly elected officers for the Federation in 1956 included the following, from left to right: (seated) Dr. Harold Schwartz, President Ira Trivers, and Jay Solomon; (standing) Louis Marks, Sam Diamond, and Meyer Siskin.

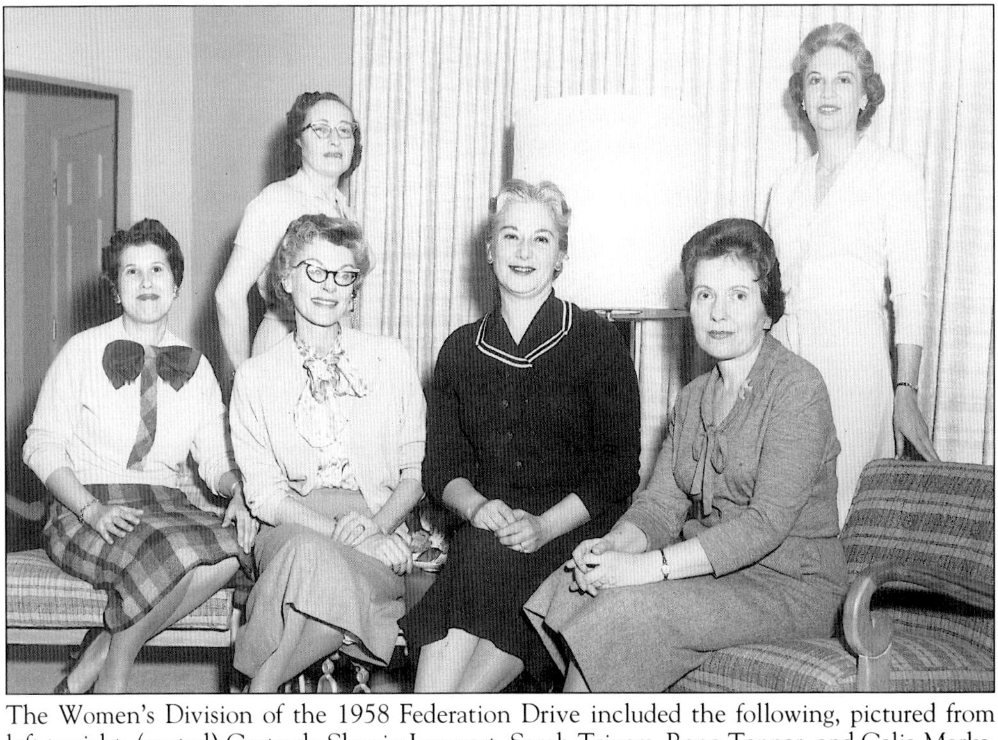

The Women's Division of the 1958 Federation Drive included the following, pictured from left to right: (seated) Gertrude Shavin Lampert, Sarah Trivers, Rene Tepper, and Celia Marks; (standing) Mollie Robbins and Rosemary Weber.

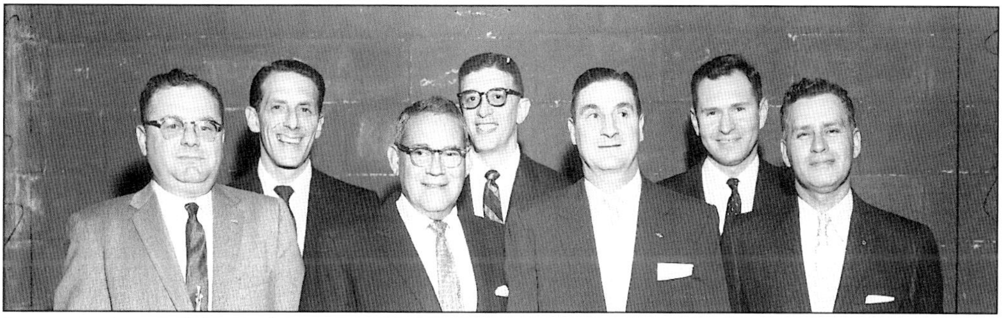

Past presidents of the Federation include Harry Miller, Henry Morris, Felix Diamond, George Berke, Sam P. Diamond, Abe Koblentz, Judge M.B. Finklestein, Louis Winer, Dr. Harold Schwartz, Ira Trivers, Jay Solomon, Louis Marks, Dr. Harold Alper, Mitchell Bush, Dr. Jack Tepper, M.B. Seretean, Ted Robbins, Mervin Pregulman, Jay Silverstein, Mark Spector, Paul Lefkoff, Thomas Trivers, Abe Feigenbaum, Robert H. Siskin, Charles B. Lebovitz, Barbara Wiston, Pris Siskin, Helen Pregulman, and Claire Siskin Binder. Officers of the Federation are pictured here in 1959. They are, from left to right, as follows: (front row) Alex Alper, Louis Marks, Mitchell Bush, and Meyer Siskin; (back row) Dr. Harold Alper, President Jay Solomon, and Jay Silverstein.

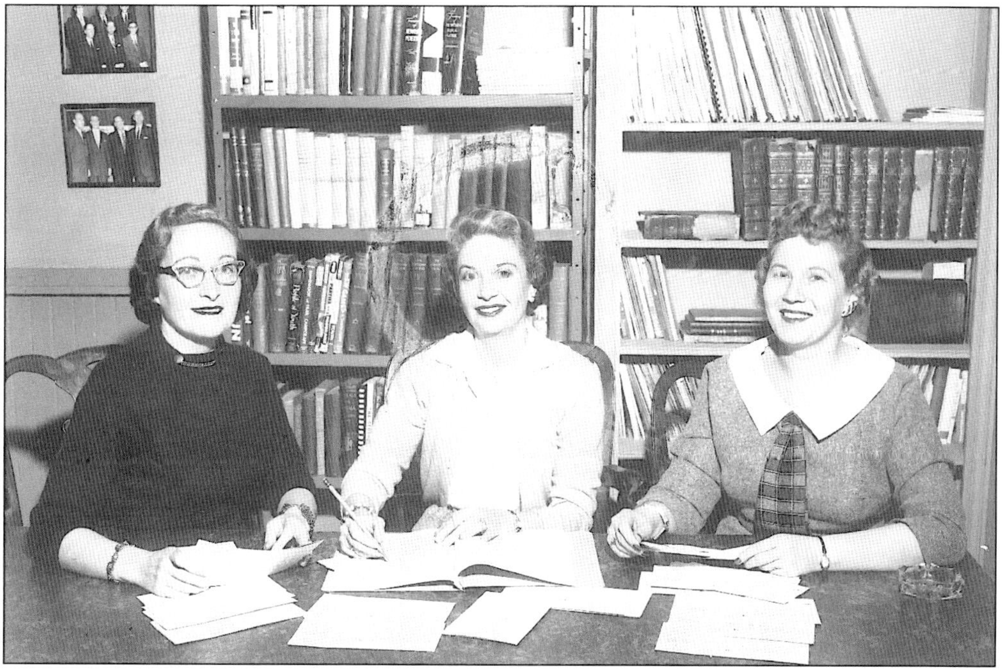

In the late 1950s, the heads of the Federation's Women's Division were busy planning their strategy to raise needed funds. Pictured here are Mollie Robbins, Rosemary (Munsey) Weber, and Mae (Greenberg) Kaset. Mollie was married to Ted, and they had one daughter, Gail (Lindsey). Rosemary was married to Harry Weber, and they had four children: Dr. Samuel C. Weber of Houston, Texas, Sally (Pearlman) of Asheville, North Carolina, Dr. Randall Weber of Philadelphia, Pennsylvania, and Susan Burt of Abilene, Texas. The Weber family first settled in Chattanooga in the early 1900s and formed the S.C. Weber Iron and Metal Company. Rosemary's in-laws, Flora (Fine) Weber and S.C. Weber, had two more children besides Harry: Maurice (married to Marie Shapiro) and Jeanne (Scull). Mae was married to Issy Kaset, and they had two children, Steve and Judy (Stahl).

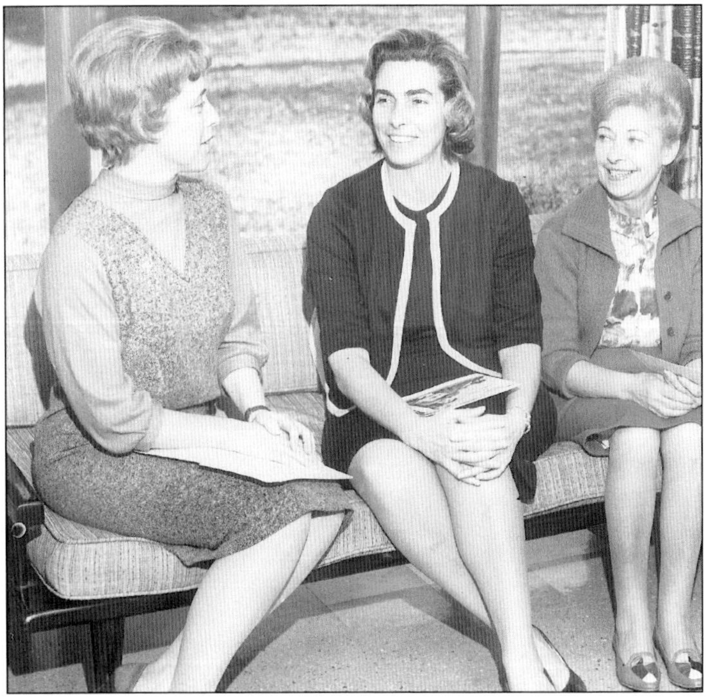

Virginia Raider (center) was the general chairman of the 1965 Federation's Women's Division. Shown here with her are Louise Kushner and Lena Berke.

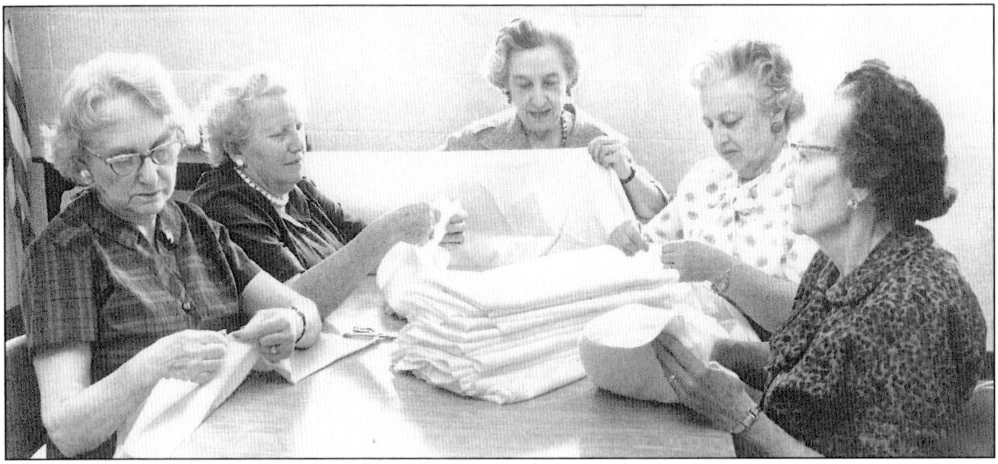

The Mizpah Sisterhood was organized by 23 women in 1877 as the Hebrew Ladies Aid Society. It was the main spring from whence most work pertaining to the congregation emanated. In 1985, the Sisterhood disbanded because of a lack of leaders, but in 1990 it was reorganized by a group of young working women into an evening Sisterhood. In 1993, daytime Sisterhood was reorganized, and monthly luncheon meetings resumed. However, by 1996, the effort of the women in both the Erev and Yom Sisterhoods failed, and the Mizpah Sisterhood disbanded again. It is believed that the efforts of the women of the Mizpah Congregation were being concentrated on "running" the congregation itself (the work of the former Sisterhood having long since been made a part of congregational responsibilities). Some of the memorable work of the Mizpah Sisterhood brings back fond memories. One of the most constant committees down through the years was the sewing committee, which sewed for local hospitals and the Red Cross during wars and disasters. Mizpah's sewing group of the 1950s is shown here. They are, from left to right, Ruth Long, Flora Shaw, Naomi Cohn, Esther Goldblatt, and Rebecca Schwartz.

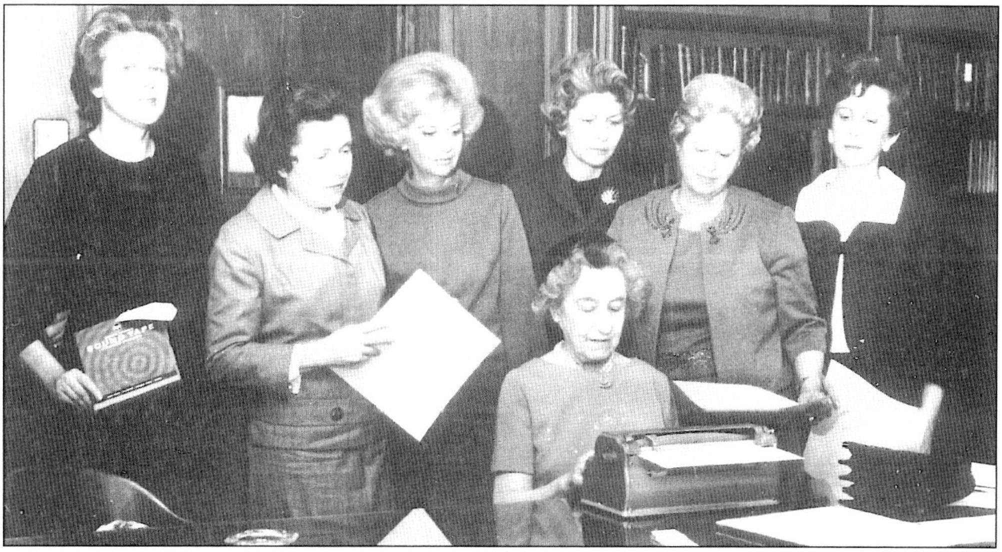

The Mizpah Sisterhood's Braille Committee was a very devoted group of ladies during the 1950s, '60s, and '70s. There were several different groups in which the work was done. First there was a group who used the Braille machines to punch the letters of the Braille alphabet onto special heavy paper. Then, another group took these sheets and painted them with a shellac to help preserve them. There was also the Talking Book Group, who used sound tapes to transcribe school lessons or whole books for the blind to enjoy. Here is a group with Naomi Cohn at the Braille machine. The others are, from left to right, Marcelle Weill, Celia Marks, Rosemary Weber, Carolyn Henning, Carol Rosenhein, and P.A. Silverstein.

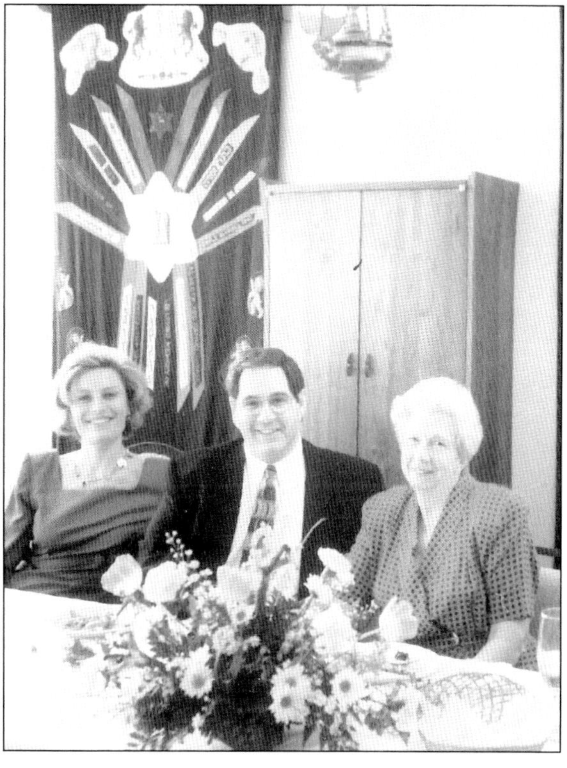

Tuesday was the day luncheons were held by the various women's organizations every month: the Mizpah Sisterhood met on the first Tuesday, Hadassah on the second, the B'nai Zion Sisterhood on the third, and the JCC Women's Auxiliary on the fourth. In the early days of the Mizpah Sisterhood, the women were completely in charge of the religious school, social events, and holiday celebrations, and had huge budgets to meet. Fund-raising was always essential. The last event the Sisterhood organized was the 130th anniversary of the founding of the Mizpah Congregation in 1996. Rabbi Ken Kanter of Nashville's Temple Micah gave a musical history of the congregation. Pictured here, from left to right, are Wendy (the rabbi's wife), Rabbi Ken Kanter, and Joy Adams, who presided.

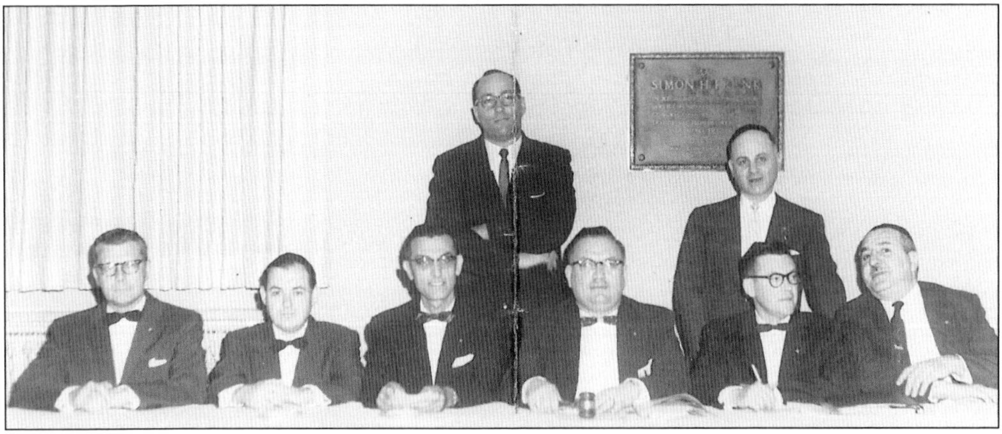

B'nai Brith, the oldest Jewish fraternity in the United States, has branches all over the world. Lodge No.446 in Chattanooga was founded in 1895. The organization maintains hospitals and technical schools, as well as homes for the aged, infirm, and orphans. It also gives immigrant aid. It sponsors the Hillel Foundations at universities and Aleph Zadik Aleph chapters, better known as AZA, for Jewish boys. The Anti-Defamation League works to eliminate slander, libel, discrimination, and hatred against Jews. Pictured at a lodge meeting are the following, from left to right: (seated) Charles Cohen, Louis Epstein, Morris Slutsky, Alex Alper, Harry Dubrow, and Harold Gross; (standing) Charles Levine and Ralph Abelman. Charles Cohen and his wife, Lorraine (Netter), moved to Houston, Texas, in 1996 to be near their sons, Roy and Joseph, whose families live there.

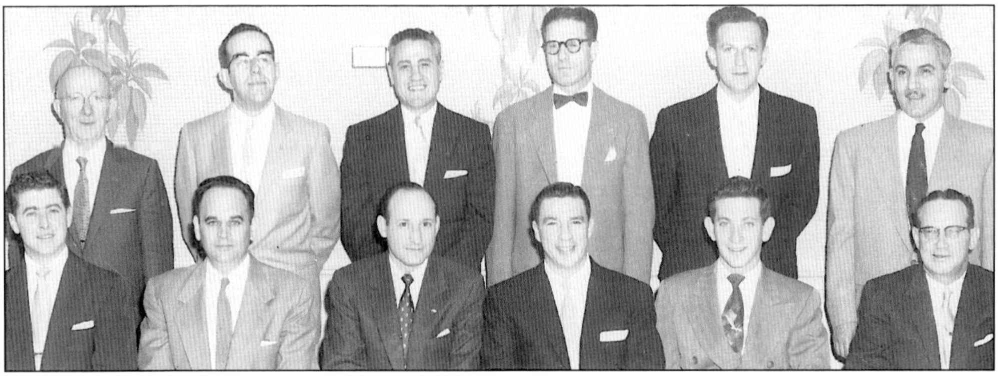

In 1949, a B'nai B'rith Chapter was organized in Dalton, Georgia, with Nathan Snow as its first president. Officers for their B'nai Brith Lodge in 1955 included the following people, from left to right: (seated) Harold Shapiro, Hi Raisin, Leonard Lorberbaum, Lester Goldberg, Paul Gottlieb, and Irvin Funk; (standing) an unidentified guest, Paul Tennenbaum, Maurice Saltzman, Bill Wisen, David Winkler, and another unidentified guest. (Ward's Photo Service, Dalton, Georgia.)

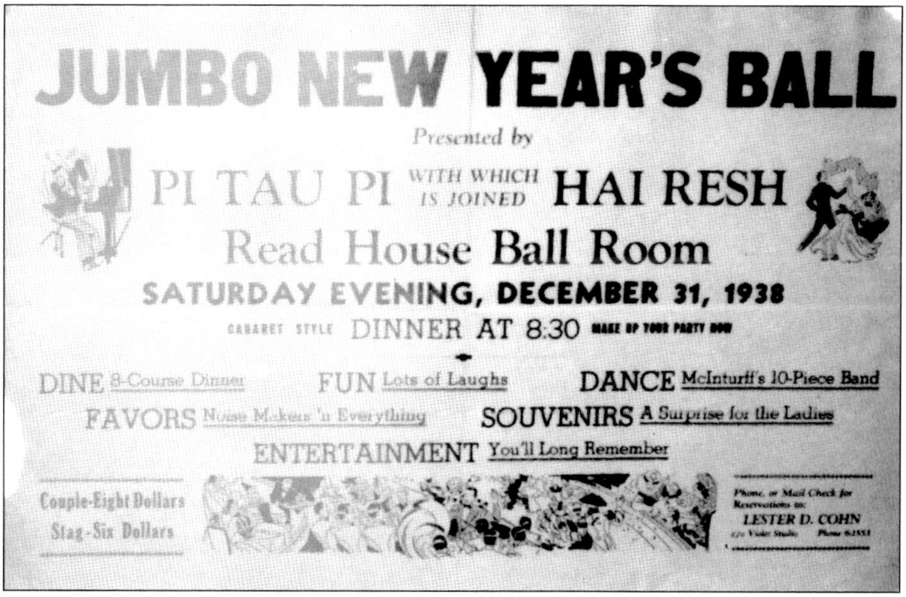

In the 1930s, '40s, and '50s, the sounds of the big bands reigned supreme! Everyone went to hear the singers and to dance. Glenn Miller, Tommy Dorsey, Jimmy Dorsey, Benny Goodman, Frankie Carle, Gershwin, Ray Coniff, Al Hirt, Xavier Cugat, and Artie Shaw, among others, were favorites. It was a dancing era, and dancing was the favorite pastime for both young and old. Pictured here is a flyer announcing a New Year's Eve Ball and Dinner to be held at the Read House in 1938. Two Jewish fraternities, Pi Tau Pi and Hai Resh, were joining together for this affair. Notice the bargain price! (The Read House.)

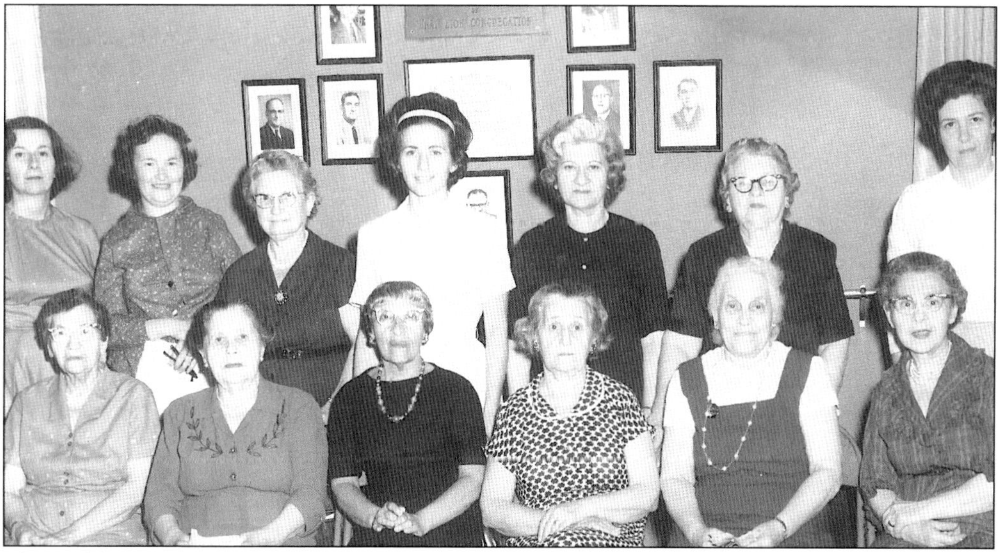

The Golden Age Club was organized in the 1950s by Dora Frumin and the JCC. Jewish seniors, both men and women, are served hot Kosher lunches and meet every Wednesday. Attending a Golden Age Planning Meeting in 1960 are the following people, from left to right: (front row) Mrs. Zavels, Nachami Laskin, Mary Rind, Fanny Reinhold, Rosa Richelson, and Dora Frumin; (back row) Louise Spector (pianist), Mitzie Cash, Bella Katchen, Myra Framm, Bertha Phillips, Eva Shavin, and Mary Spector. (John Goforth.)

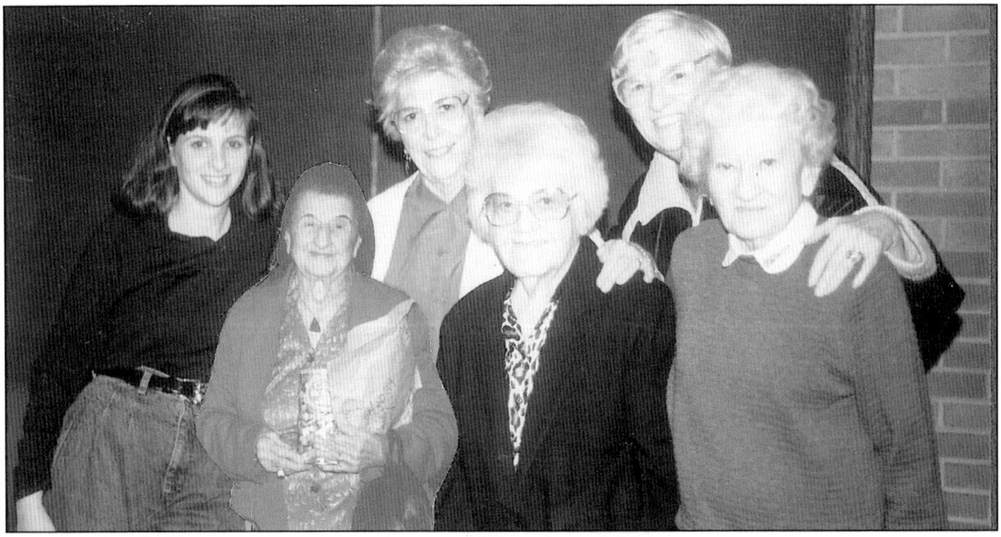

This group of Golden Age participants in 1996 includes Marcy Pellegrino (program director), Fannye Wise, Mary Spector, Polly Pressman, Helen Schwartz, and Bertha Philips.

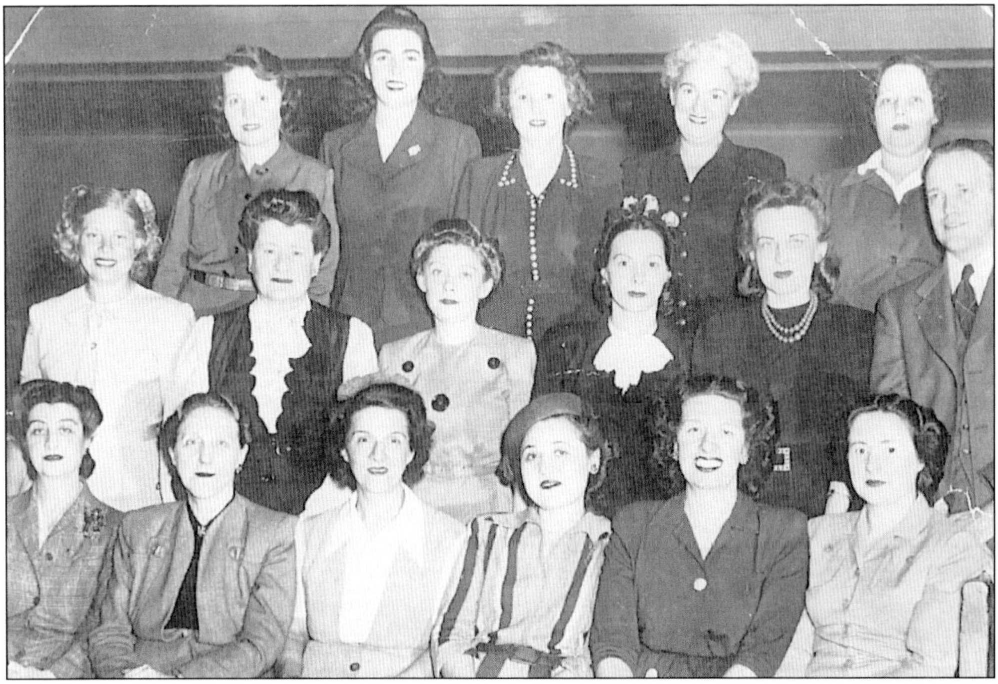

The Senior Hadassah, the women's branch of the Zionist movement, was organized in Chattanooga in 1915 in the home of Mrs. Harry Winer. It was the first one organized in the entire South. The building up of Palestine, and then of the State of Israel, were their primary objectives. Chattanooga has a very strong group of devoted women who give to various causes in Israel. Pictured here, in 1943, are a group of Hadassah Singers. They are, from left to right, as follows: (front row) Ann Guerry, Rae Graff, unidentified, Rose Tabb, Sylvia Solomon, and Rachel Winer; (middle row) Sylvia Frumin, Syd Shinbaum, Lena Berke, Rose D. Winer, unidentified, and Jim Mahoney (choir director); (back row) Celia Marks, Virginia Weitzner, Ann Horowitz, Rae Heller, and Hannah Blacker.

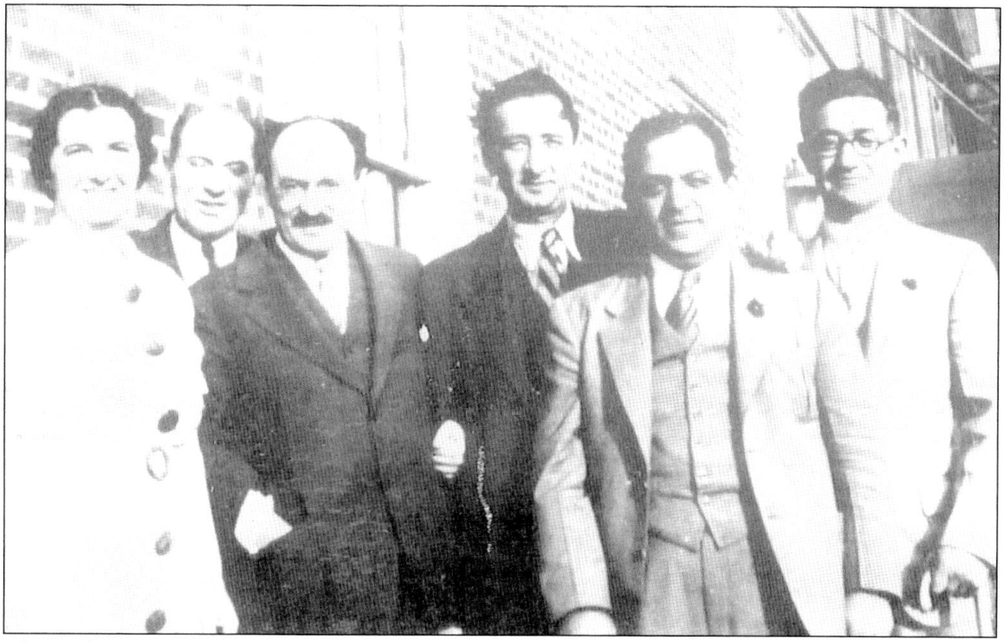

The Chattanooga Farband Branch 157 was a Zionist organization that was very active in Chattanooga raising money for Palestine, even before the State of Israel was established. Pictured is Golda Meir, in 1943, visiting in Chattanooga and raising money for the homeland. Traveling with her were three officials and Chattanoogans Wolf Gordon and Nathan Hofferman.

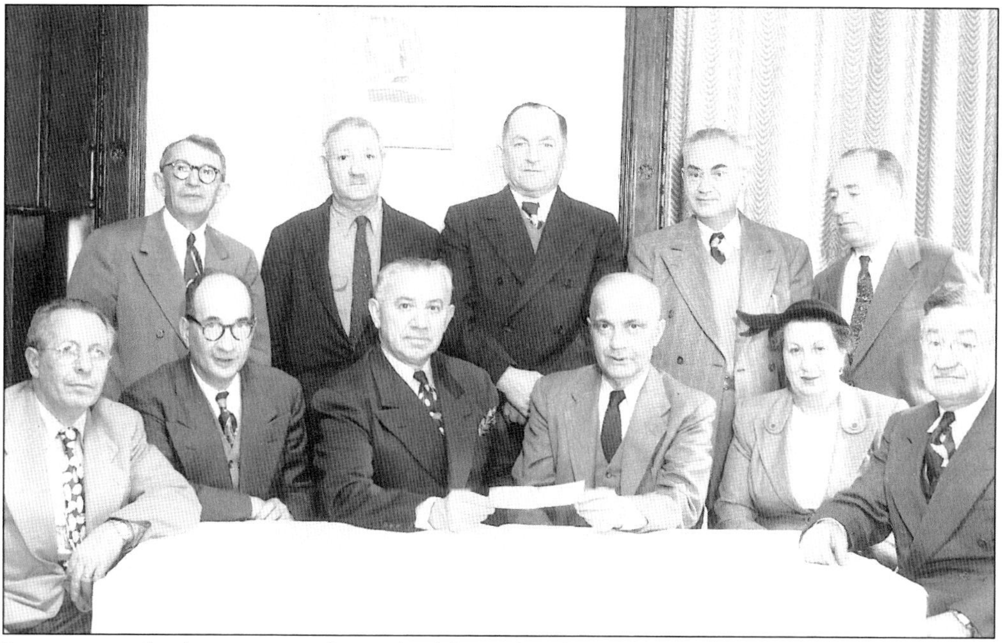

Presenting a check to carry on the work of the Farband in the 1940s were the following, pictured from left to right: (seated) Noah Brouner, Abe Sugarman, Morris Gill, an unidentified guest, Bessie Gordon Dubrow, and Nathan Hofferman; (back row) Harry Sulman, Ben Susman, Paul Dubrow, Abe Zuckerman, and Joe Cherney.

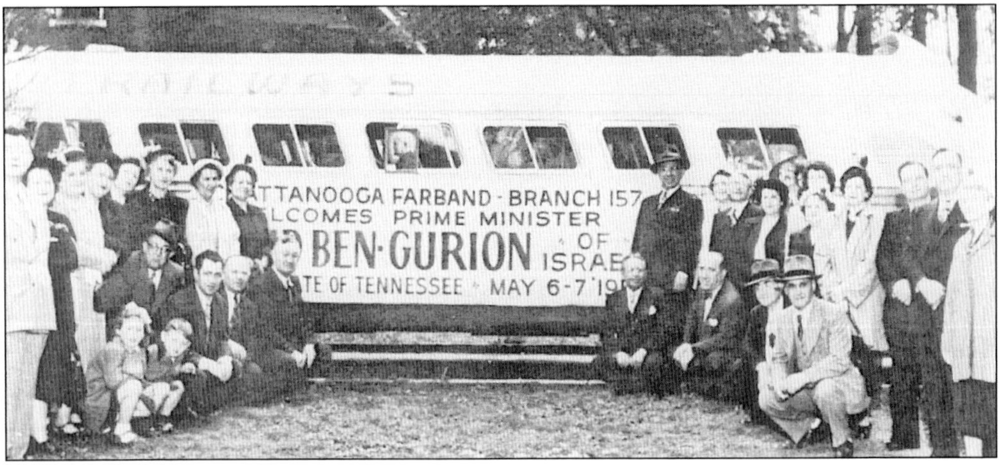

In 1960, David Ben-Gurion, the prime minister of Israel, came to Tennessee to study the TVA and to help sell State of Israel Bonds. A dinner was held in Knoxville to honor him. Busloads of people came from all over the state to attend this affair, including a large group from the Chattanooga Farband Branch 157.

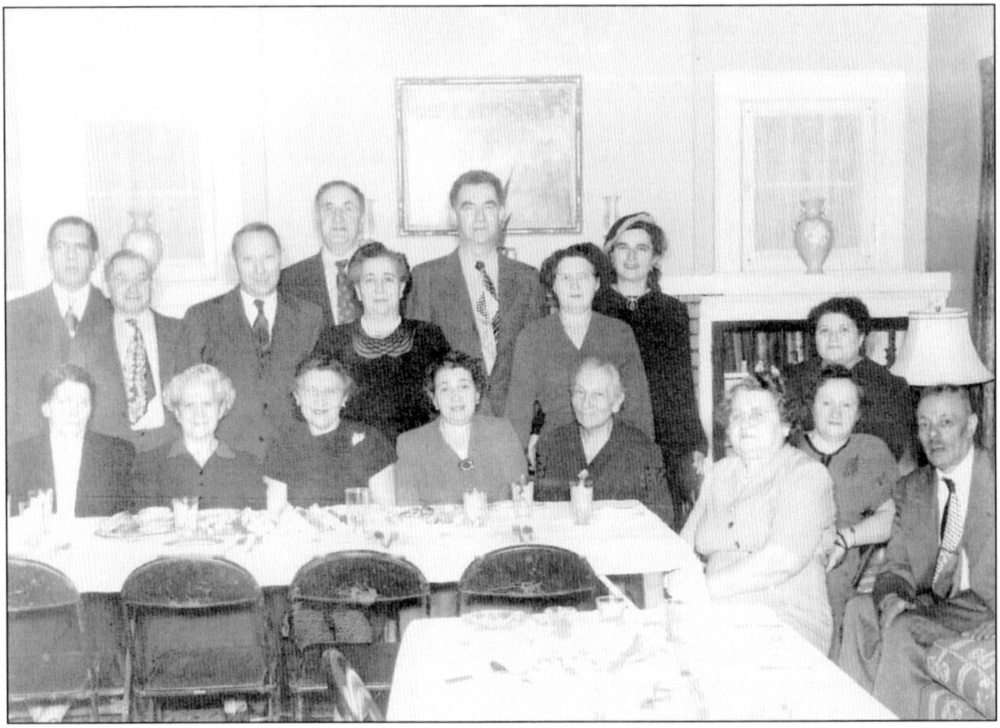

Members of the Workmans' Circle (or "Arbiter Ring"), Chattanooga Branch 495 consisted mostly immigrants from Eastern Europe and Russia. They had lived under communism, and their second language was not Hebrew, but Yiddish. They were mostly secular and were not generally Zionist. Pictured at an early Workmans' Circle Dinner are the following, from left to right: (front row) Sonia Abramson, Annie Shavin, Ann Kopkin, Rose Simonoff Solomon, unidentified, Eva Shavin, unidentified, and Max Pressman; (back row) Meyer Solomon, Sol Kopkin, Louis Shavin, Jerome Zavels, Rose Press, Ben Zion Harriton, Miriam Harriton, Esther Chaya Sir, and Ray Page.

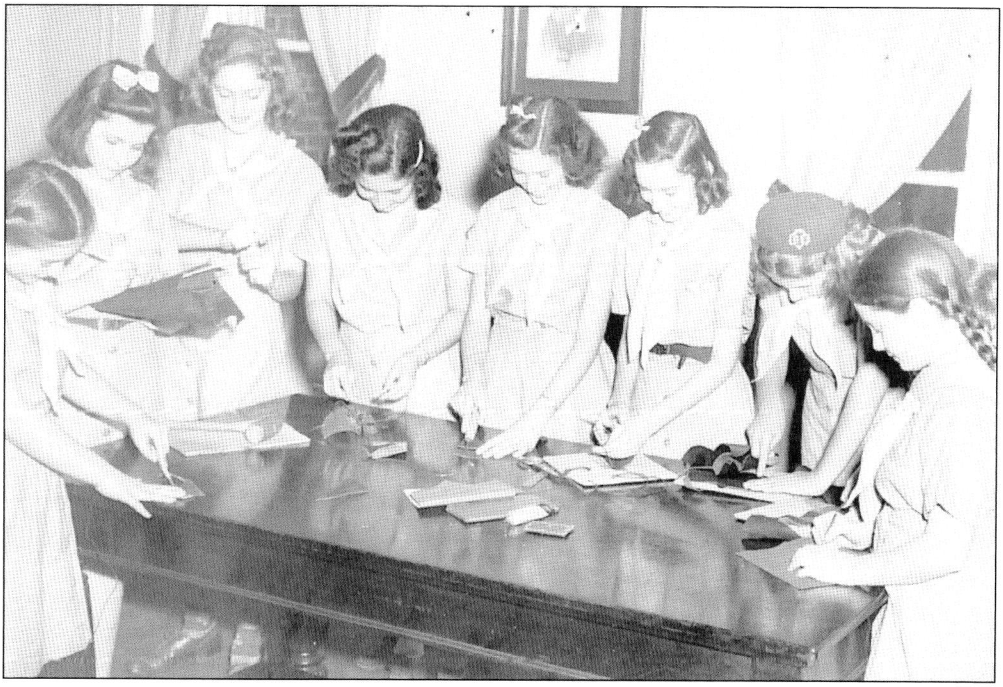

Many Jewish youths of Chattanooga actively participated in the Boy and Girl Scouts. Girl Scout Troop #5 is shown here busy working on a project in 1940. From left to right are Ruth Sadikoff, Jo Ann Effron (Richelson), Jerry Daneman (Sadow), Jeanne Hene, Florine Gould, Jeanne Angel (Weil), Farol Faye Finkelstein (Seretean), Jane Kalman (Ginsberg), and Clara Freedman (Shoenig).

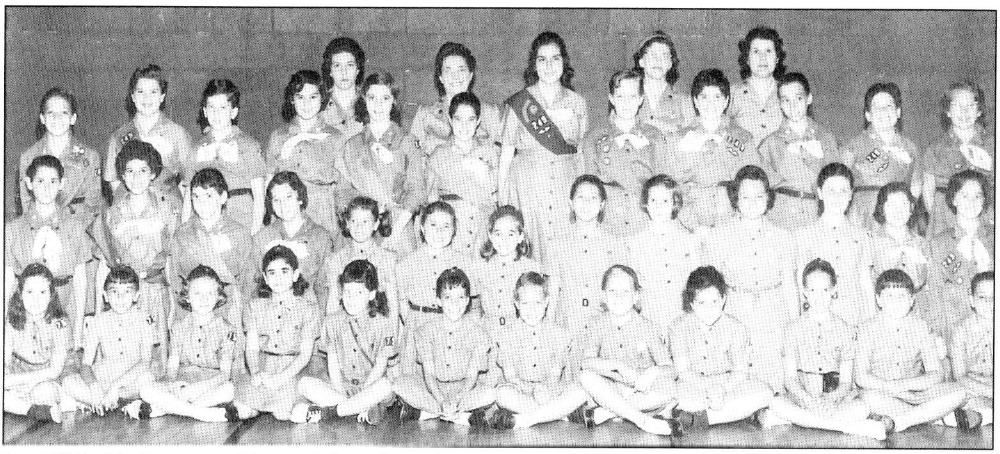

In 1955–56, Brownie Troop 75 and Girl Scouts Troop 249 held their meetings at the JCC. From left to right are as follows: (front row) Jan Collins, Robin Nash, Ziva Perchik, Carol Porter, Marilyn Charp, Jo Ann Jaffe, Myra Richelson, Ella Mirkin, Sherry Richelson, Pat Abelson, and Rita Raider; (middle row) Elaine Kaset, Joy Ulin, Marcia Shulman, Sharon Polsky, Leslie Norman, Monique Scheine, Ellen Porter, Ellen Shavin, Eleanor Spector, Joyce Dubrov, Josephine Cross, and Bertha Monette; (back row) Linda Kaset, Terry Menuskin, Janis Greenberg, Roz Ulin, Mary Spector (leader), Harriette Fanburg, Rae Jaffe (leader), Ann Streiter, Claire Binder, Sandy Spector, Freda Charp (leader), Sherry Phillips, Gert Shavin (leader), Bobbie Raider, Paula Brandman, and Roz Goldstein.

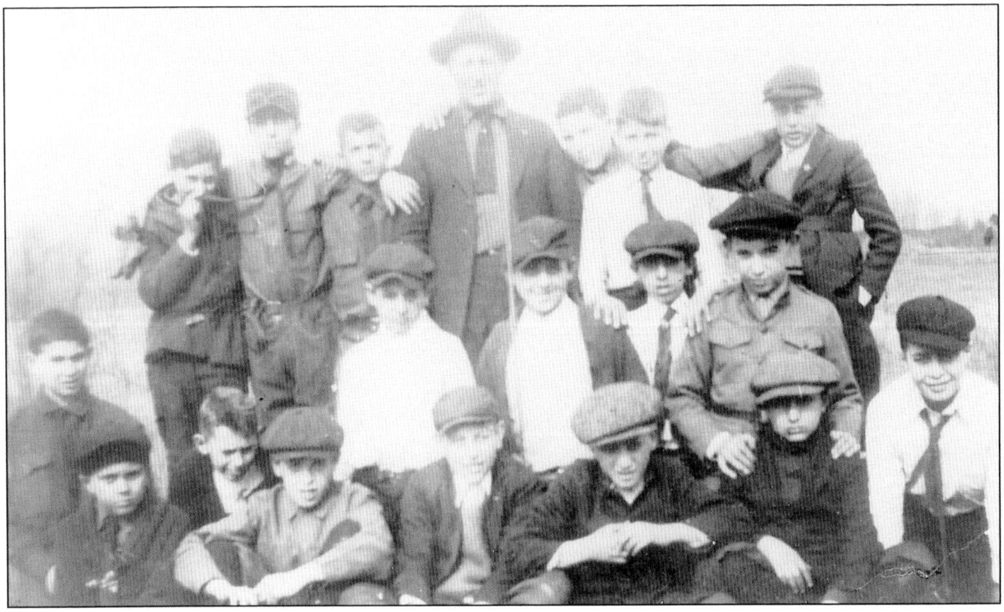

The Jewish Boy Scouts of America, Troop #8, led by Scoutmaster Sam Diamond, are seen here in a 1920 gathering. From left to right are as follows: (front row) Beryl Block, Isadore Silverman, Dave Brandman, H.C. Perlman, Abe Frumin, and Aaron Diamond; (middle row) Louis Silverman, Sam Pressman, Louis Lebovitz, Bennie Dubrow, "Mitty" Deitch, and Harry Fanburg; (back row) "Pik" Katchen, Abe Wise, "Sonny" Deitch, Sam Diamond, Herman Silverman, Joe Diamond, and Lou Brandman.

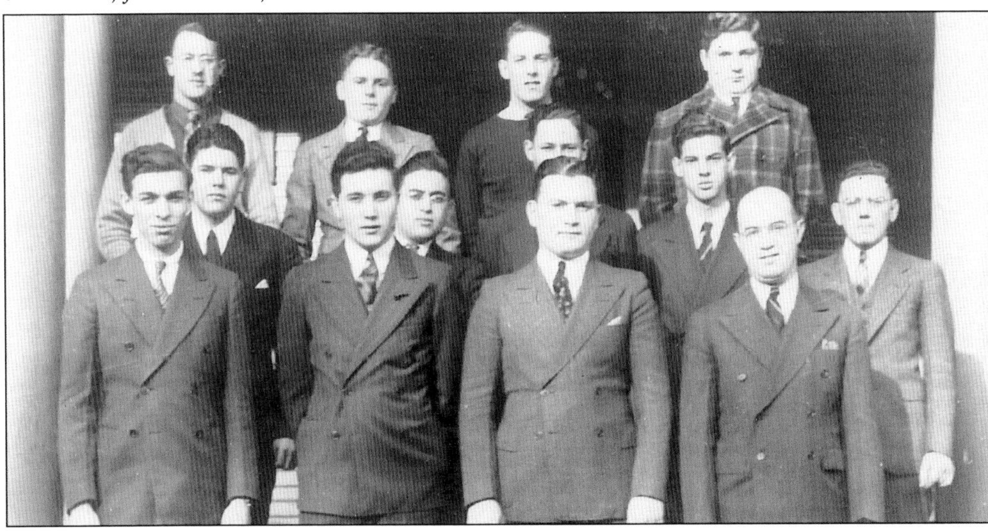

The Adolph S. Ochs Memorial Chapter of AZA, Junior B'nai B'rith, was organized in the fall of 1935 in Chattanooga. This is an international youth fraternity, which has for its program the mental, moral, and physical development of its members while strengthening their Jewish affiliations. Some charter members of the group are pictured here. They are, from left to right, as follows: (front row) Raymond Weitzner, Herbert Abelson, Alex Alper, and Mr. David Slabosky (sponsor); (middle row) Leo Mennen, Billy Raider, Harold Goldstein, Morton Schwartz, and Morris Tandeta; (back row) Sam Shavin, Harold Shoenig, Harold Alper, and Barney Solomon.

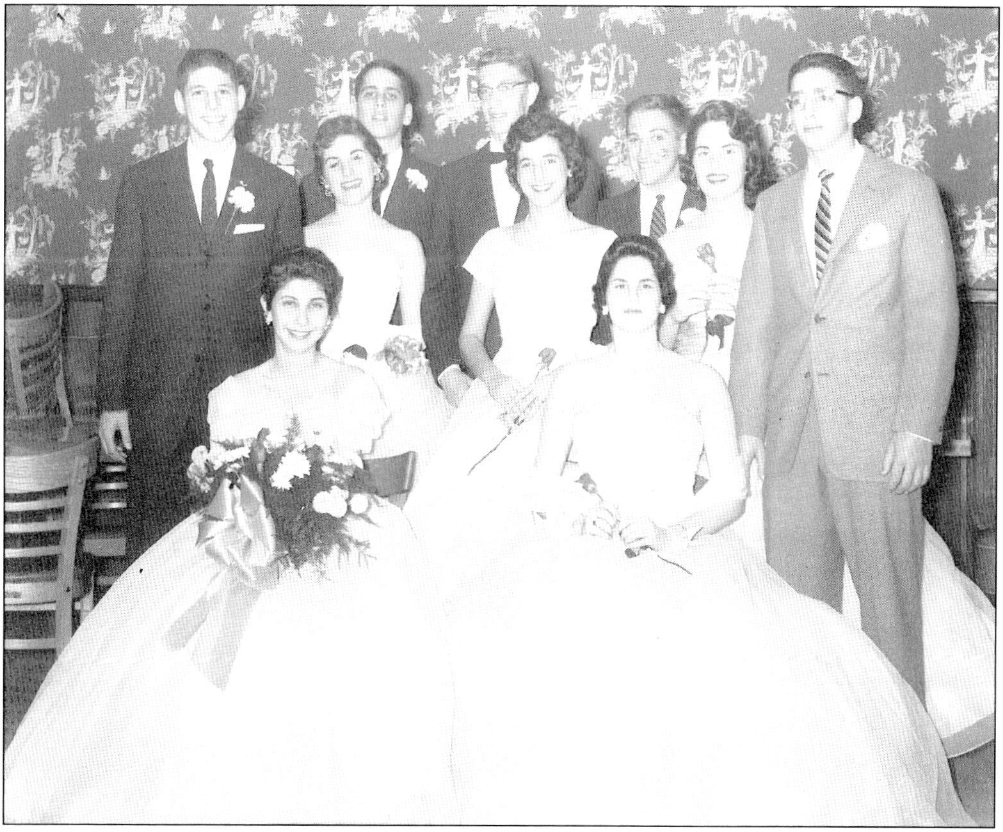

In 1955 the B'nai Brith Girls, the BBG, had a formal dance. Some of those attending are pictured here. They are, from left to right, as follows: (front row) Lynn Brandman (Hochman) and Barbara Siskin (Brook); (middle row) Larry Sauer, Reah Polsky (Friedman), Doris Winer (Greenberg), Robbie Kaset (Hershkovitz), and Alan Koplan of Dalton; (back row) Paul Berz, Harvey Frumin, and Alan Saturn of Nashville.

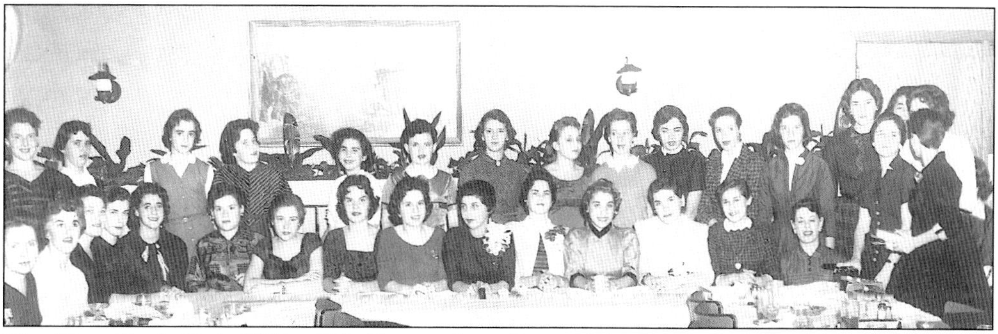

The B'nai Brith Girls FDR #179 Chapter Installation of 1956 was a gala dinner party. From left to right are as follows: (front row) Celia Marks, Lydia Kaset, and Fanny Polsky (advisors to the group), Faye Lebovitz, Doris Winer, Sydney Marks, Judy Marks, Robbie Kaset, Anita Friedman, Lynn Brandman, Barbara Siskin, Rhoda Bock, Rhea Polsky, Doris Effron, and Betty Sacks; (back row) Michelle Morris, Marion Ludsky, Carolyn Sear, Jane Kaset, Alicia Rhodes, Judy Henning, Iris Kaplowitz, Elaine Pearlman, Sandi Siskin, Shoshana Winer, Doris Bolton, and Rita Gayle Andrews. The women to the far right huddled together remain unidentified. (Jimmy's Photo, Fort Oglethorpe, Georgia.)

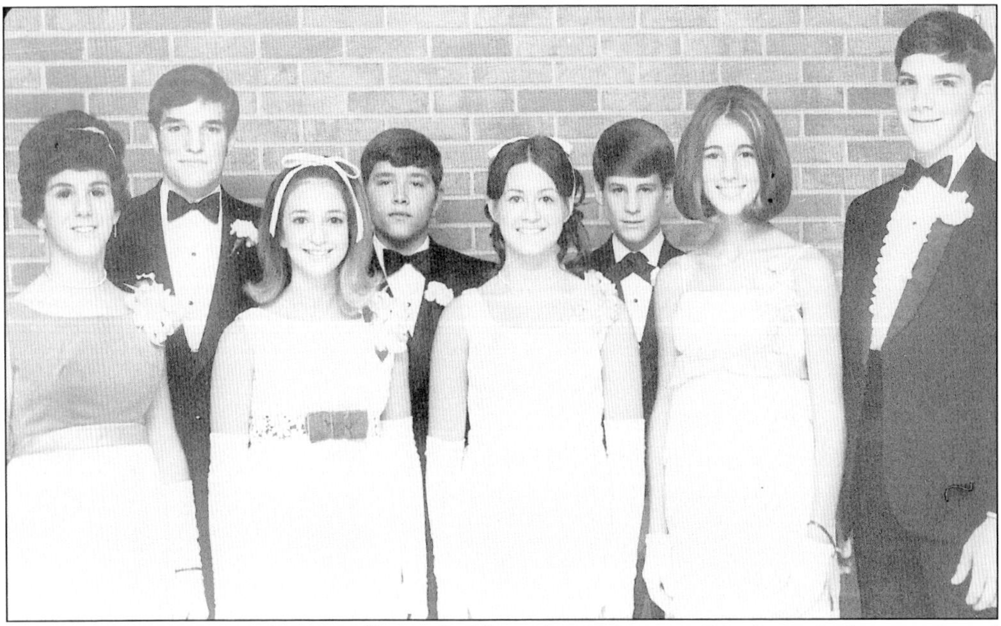

The annual Beau-Sweetheart Ball was held at the JCC in 1970. Gina Lieb was elected Sweetheart and Lee Abelson was elected Beau. Here are a few people taking a pause from the dancing. From left to right are Adele Lander, Gary Gropper, Gina Lieb, Donnie Wise, Mimi Rothman, Alan Stein, Barbara Mendel, and Lee Abelson.

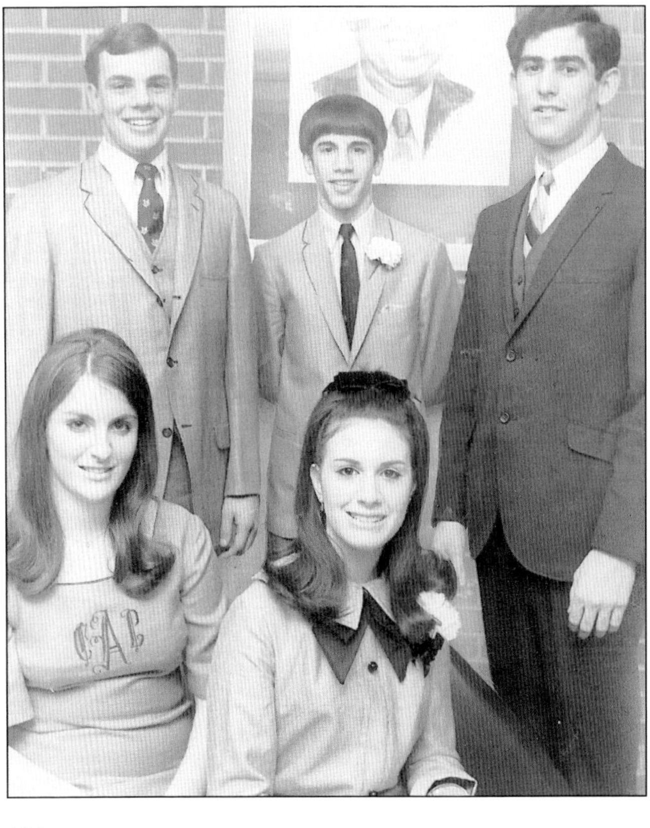

Some of the officers attending a state meeting at the JCC in Chattanooga in 1968 are pictured here. From left to right are as follows: (front row) Carole Allen, Birmingham District #7 BBG, and Lily Prebul, Chattanooga president of the Moccasin Bend BBG; (standing) Bobby Goodfriend from Athens, Tennessee, vice president of the Cotton States AZA; Jerry Finkle, Chattanooga president of the Adolph S. Ochs AZA; and Jay Herman from Memphis, Tennessee, the social awareness chairman of the Cotton States AZA.

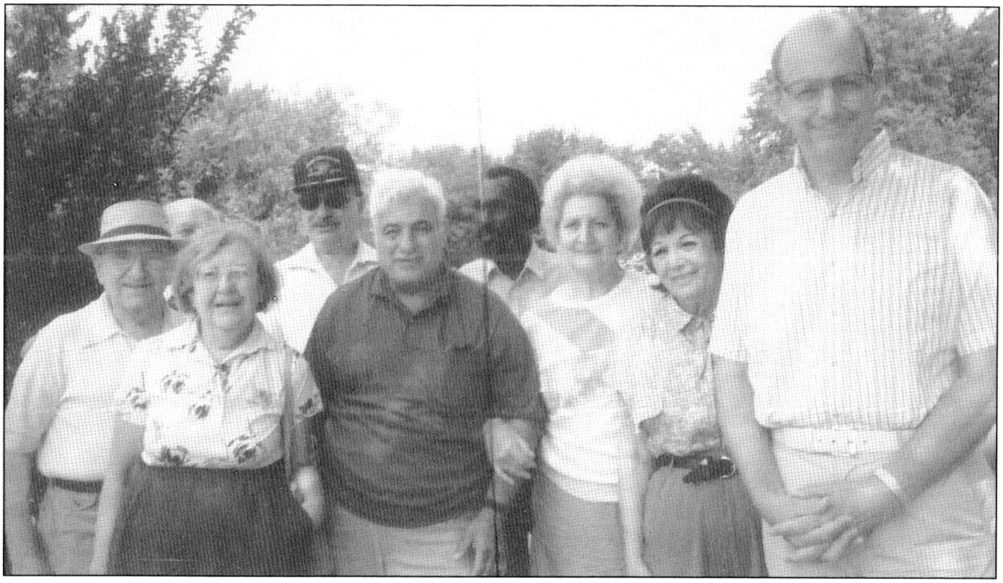

The In-Between Social Club, organized by Dr. Howard and Ida Gault and Ella Tyber Chunowitz, operated from 1978 until 1994. It usually met on Sundays, once a month, and took numerous trips to surrounding cities. Pictured here, from left to right, are Manny and Isabelle Feintuch, Al and Ruby Page, Mollie Kleiman, Ida and Howard Gault, and Walter Adams. Other clubs that were organized in Chattanooga included the Quarter Century Club, the Colonial Club, and the Emanon Club, whose members, in 1940, bought acreage on Chickamauga Lake and built summer cottages, a clubhouse, and a swimming area.

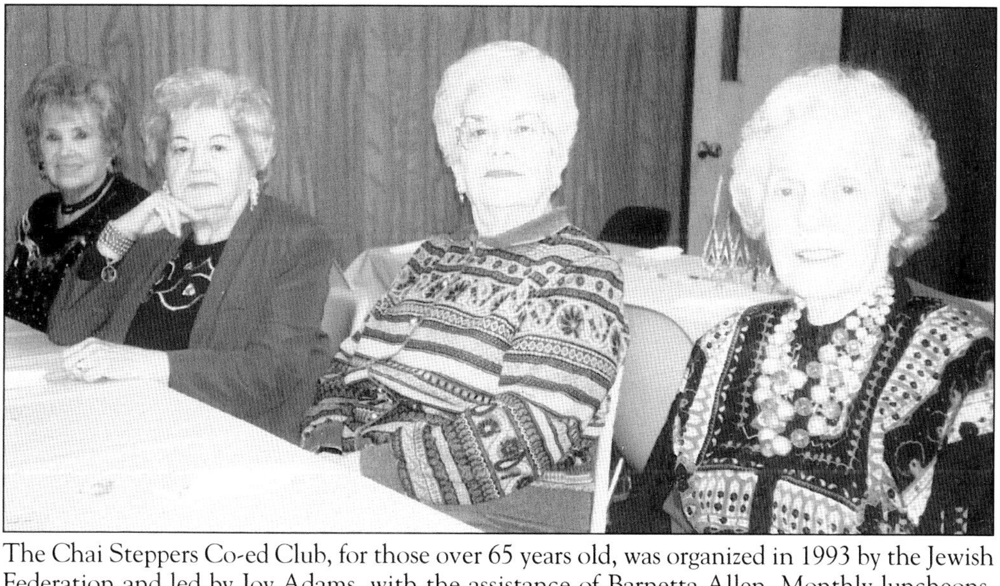

The Chai Steppers Co-ed Club, for those over 65 years old, was organized in 1993 by the Jewish Federation and led by Joy Adams, with the assistance of Barnetta Allen. Monthly luncheons, special events, and trips, plus bi-weekly exercise classes, were the main activities of the group. They spearheaded the creation of the Jewish Reflections Exhibit of 1996, depicting pictorially the history of the Jews of Chattanooga from 1865. The club is also collecting data, such as family trees, histories, and pictures, for the Chattanooga Jewish Archives. Pictured at a monthly luncheon, from left to right, are Reba Bock, Erma Lebovitz, Ruth Jacob, and Rae David.

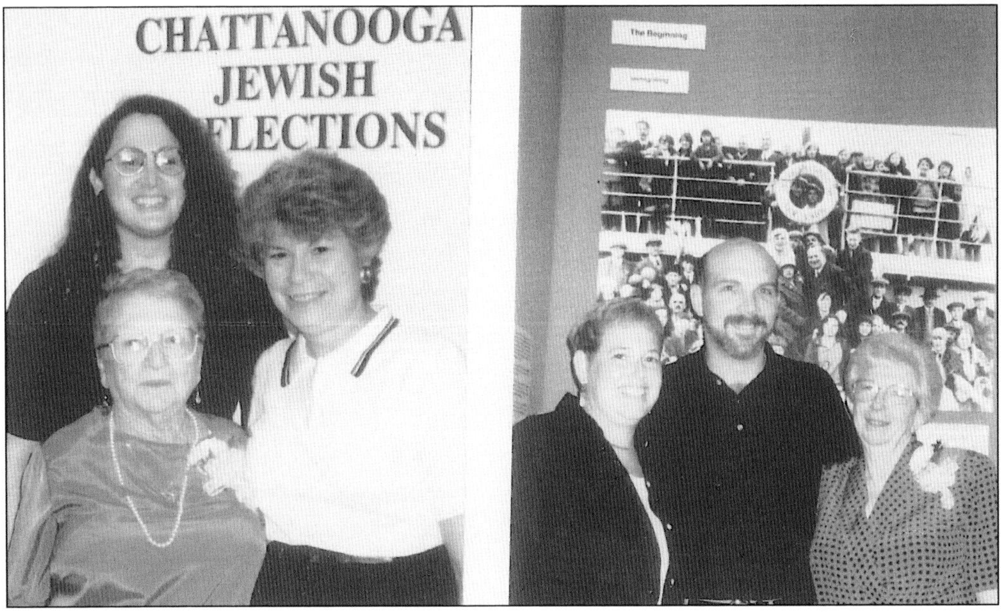

The "Jewish Reflections Exhibit—Chattanooga, 1865 to the Present" opened in August 1996 at the Chattanooga Regional History Museum for a three-month run. Pictured here on opening day, from left to right, are Barnetta Allen (co-chairman), Trudy Trivers and her daughter Laura (Harkins) of Washington D.C., Iris and Lee Abelson, and Joy Adams (curator and chairman of the exhibit).

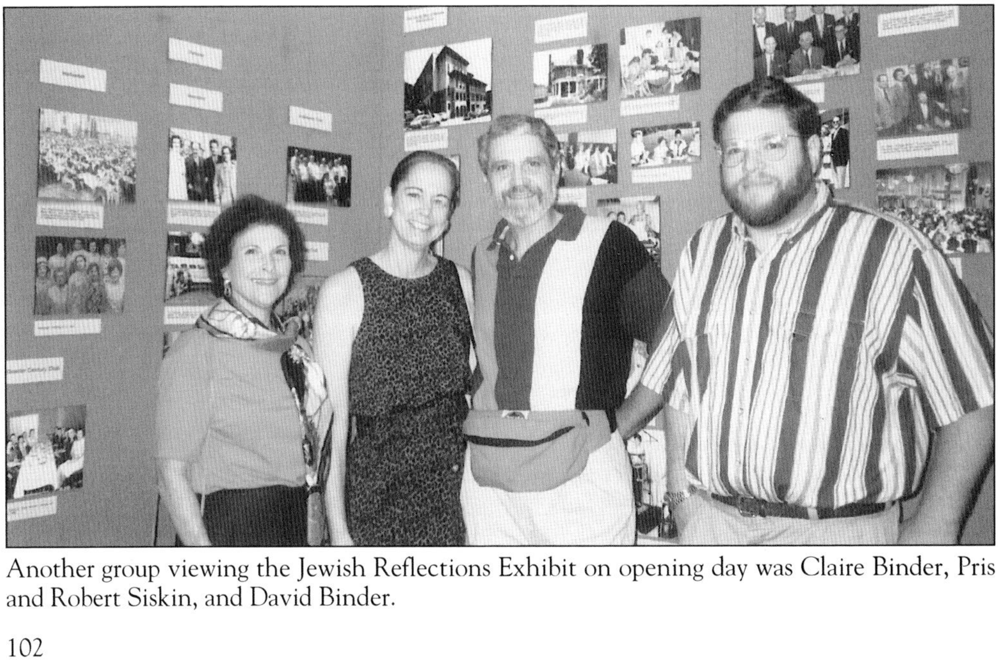

Another group viewing the Jewish Reflections Exhibit on opening day was Claire Binder, Pris and Robert Siskin, and David Binder.

Seven

INTERACTING IN THE COMMUNITY:

Military, Government, and the Arts

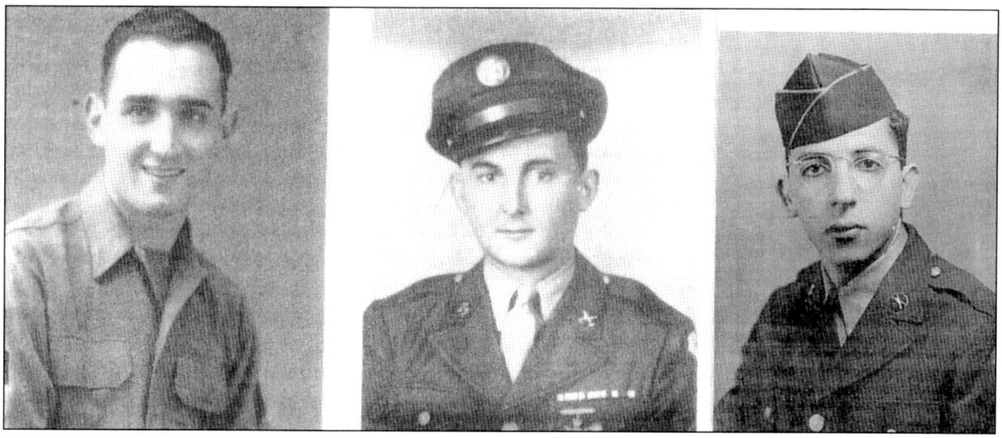

The Hebrew word tikkun olam means "repairing the world." The Torah commands Jews to commit themselves to creating a more perfect and just world. Chattanooga Jewish citizens have always and are continuing to work with the community to build an ever more perfect Chattanooga. One example is Chattanooga's young Jewish men serving in the War between the States, World War I, and World War II. Pictured here, from left to right, are Sam Spector, David Dubrow, and Harris Gould, three of Chattanooga's young men who gave their lives serving in World War II. The paneled library at the Mizpah Congregation was created soon after Harris' death in the late 1940s. It was built by Mr. and Mrs. Gus Gould in memory of their son. Another young person, Paul Fisher Goodman, also lost his life in World War II. Rosemary Wolff has been the librarian at the Mizpah Library for years, and she and her husband, Al, also headed the Adult Education Committee. Their children are Stephanie, Barbara, and David.

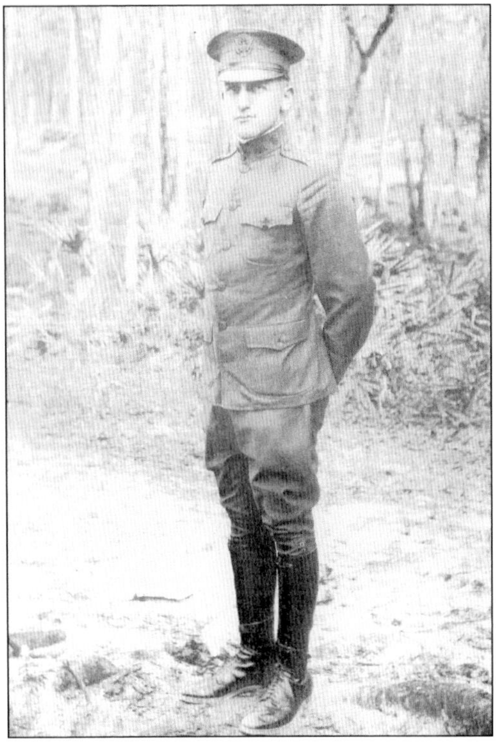

Captain Maurice Poss served in World War I from 1914 to 1918. He was the son of Ike Poss, who was born in Fremont, Ohio, in 1862. Ike moved to Chattanooga at the age of ten with his parents. Upon arriving in Chattanooga, the family entered the real estate business. Ike Poss was succeeded by his sons, Maurice and Henry, and the firm came to be known as Poss Bros. In the 1950s, the Maurice Poss Homes Housing Project on East Twenty-fifth Street was built for underprivileged families and was named for him. Maurice's son, H.M., and H.M's sons, Henry and David, operate the Tennessee Hotel Supply. H.M. was married to Ann Brown, and they had two more children: Charles, an attorney, and Cecil (Kollmansperger). Some other developers and builders in Chattanooga include Ival Goldstein, Colman Hochman, Tom Traub, and Herman Trotz.

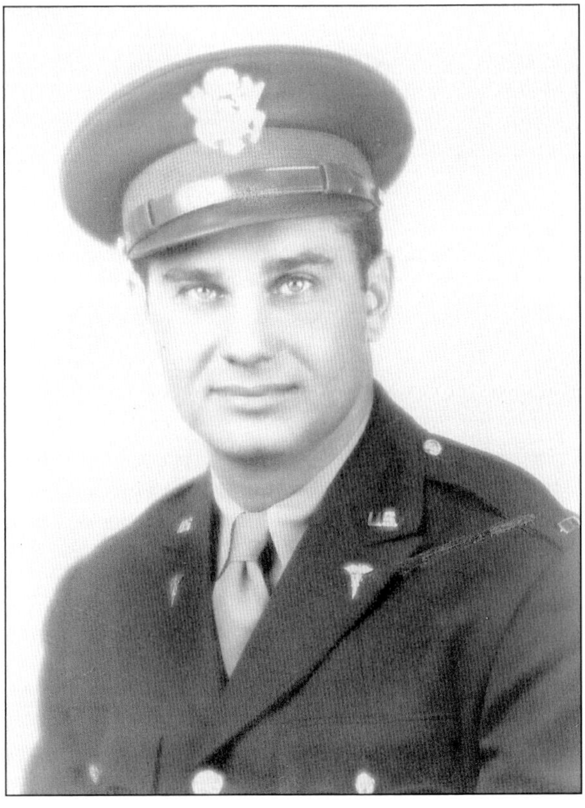

Before his army service from 1942 to 1945, Lt. Col. Jay Sadow practiced veterinary medicine in his hospital on Cherokee Boulevard in Chattanooga. In 1942, he married Sylvia Solomon and left for Iran for army duty in World War II. While there, he was in charge of building three movie theaters for the army to entertain the troops. After the war, he returned to Chattanooga and founded two radio stations, WRIP and WLMX, and a television station, WRIP-TV, which has evolved into FOX 61 Network. He was a pioneer in starting the first religious gospel broadcasting in the nation in 1958, for which he received great criticism at the time. He and Sylvia had one son, Dr. Samuel H. (Chip) Sadow, a heart surgeon in Palm Beach, Florida. He is now married to Gerry (Daneman Haber).

Sam Jaffe served in the U.S. Navy in World War II. Some other Chattanoogans who were in the service during World War II were Colonel Harry Miller, Bernard and Sam Shavin, Captain Raymond Effron, Ben Steinau, Sol Klaus, and Jack Cassell, among many, many others. Practically every family had sons in the service.

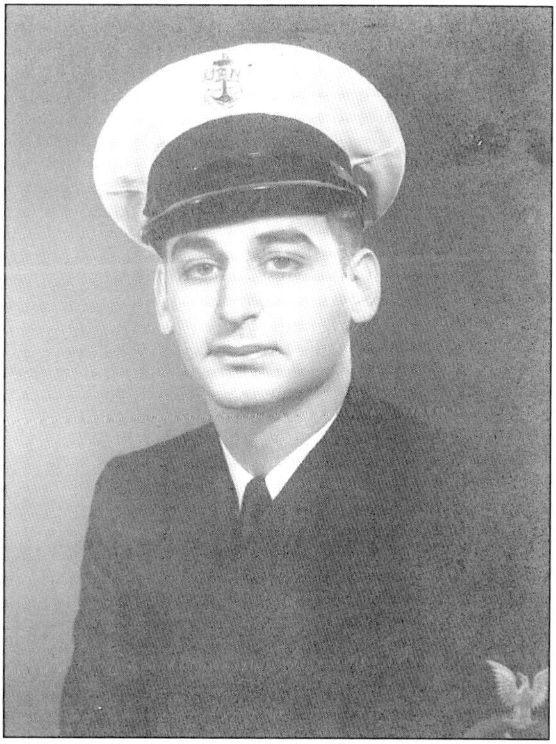

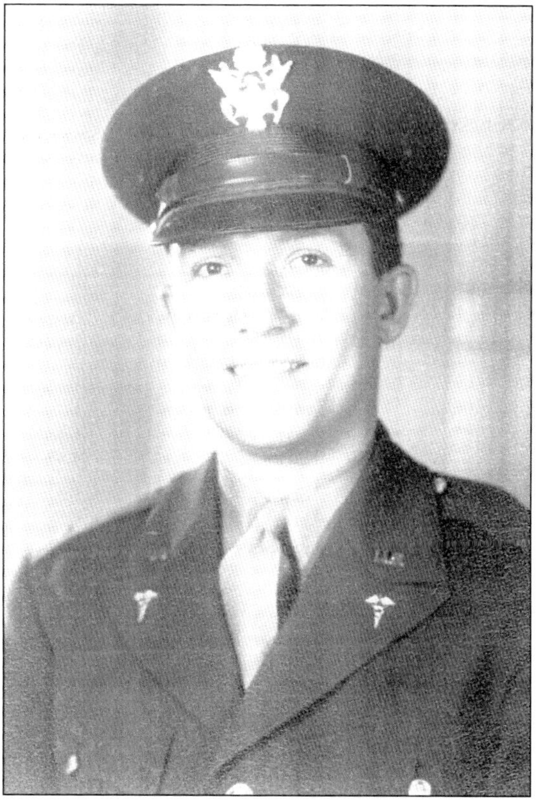

Captain Dr. Harold Schwartz served in World War II from 1943 to 1945. He was a leading obstetrician/gynecologist in Chattanooga after the war. In 1937, while in residency at Bellevue Hospital in New York City, Dr. Schwartz did some of the original research on the Rh factor. He married Eleanor Miller, and they had three children: Patricia, Harold Jr.(married to Elwynn), and Ellen (Yellin) of New Orleans. Harold Jr. has a son, Harold III, whose mother is Judy Schwartz. Eleanor and Harold Sr. have made a major contribution to the Ochs Memorial Temple Sanctuary in memory of their parents, Harry and Ethel Miller and Julius and Rebecca Schwartz. They gave eight exquisite stained-glass windows depicting eight of the major Jewish holidays. Erin Yon was commissioned to design and create these windows in 1997.

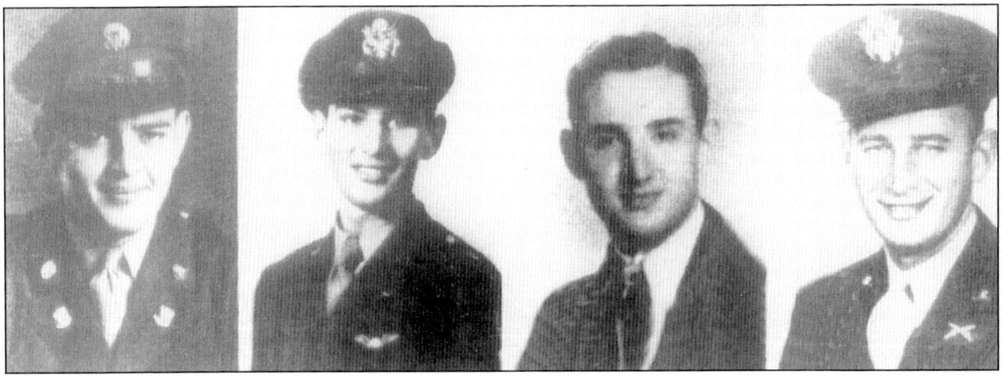

Abraham and Ella Spector had four sons who served during World War II: Marvin, Sam, Mark, and Joseph, certainly a record for any family! The Spectors had three more children: Freda, Bessie, and Julius (who too young to serve). Some of the Spector sons continued to live in Chattanooga and participated in all kinds of worthwhile activities. Marvin married Maxine, Mark married Mary (Richelson), Freda married Harry Cure, and Julius married Louise (Effron).

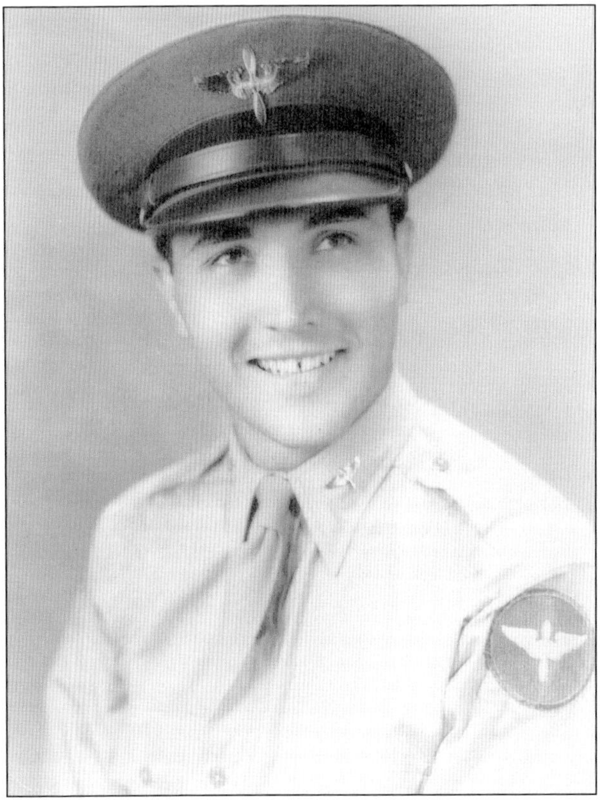

Herbert Abelson (pictured) served in the USAF in the Pacific. He has three children—Patricia (Maner), Lee, and Richard—and four grandchildren: Alan, Robert, Scott, and Blair. Charles Levine served on the USS *Queenfish* as a radio and sonar operator during World War II in the South and East China Seas, the Yellow Sea, and the Sea of Japan. Charles, a CPA, is married to Miriam Litoff and they have two children, Robert and Susie. Fred Rosen of Dalton was a PT Boat Commander in the navy. He was CEO of the Enduro Carpet Mills after the war.

The earliest of Chattanooga's Jews to serve in the government was Prosper Lazard, from Lorraine, France. He was appointed as the police commissioner in 1887 and then was elected city treasurer. He was president of the Mizpah Congregation from 1886 to 1889 and again in 1897. Prosper was a colorful person. In 1867, at the foot of Market Street on the Tennessee River, he opened a "floating bathhouse" that was swept downstream in the flood of 1867. He was rescued by a steamboat crew and towed back to Chattanooga. After that episode, Lazard opened a "drug, oil, and lamp" store on Market Street in partners with his brother-in law, Dr. Marx Block. They also offered "Concordia" wine, made from grapes from Dr. Block's farm on Missionary Ridge.

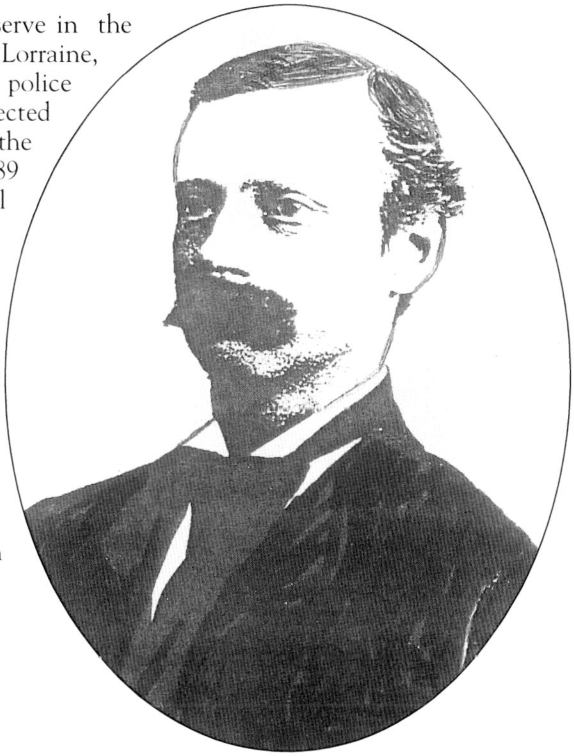

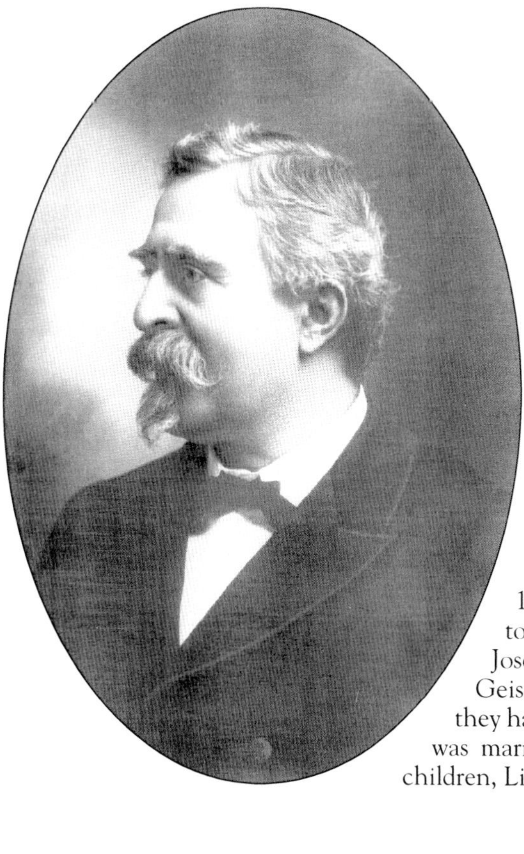

Joseph Wassman (pictured) was mayor of Chattanooga from 1901 to 1902 and was the first recorded president of the Mizpah Congregation from 1880 through 1885. From 1963 to 1964, Arvin Reingold served in the Tennessee State Legislature. Abe Prebul served as a commissioner to the town of East Ridge, Tennessee, from 1969 through 1972. Lee Abelson served as vice-mayor of the town of Signal Mountain, Tennessee, in 1995. Joseph Wassman's great-grandson is Robert Geismar. Arvin Reingold was married to Lil, and they had two children, Gail and Arthur. Abe Prebul was married to Esther (Stein), and they had three children, Lillie, Joyce, and Joe.

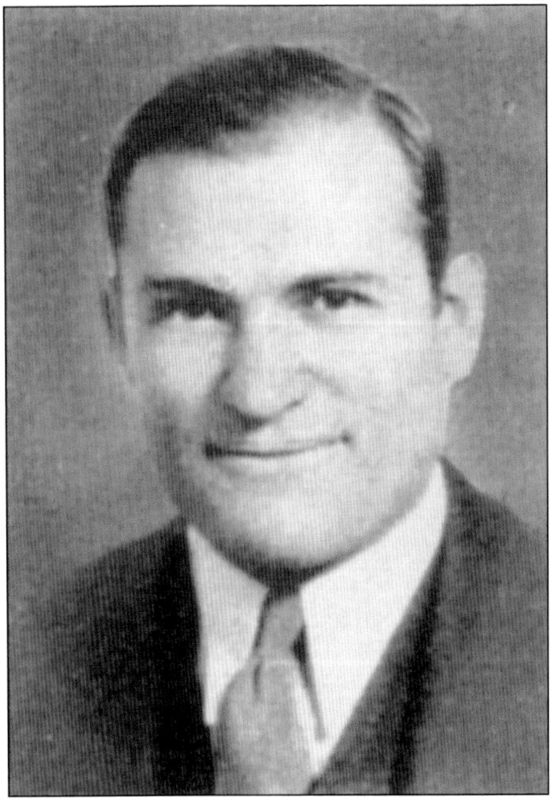

Judge Morris Finkelstein presided over the Chancery Court, Part II. He was appointed to the bench by Gov. Frank Clement in 1955, and was the elected by the people in 1956, 1958, and 1966 before retiring in 1972. He was very active in the B'nai Zion Congregation. His wife was Rose Baras, and his children were Marvin and Farol Faye. Other attorneys include Ralph Shumacker, Harry and Flossie Weill, Harry, Marvin, Ronald, and Andrew Berke, Robert Kiselik, Howard Levine, Jon and Judy Bloom Minnen, Ben Tabb, Bernie Cohen, Hal Schwartz Jr., Arvin Reingold, Charles Poss, Selma Paty, Pam Rymer, Allison Ulin, Stephen Goldstein, Louis and Eron Epstein, Michael Mallen, Carol Berz and Charles Dupree, Richard Schulman, Don Spiegel, and Hallie McFadden, among others.

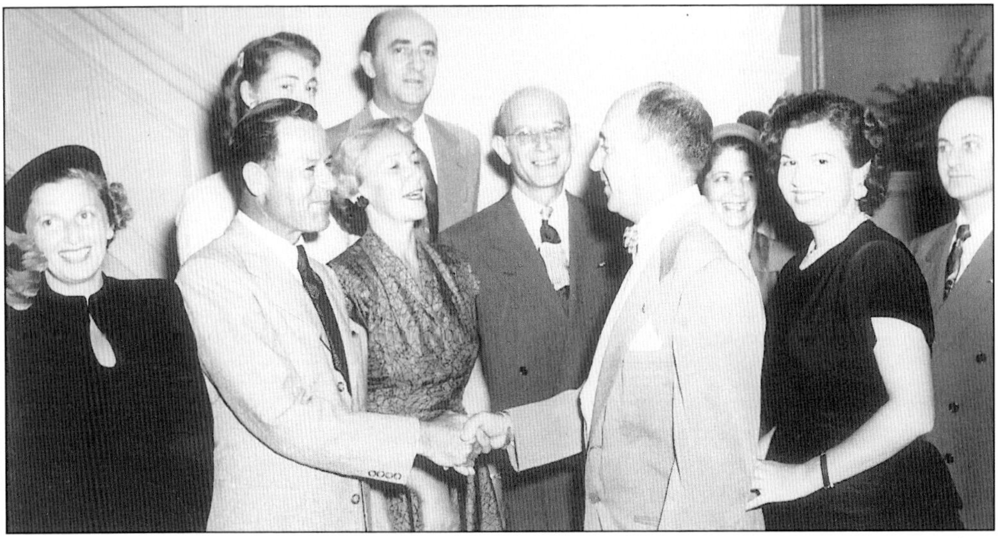

Judge Benjamin Louis Cash sat on the General Sessions Court Bench. He was appointed in 1968 by Governor Buford Ellington. In 1970, Cash was elected by the people to the Criminal Court Bench. He is pictured here with his wife, Rose, at a reception at the Jewish Edgewood Country Club in 1949. Ben and Rose had two daughters, Pat and Antoinette. Others in the picture include Klari and Abe Koblentz, Ben and Florence Block, Ada and Ralph Abelman, and Manny Russ and his daughter Rita. Some of Chattanooga's bankers are Sandy Chambers, Warren Dropkin, Stanley Leventhal, and Paul Stahl.

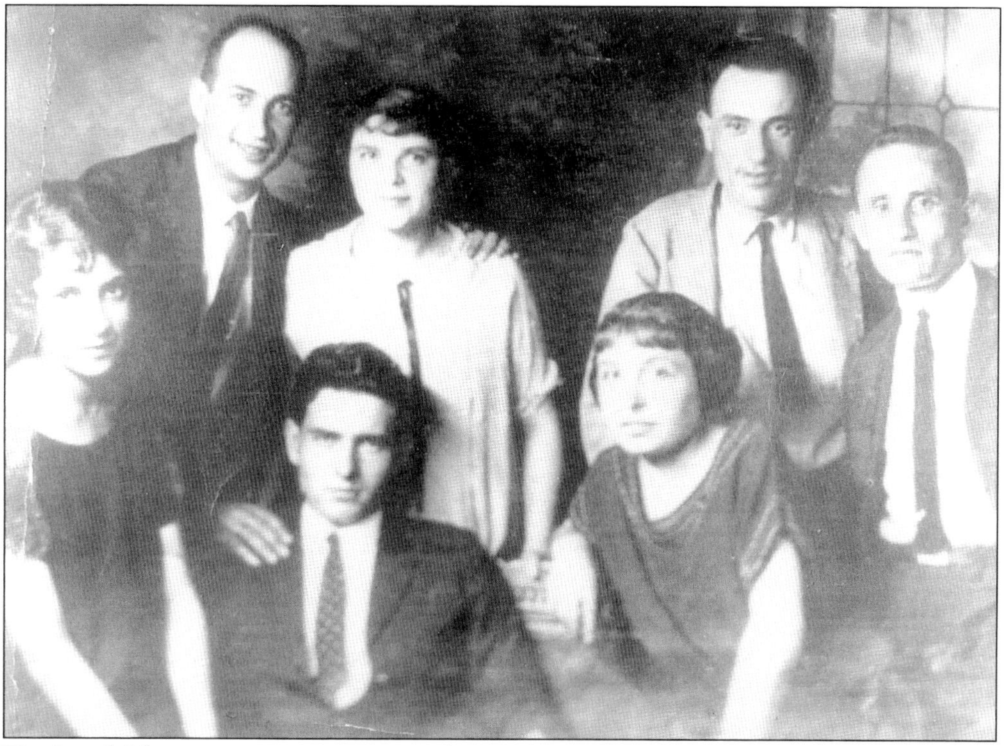

The Jewish Theater group in 1923 was under the auspices of the YMHA. All performances were in Yiddish. The group called itself the Jewish Culture Club. Pictured, from left to right, are as follows: (front row) unidentified, Mr. S.J. Rodman (executive secretary of the YMHA), and Eva Shapiro; (back row) Abe Shugarman, Tammie Shugarman, Wolf Gordon, and Max Sadikoff. Wolf Gordon was married to Bessie (Effron), and they had three children: Anna (Jacobson), Sara (Radin), and Max (married to Bella Shavin).

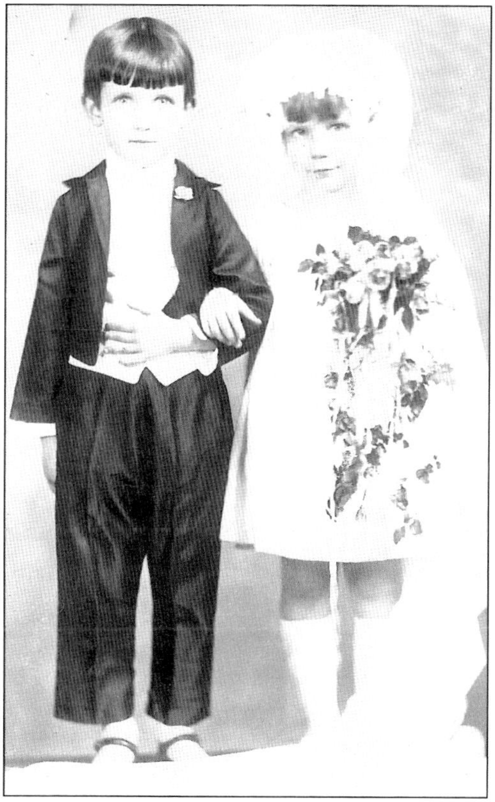

In 1927, the Mizpah Sisterhood planned a Tom Thumb wedding featuring two of the congregation's children. Pictured are groom Elinor Angel (now Mrs. William Breman of Atlanta) and bride Joy Effron (Adams). The story goes that Herman Geismar Jr. was originally to be the groom but caught the grippe (flu) and could not perform. So, Sadie Angel took her daughter to the barbershop, had her hair cut off, and dressed her in the groom's outfit. The show did go on!

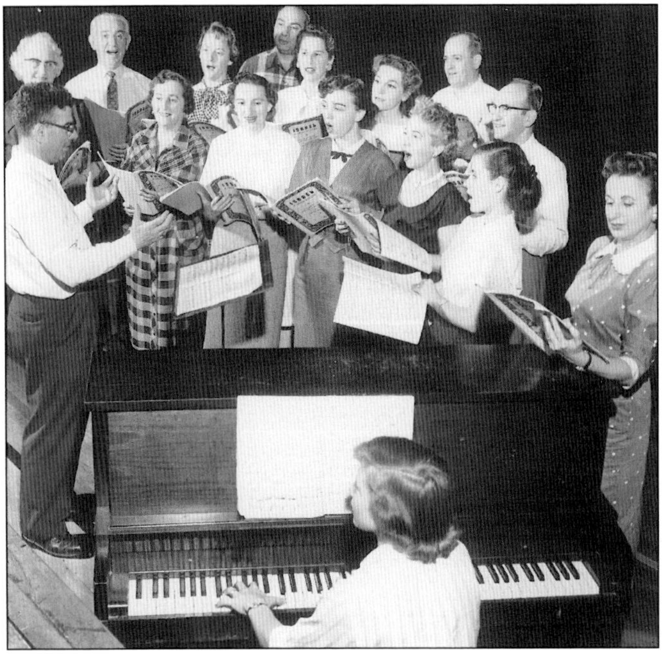

For many years, Sylvia Eidex (standing on the right) served the Chattanooga community as a voluntary play director and producer at the B'nai Zion Congregation and the JCC. In 1958 she directed a cantata celebrating the tenth anniversary of the State of Israel. Her husband, Harry, was extremely active in the B'nai Zion Congregation, serving as chevra kadisha (one who prepared bodies for burial) for over 30 years and as a teacher of young people. Their twin sons, Drs. Maxwell and Marshall Eidex, live in Atlanta.

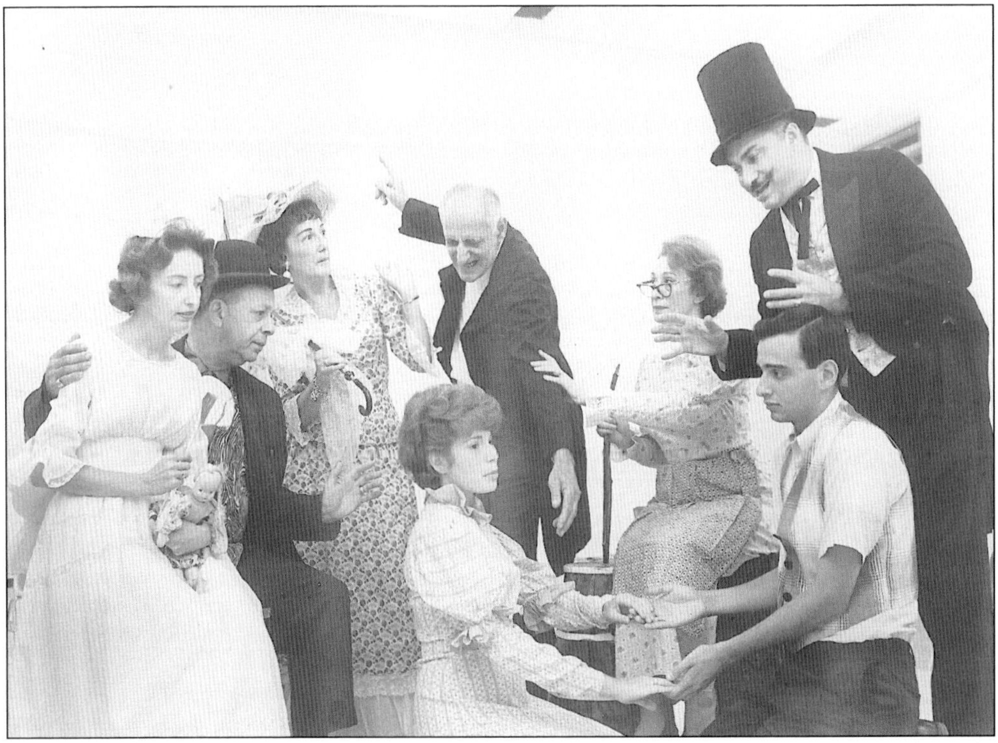

In 1963, the JCC produced a play, an old-fashioned melodrama featuring Dr. Howard Gault, Trudy Gault, Harry Fox, Dorothy Abelson, Harry Cure, and Ruth Chazen, among others. Howard's children are Trudy (Trivers) and Mark Gault of Atlanta. Dorothy's children are Iris and Trudy.

Monte Jaffe, the son of Izzy Jaffe, was born and raised in Chattanooga. He is shown here with his wife at a function during which he was honored in the 1990s. Monte lives in Germany and sings in opera houses all over Europe. Many in the Chattanooga Jewish community have been closely involved in the arts through the years. Melvin Margolin was one of the founders and the first conductor of the Chattanooga Symphony in 1933. Since 1993, the conductor of the symphony has been Robert Bernhardt. Jewish instrumentalists include violinists Kerren Berz, Alvin Blumberg, Jacinto Cobos, Lester Cohen, Solly Fott, Isadore Kaset, and Jacob Radin; concert masters Edward Shalett, Seymore Shavin, and Louis Slabosky; cellist Dr. Sam Binder; and French horn player Robert Shinbaum. Board members of the Chattanooga Symphony and Opera include Dr. Clarence and Edna Shaw, Rosalyn Reisman, Dr. Philip Livingston, Ruth Holmberg, Dr. Samuel and Claire Binder, Hal Schwartz Jr., Dr. David Tepper, Sonia Young, Priscilla Siskin, Karen Diamond, Gary Lander, Lawrence Levine, Ann Belkov, Candy Kruesi, Marilyn Center, and Eleanor Schwartz.

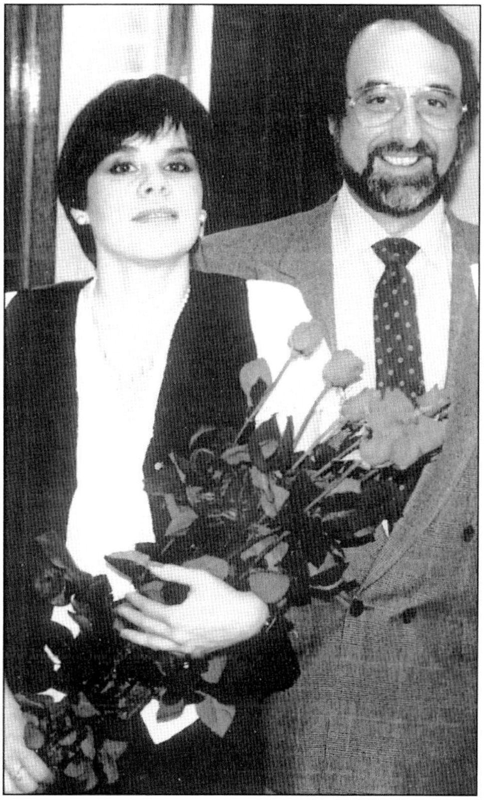

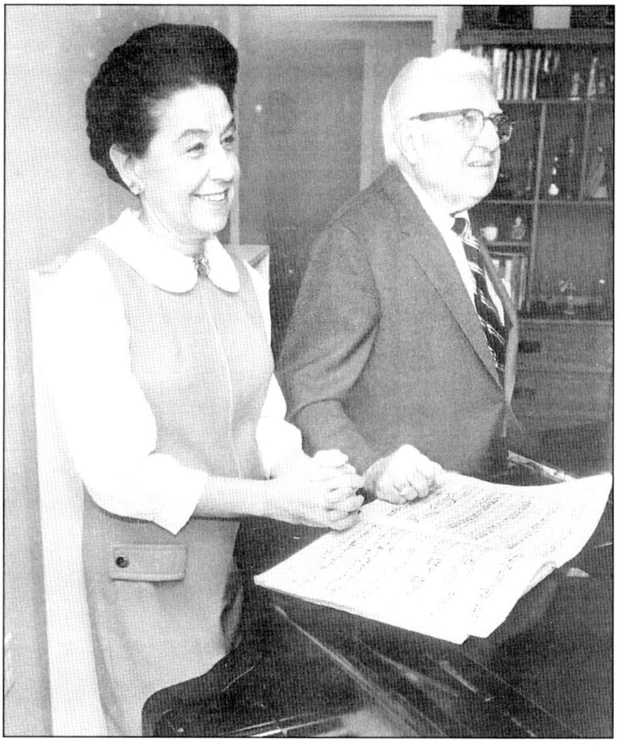

Edward and Bernice Shalett, a husband and wife team, are remembered for their violin and piano performances. They played at weddings and all kinds of events in Chattanooga. Ed and Bernice had two children, Teddi (Mendel) and Harold. Jewish supporters of the arts include Ruth Holmberg and Merv and Helen Pregulman (board members of Allied Arts); Marilyn Center, Karen Diamond, Nancy Ulin, and Cheri Spitalny (former board members of the Hunter Museum of Art); and Ann Belkov, Abe Borisky, Judge Morris Finklestein, Rabbi Kenneth Kanter, Candy Kruesi, Norman Moore, Judy Schwartz, Farol Seratean, and Sonia Young (former board members of the (Little Theater) Chattanooga Theater Center).

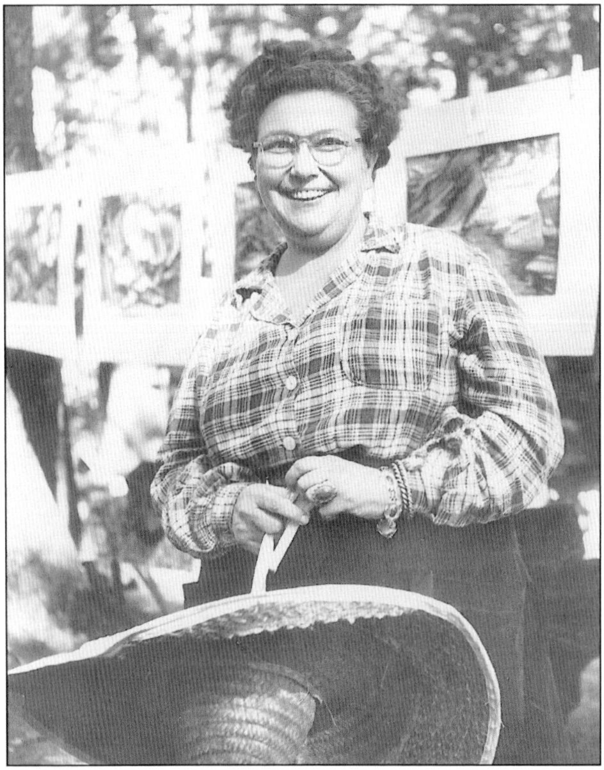

Frances (Fannye) Mennen is the genius who first introduced the idea of the Clothesline Art Show in 1946, an annual, highly acclaimed event for 27 years. She named her show Plum Nelly because it was held "*Plum* out of Tennessee and *nelly* (nearly) in Georgia." The shows were held in the New Salem Community between Trenton and Lafayette on Georgia Highway 143. The paintings were displayed out in the woods on clotheslines attached to tree trunks. Food and crafts were also offered at these events. A skilled craftsman and artist herself, Fannye carefully selected the work to be shown and screened out all but the finest and best artists. (Chattanooga/Hamilton County Bicentennial Library.)

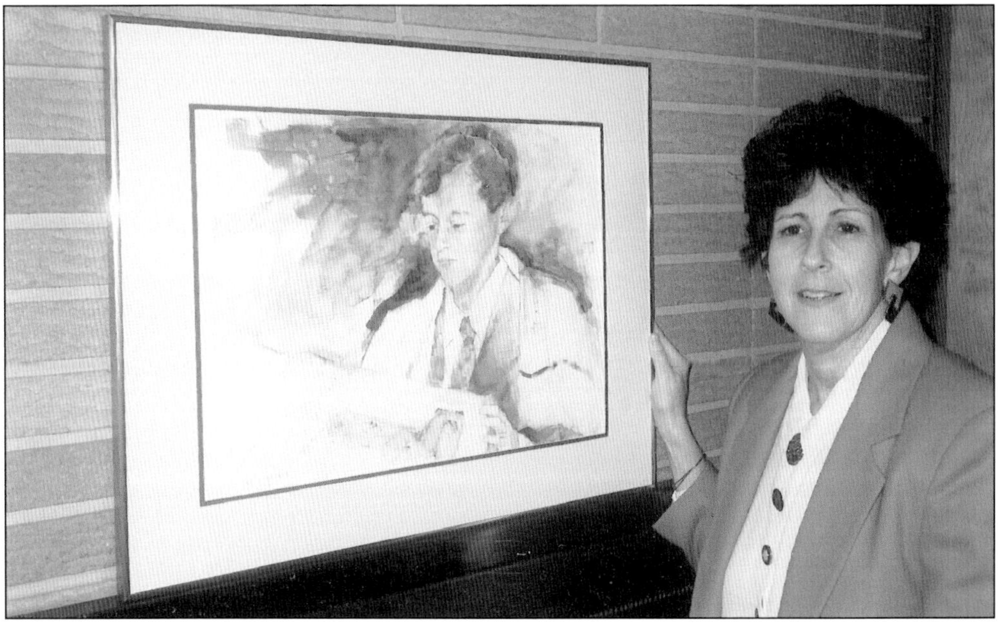

Watercolor artist and instructor Jan Greenwald of Atlanta (the daughter of Jo Ann and Maurice Richelson) was born and raised in Chattanooga. Her work is exhibited and sold throughout the Southeast. The painting in this photograph is of her son Michael when he was reading from the Torah, at the time of his bar mitzvah in 1994. Jan has two brothers in Chattanooga, Steven and Robert.

Lillian Brown Feinstein, the much beloved wife of Rabbi Abraham Feinstein, was a painter and sculptress for over 40 years. Her sculptures were made in both wood and metal and are shown in museums around the country.

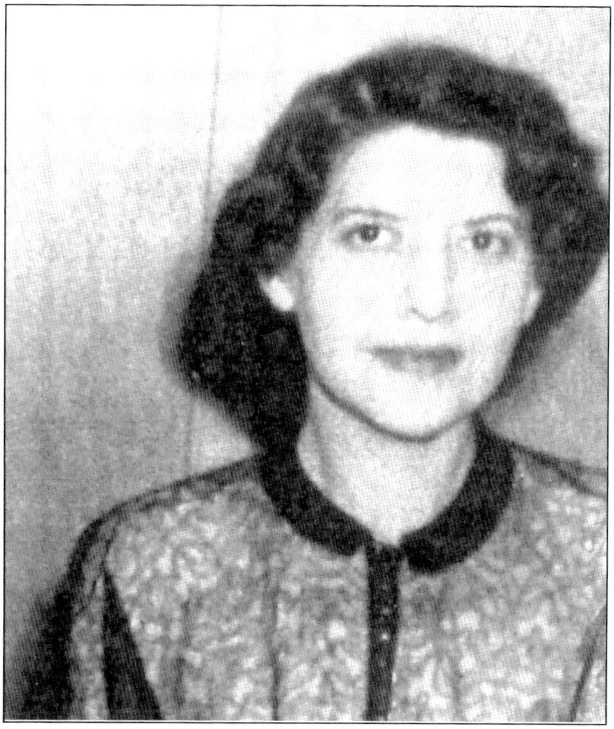

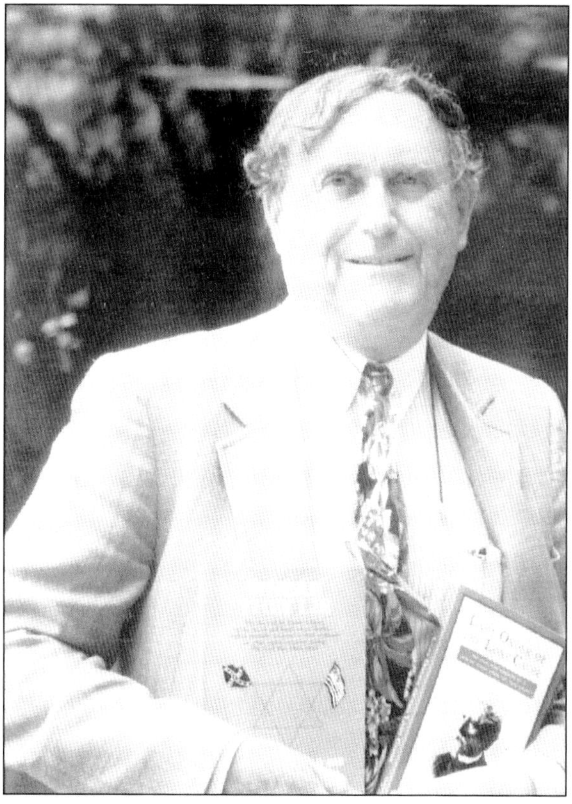

CPA Mel Young is the author of two books (in the 1990s) on the Civil War: *Where They Lie* and *Last Order of the Lost Cause*. He is an expert on Jewish soldiers who fought in the War between the States. He discovered that Jews fought against one another for both the North and the South. There were 9,000 Jews in the Union Army and 2,000 Jews in the Confederate Army. Another Chattanooga writer is Julius Parker, who was city desk editor at the *Chattanooga News Free Press* and wrote *Grab Life and Hold On*. His son, Barry Parker, has written several books, two of which are *The Tennesseean* and *The Tennesseeans Revisited*.

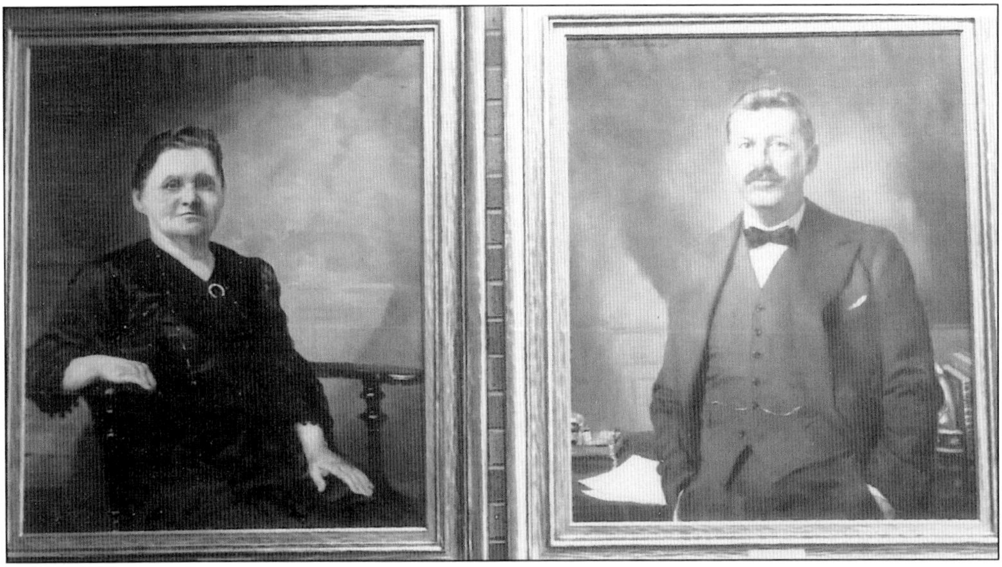

Mose and Garrison Siskin and their heirs are Chattanooga's most outstanding philanthropists. They created the Siskin Museum, the Siskin Foundation, the Siskin School, and the Siskin Rehabilitation Hospital in memory of their parents, Robert and Anna Siskin (pictured). The Foundation was created in 1950 to realize a triple ambition of Mose and Garrison: to characterize and render channels for religious, philanthropic, and social causes.

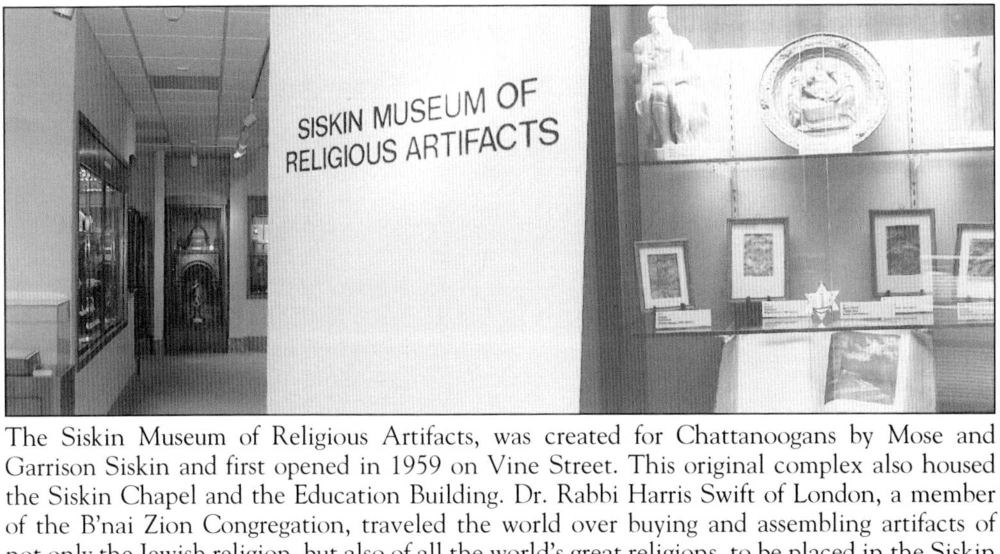

The Siskin Museum of Religious Artifacts, was created for Chattanoogans by Mose and Garrison Siskin and first opened in 1959 on Vine Street. This original complex also housed the Siskin Chapel and the Education Building. Dr. Rabbi Harris Swift of London, a member of the B'nai Zion Congregation, traveled the world over buying and assembling artifacts of not only the Jewish religion, but also of all the world's great religions, to be placed in the Siskin Museum. The exhibit was moved to a new location in the new Siskin Complex off East Third Street in 1990. Pictured are some of the magnificent treasures in the new Siskin Museum.

Eight

BUILDING COMMUNITY: *Welfare and Special Achievers*

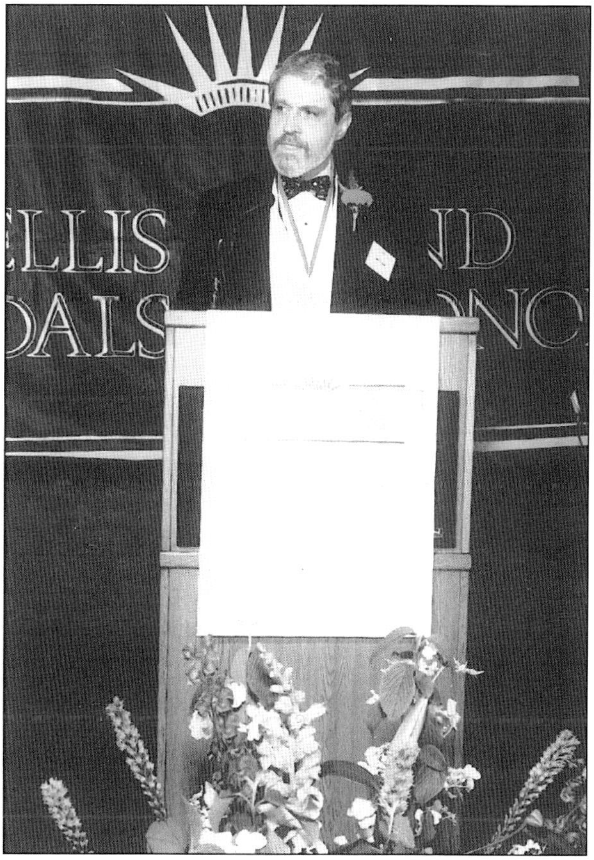

Robert Siskin received the Ellis Island Medal of Honor for the Siskin family in 1995. The award is given to immigrant families "who made a difference in America." His wife, Priscilla (Flasher), a native of Beverly Hills, California, and their two sons, Johathan of Washington, D.C., and Daniel of Los Angeles, were present.

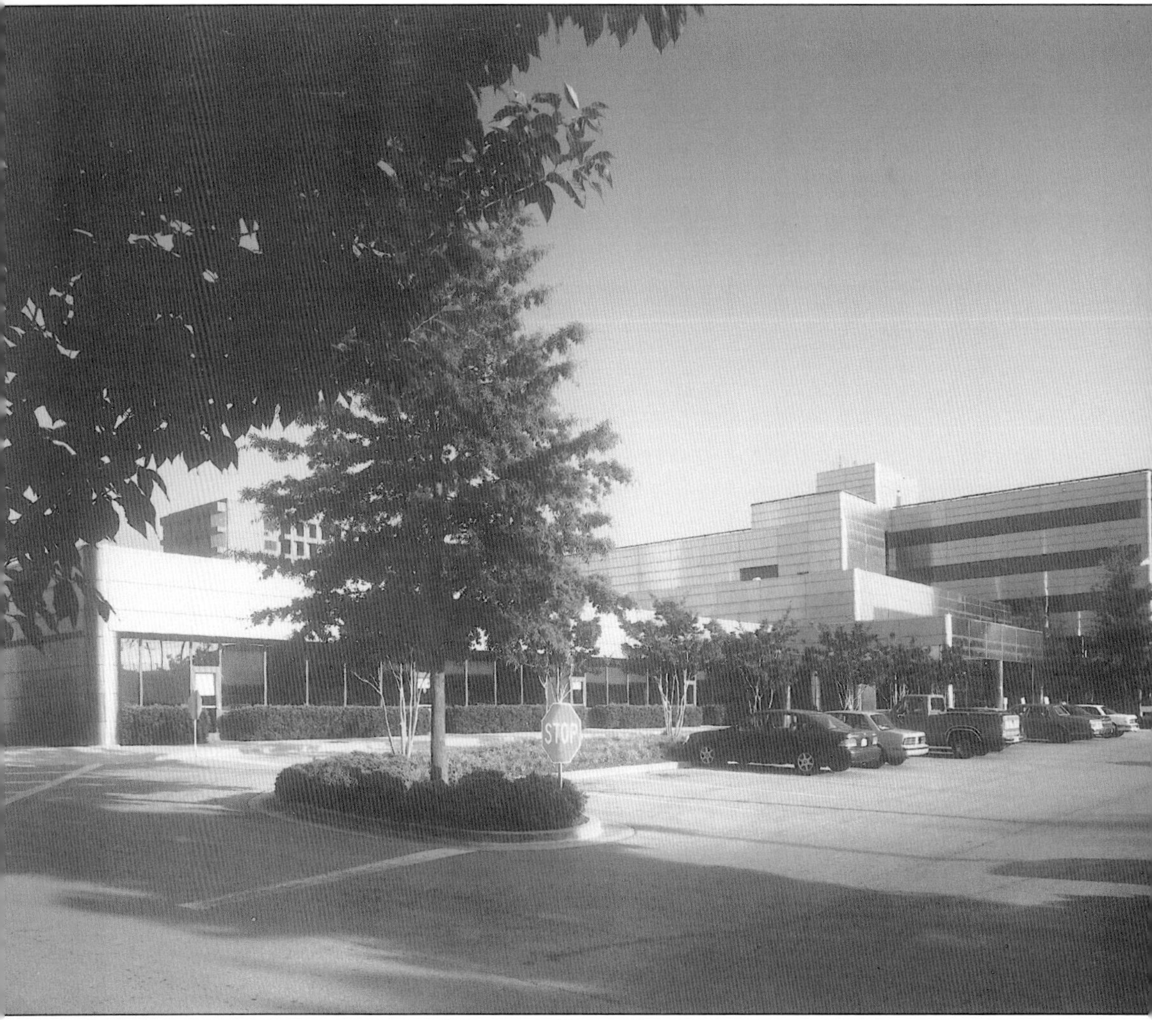

The new Siskin complex opened in 1990 off East Third Street on Siskin Road. It is Tennessee's first free-standing hospital dedicated solely to physical rehabilitation. It contains the Siskin Hospital for Physical Rehabilitation, the Siskin School for individuals with one or more disabilities, the Siskin Foundation offices, and the Museum of Religious Artifacts. Other Siskin Foundation programs are the Westside Child Development Center and the Children's Wellness Center. "For nearly 50 years the Siskin Foundation has helped children and adults with disabilities and special needs."

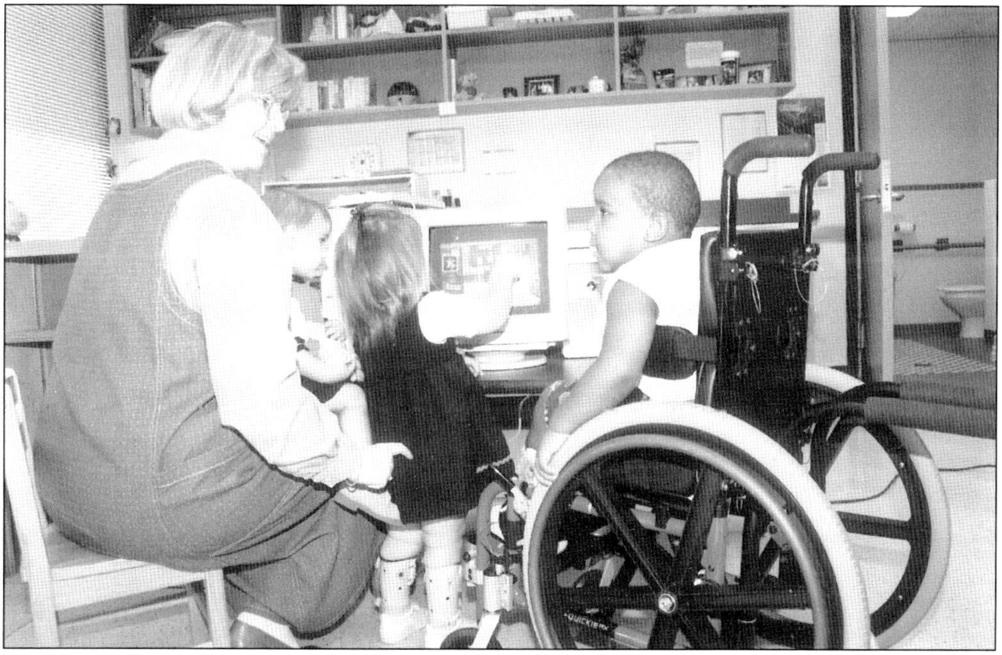

The Siskin School, accredited, licensed, and approved by five Tennessee commissions and departments, "is an early intervention and educational program for children between the ages of birth and 21 who have one or more developmental disabilities." There are three main components of the school: evaluation, early intervention with a combination of home/school based programs, and the school program that modifies the curriculum for each child according to individual needs. "With a low teacher/student ratio and intensive structured teaching, the students are provided with opportunities to develop self-confidence, intellectual, communication, and relational skills."

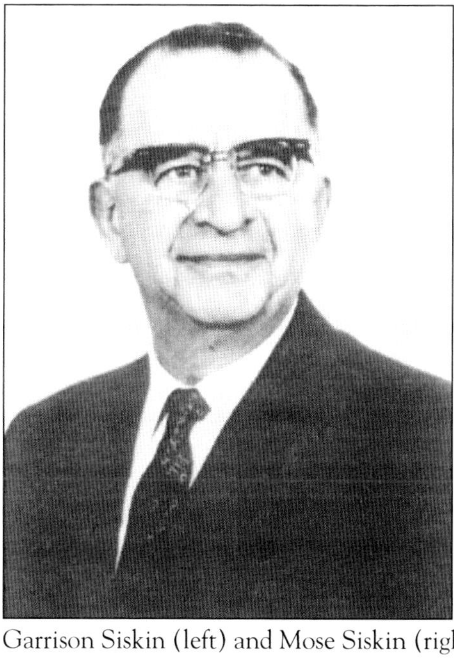

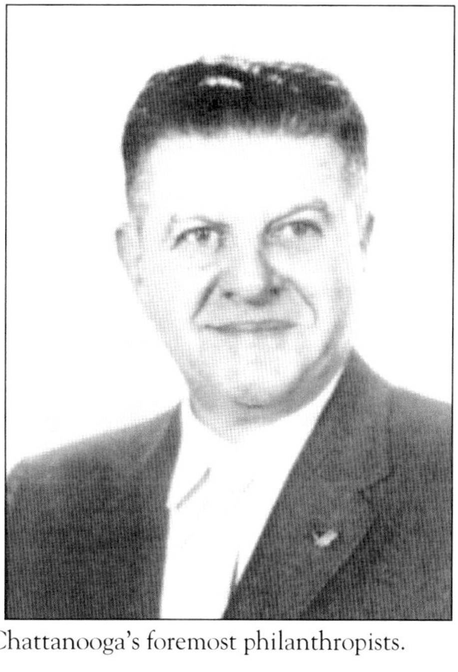

Garrison Siskin (left) and Mose Siskin (right) are Chattanooga's foremost philanthropists.

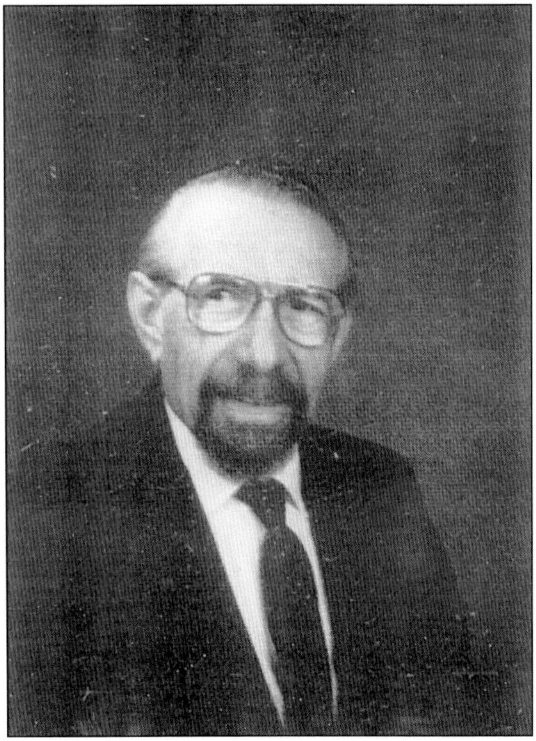

Dr. David Dzik, an optometrist and pioneer in the vision training of children, won the Southeast Tennessee "Optometrist of the Year" Award in 1970 because of his thesis and research on "Vision and the Child in Tennessee." The paper analyzed the visual status of children as it related to overall behavior. Dzik's son, Dr. Joseph Dzik, is an optometrist in Chattanooga and holds classes in vision training. David's older son, Johnny, lives in New York and teaches music. Other optometrists in Chattanooga were Al Rhodes and his son Clayton, Murray Porter, Max Yagoda, and Charles Rosenthal.

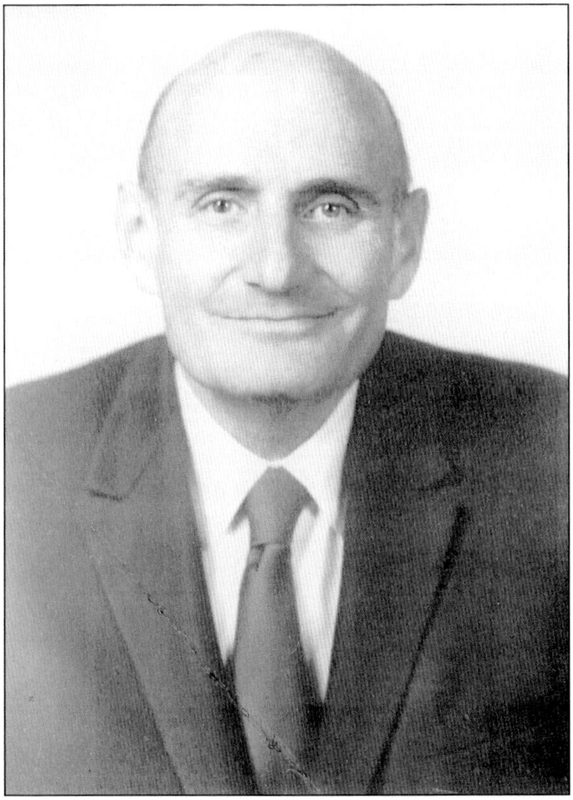

Alvin Blumberg, a native Chattanoogan, was a man of four successful careers: he was a violinist (having studied at the Julliard School of Music, he played in the Chattanooga Symphony), a Chattanooga public school teacher, a businessman (he owned six discount chain stores), and an Army officer. After serving 30 years in the U.S. Army and 5 years on active duty during World War II, he was discharged as a Lt. Colonel. He then served in the U.S. Army Reserves until retiring as commanding officer of the 3397th U.S. Army Garrison in Chattanooga, at which time he was awarded a Legion of Merit Citation for exceptionally meritorious conduct in the performance of outstanding services. Alvin married Peggy (Steinfirst) of New Orleans, and they had three children: Alvin Jr., William, and Janet. Alvin Jr. and William graduated from the Air Force Academy.

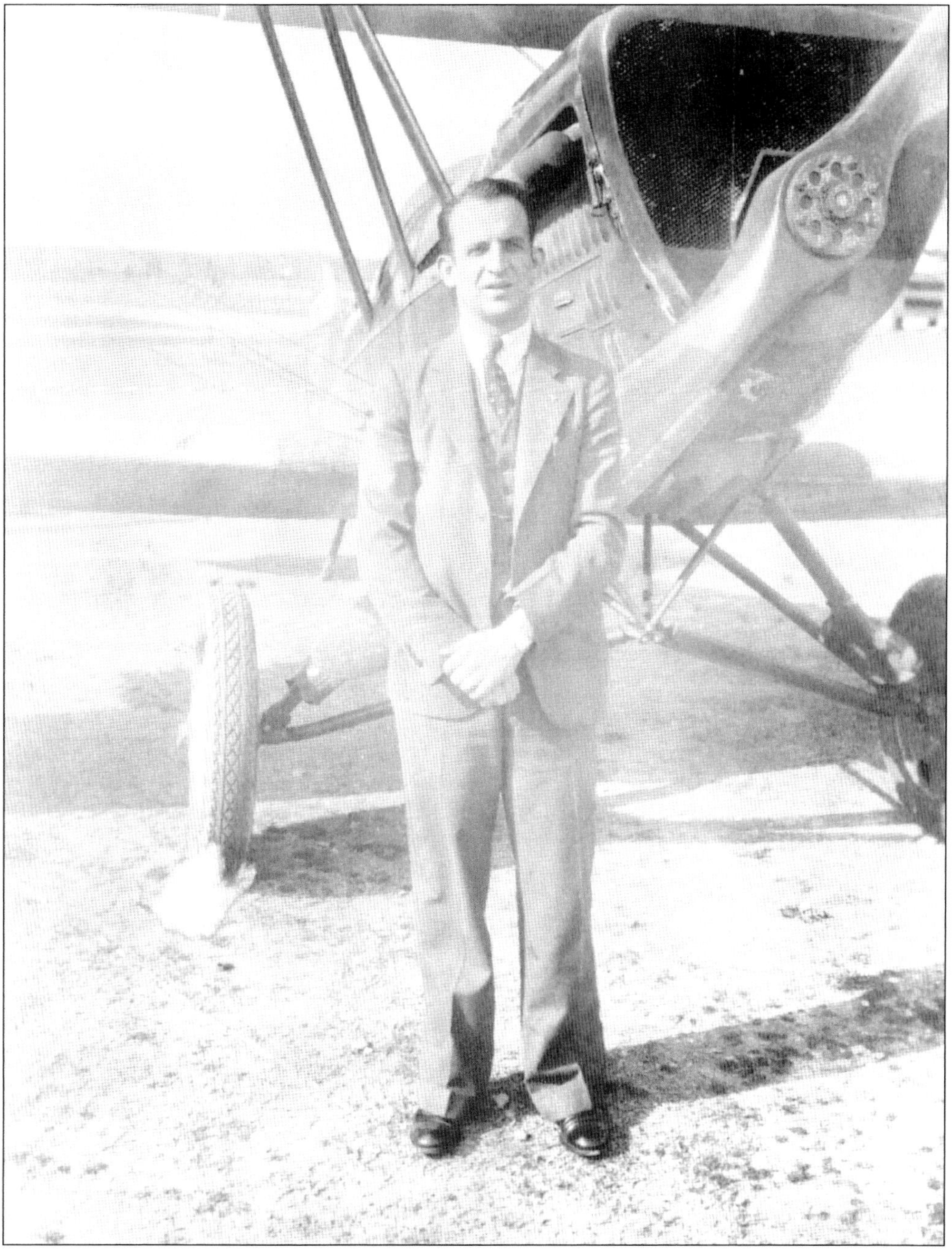

Myer H. Winer was Chattanooga's first Jewish aviator! He was taught to fly by Harry Porter, a Chattanooga pioneer in the flying industry. Myer is pictured with his French-made, open-cockpit biplane in the early 1930s. He loved to participate in air races, which he kept very secret from his mother. When he became engaged to Rose Prince, she made him sell his plane before she would agree to marry him. He was very active in the B'nai Zion congregation, serving as chairman of the chevra kadisha (the ritual preparer of bodies for burial) for many years. Myer and Rose had three children: Lois (Kiselik), Sanford (Elaine Brukner). and Minna Ree (Ed Miranne).

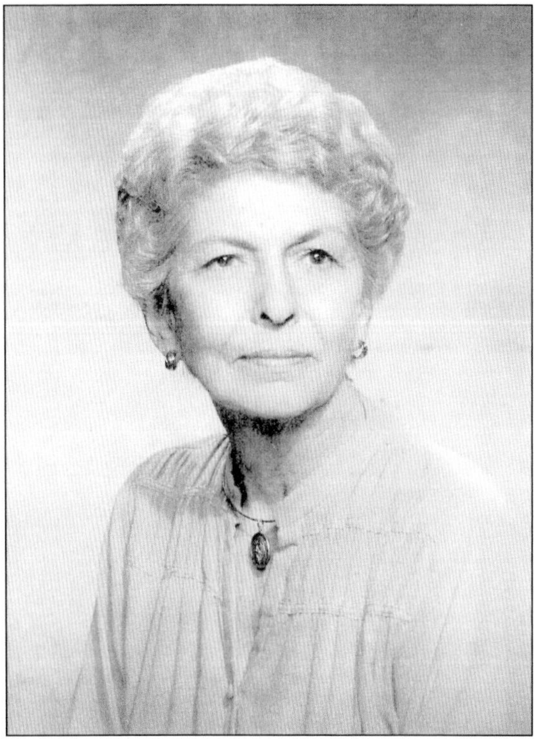

Carolyn Prendergast Henning distinguished herself in activities at the Mizpah Congregation as well as in the community at large. She was the first woman president of the Mizpah Congregation, and served in that position two different times in the 1980s. She was the director of the Chattanooga Volunteer Bureau for ten years, assistant director of the Chattanooga Metropolitan Council, served on the Chattanooga-Hamilton County Regional Planning Commission for 23 years, was chairman of the board of commissioners of the Chattanooga Housing Authority for a total of 19 years, and was one of the original board members of the Chattanooga Neighborhood Enterprise. She was married (and later divorced) to Dr. Harold Henning, and they had three children: Judy (Gehr) of Cincinnati, Ohio, William (Bill) of Colombia, Missouri, and Robert (Bob) of Memphis.

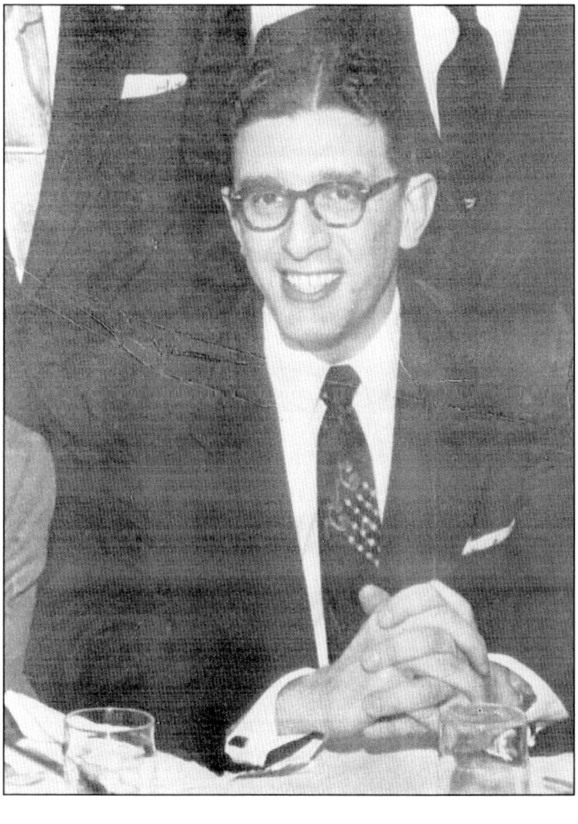

Joel W. "Jay" Solomon was appointed by President Jimmy Carter as director of the General Services Administration in Washington, D.C. A graduate of Baylor and Vanderbilt University, he was connected with the Independent Enterprises and Arlen Shopping Centers and was involved in shopping mall and office complex development. The old Main Post Office on Cherry Street was renamed in his honor, becoming the Joel W. Solomon Federal Building. He was married to Rosalyn, and they had two children: Joel Jr. of Nashville and Linda of New York and Connecticut.

Charles B. Lebovitz, chairman of the board and chief executive officer of CBL & Associates Properties, Inc., and past chairman of the International Council of Shopping Centers, poses with his wife, Betty, as he receives the McCallie School's distinguished Alumnus Award in 1995. Eastgate, Northgate, and Hamilton Place have been developed by the Lebovitz family over the past 35 years. As of April 1, 1999, the firm owns/manages 140 shopping centers in 25 states, totaling 33.5 million square feet. He has four children, Stephen, Michael, Alan, and Beth, three of which are active in the operation of the company—Stephen was named president in February 1999, Michael is senior vice president of mall projects, and Alan is an executive in the mall development division. Beth, a resident of Brookline, Massachusetts, is employed by the Timberland Corp. Isaac Lebovitz (Charles' grandfather) came to Chattanooga from Russia at the turn of the 20th century. He and his wife, Fannie, had seven children: Abner, Dave, Edith, Louis, Moses, Rae (Charles' father), and Robert. The Lebovitz family has made very generous contributions to local endeavors and the Israeli community.

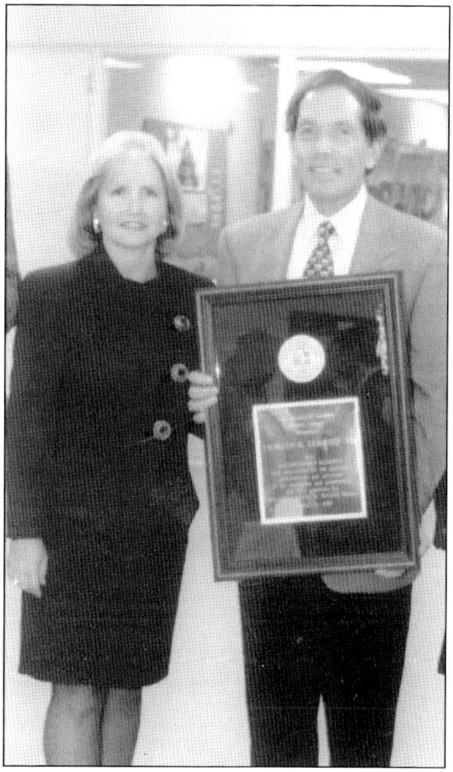

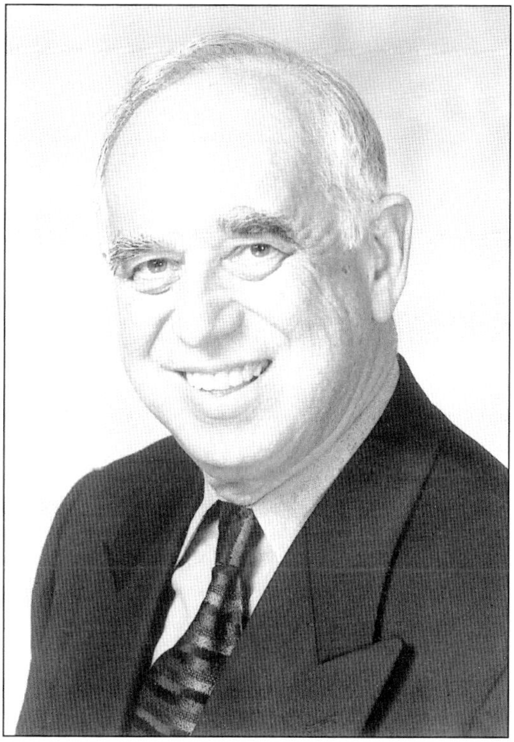

S. David Freeman was reared and educated in the Chattanooga public schools. He is known for implementing energy efficiency and the environmentally compatible production of electricity. As such, he has served in high-level government positions as an energy advisor to the White House, to the Senate Commerce Committee, and to the Federal Power Commission. His home now is in Los Angeles, California, where he is the general manager of the nation's largest municipal utility, the Los Angeles Department of Water and Power. Formerly, he was chief executive officer of power authorities in New York, in Tennessee (the TVA), in Texas, and in Sacramento, California. He was director of the Ford Foundation's landmark Energy Policy Project. His father was one of the early merchants in Chattanooga and operated a clothing and umbrella shop on Ninth Street.

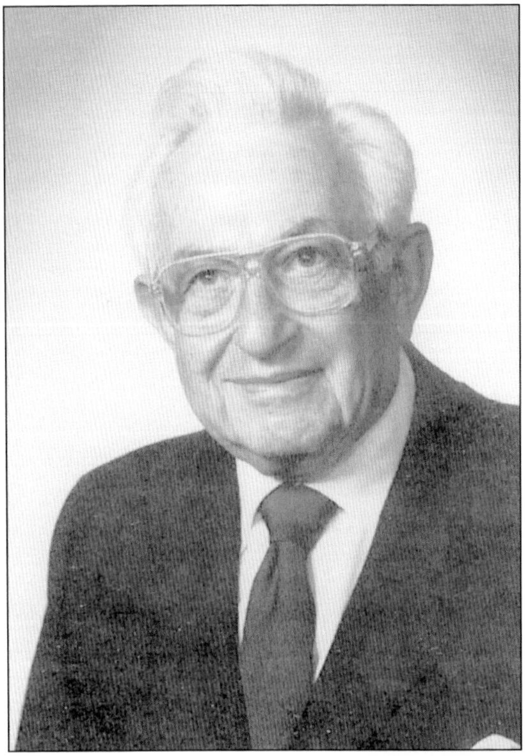

Dr. Sidney Edelstein, born and reared in Chattanooga, was founder of the Dexter Chemical Corporation in New York City. Described as a "citizen of the world," he was one of the world's leading authorities in textile dyes and created the formula for Stone Washed Blue Jeans. He pioneered the research in Israel on the origin of ancient royal purple dye, and founded the Edelstein wing of the Hebrew University in Jerusalem, which houses all the Edelstein papers, along with an incredible collection of books on the history of dyes. Because he believed that "Science must work with a sense of History, or we shall destroy ourselves," he created a new department in the Hebrew University called Philosophy and Science. Sidney's grandparents came to Chattanooga in 1891. His sister was Miriam Edelstein (Effron), whose children are Doris Effron (Goldstein) and Dr. Morris Effron of Cambridge, Maryland.

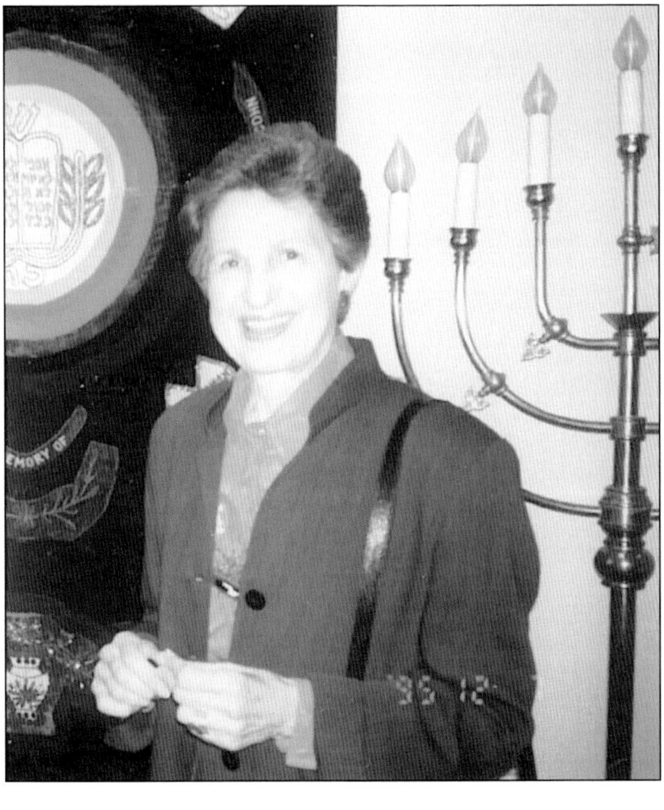

Ruth Sulzberger Holmberg, a granddaughter of Adolph S. Ochs, has been the Publisher and President of *The Chattanooga Times*. She is a member of the Mizpah Congregation and has continued to contribute to the welfare of the Ochs Memorial Temple, which her grandfather built and gave to the congregation. More than this, she has contributed greatly to the welfare of Chattanooga, Tennessee. Native Wes Hasden served Ruth Holmberg as assistant to the publisher. Wes is married to Nikki Cohen, a reviewer/critic for the *Times*, and they have one daughter, Kaysi Dixon, who lives in Greenville, South Carolina.

Ted Mallen, president and CEO of Intera Corporation in Chattanooga, developed the original process for treating man-made fibers to make them comfortable and absorbent—to "wick away moisture," resist odor, mold, mildew, fungus, yeast, and bacteria. He registered the trade name "Intera" for this product and holds many patents on the process. Now licensed and marketed on a global basis, Intera is also sold under other brand names and is the world's only proven permanent moisture transport technology. Ted's sons are Richard (Rick) and Brian.

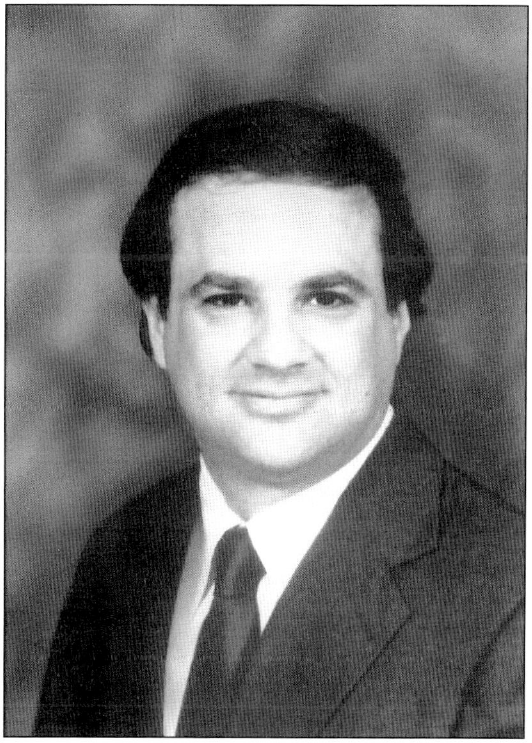

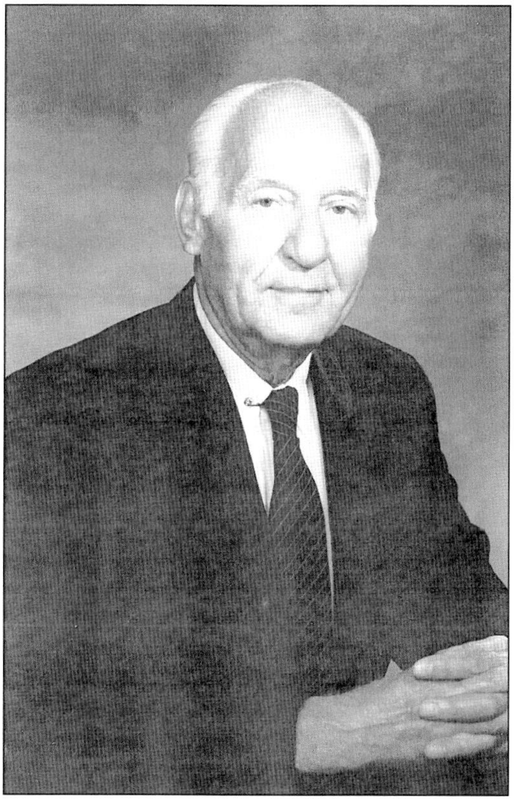

Felix Diamond founded the Felix Diamond Company, a general insurance agency, which celebrated its 60th anniversary in 1990, and the Reliance Mortgage Company. He was a founding partner and charter board member of WDEF-TV Channel 12. He served as president of the Mizpah Congregation, the Chattanooga Jewish Welfare Federation, the Insurors of Chattanooga, and as chairman of the board of directors of St. Barnabas Nursing Home. Felix married Estelle Moore, and they had three children: Sally (Rosenberg) of Greenwich, Colorado, Norma (Perlman) of Westport, Colorado, and David, who carries on the insurance/mortgage business with his son Sam. David's wife, Karen, won the 1999 Woman's Community Service Award from the Pilot Club for her tireless dedication to improving the quality of life in her community, from historic preservation to the arts. Karen and David also have a daughter, Sarah.

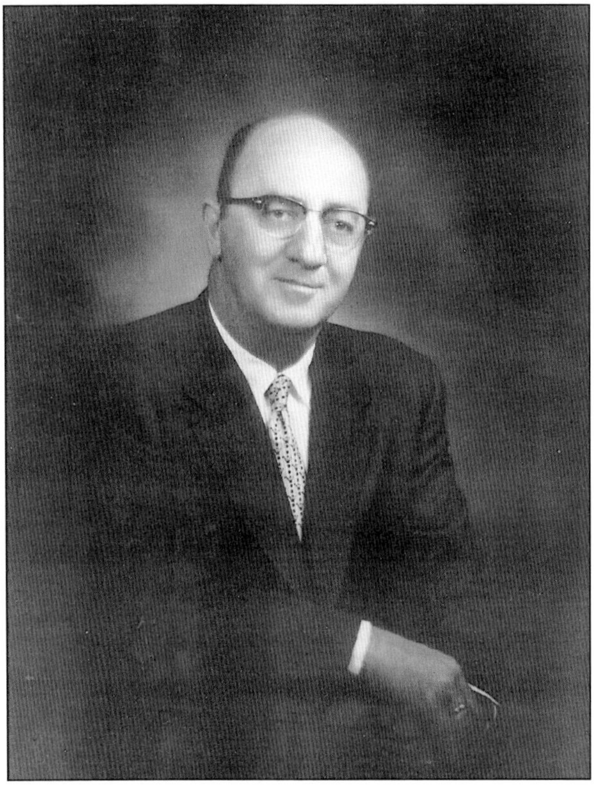

Manuel Russ came to Chattanooga from Atlanta as a young man and lived with his sister, Ida Leventhal. He went to work for L.B. West and Marvin Leventhal, Ida's husband, in the Wesco Paving Company, which he purchased in the mid-1940s. Further along in his career, he founded Chattanooga Rock Products, the Chattanooga Asphalt Terminal, and the Chattanooga Asphalt Haulers. About 1957, the Vulcan Materials Company purchased Wesco Paving and Chattanooga Rock Products. Manny married Josephine Diamond, and they had two children, Rita and Philip. Philip, a real estate appraiser, lives in Nashville. He and his wife have two children, Benjamin and Johanna.

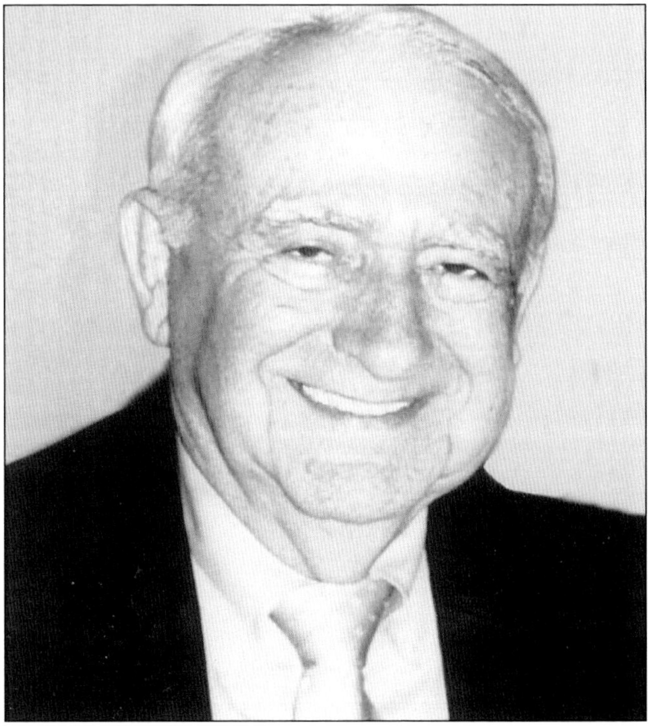

Sam Speer, a practicing optometrist who married Manny Russ's daughter Rita, became associated with the Chattanooga Asphalt Haulers. Sam later changed the name to the Russ Transport Company and founded Producers Transport. These companies hauled not only asphalt, but also heating oil, cement, and various other dry products. Sam and Rita had three girls: Sheryl (Blechner) of Atlanta, Rae (Hirsch) of Nashville, and Jan (Fox) of Birmingham.

Dr. Jack Tepper revolutionized the pediatrics service in Chattanooga by opening an office in the early 1950s with a lab. His practice grew until he built the Tepper Clinic on McCallie Avenue, which soon became the Tepper Pediatric Hospital. Jack was married to Rene, and they had two children, David and Cynthia Kusnetzky of Kansas City, Missouri. Rene's brother, Floyd Kaplan, was the administrator of the hospital, and another of Jack's brothers, Lou Tepper, was a financial advisor. Floyd's wife was Beatrice, and they had two children, Ellen and Ronnie. Lou's wife was also named Beatrice, and they had two sons, Gary and Daniel. Jack's sister Margaret married David Winkler, a Dalton stockbroker. The parents of the Tepper family, William and Anna, also lived in Chattanooga.

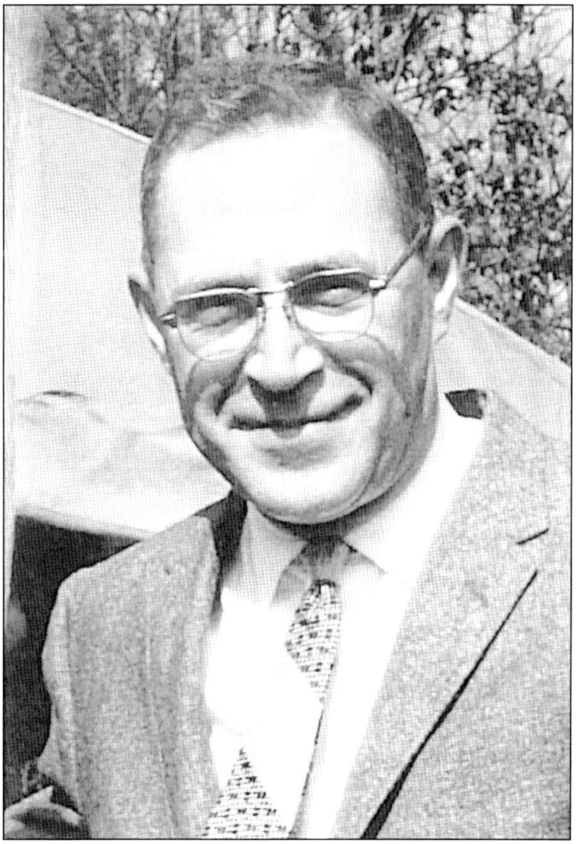

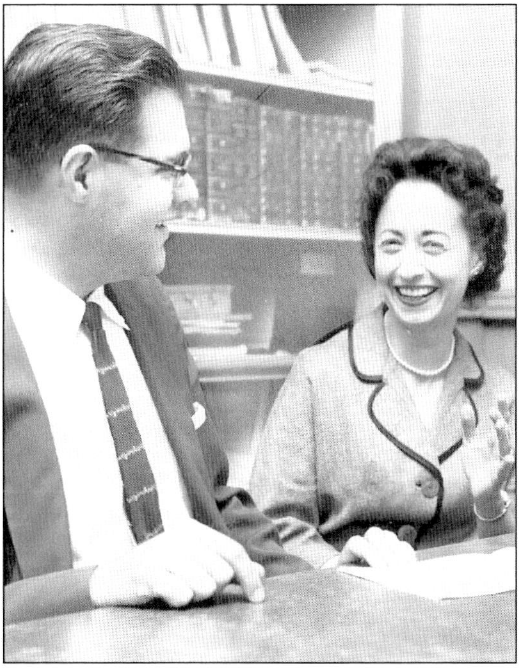

Drs. Sam Binder and Marjorie Tepper are shown at a JCC Human Growth Planning Meeting in 1959. Marjorie and her husband, Dr. Bernard Tepper, had two children, Eric and Patricia. Sam and his wife, Claire (Siskin), had three: Wendy, Ellen, and David. Other physicians who have practiced in Chattanooga include Drs. Jerome Abramson, Allen Lewis, Sam Banks, Stanley Dressler, David Drucker, Stuart Frank, Joel Ginsberg, Hyman Kaplan, David Karr, Richard Lasky, Deane Leventhal, Harold Levine, Phil Livingston, Sam and Ira Long, Frank Miller, Rick Rader, Edward Reisman Sr., Richard Roberts, David Rose, Marty Scheinberg, Clarence Shaw, Leo Shumacker, Neil Spitalny, Louis, Steve, and David Ulin, and Joe Zuckerman. Dentists Max Brener, Howard Gault, David Monen, A.H. Resnick, and Alan Stein had offices here as well.

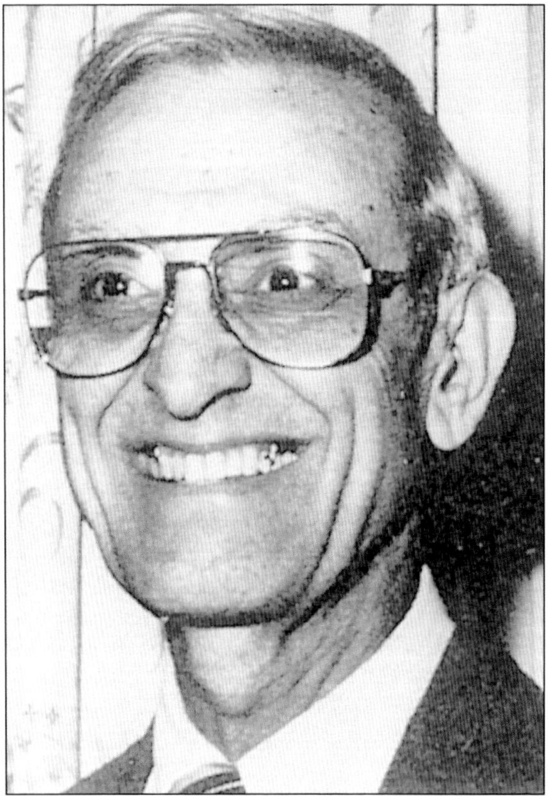

Morris Slutsky is one of Chattanooga's most ardent volunteers. He is the "father" of the 911 emergency system in Chattanooga and Hamilton County. He worked for 15 years, from 1979 to 1994, to bring this about! In 1990, the Hamilton County 911 communication district named him "911 Man of the Decade." Morris was reared in Nashville but moved to Chattanooga and was engaged in the grocery business, in real estate, and in casualty insurance. He was president and active in the B'nai Zion Congregation, the B'nai Brith, the Hamilton County Taxpayers Association, and the Crime Alert Commission. His has received awards from the Bar Association, the International Lions Clubs, and the Chattanooga Police Department. He is married to Anetha Pavlow of Chattanooga and has one son, Dr. Morton Slutsky, a plastic surgeon in Atlanta, Georgia.

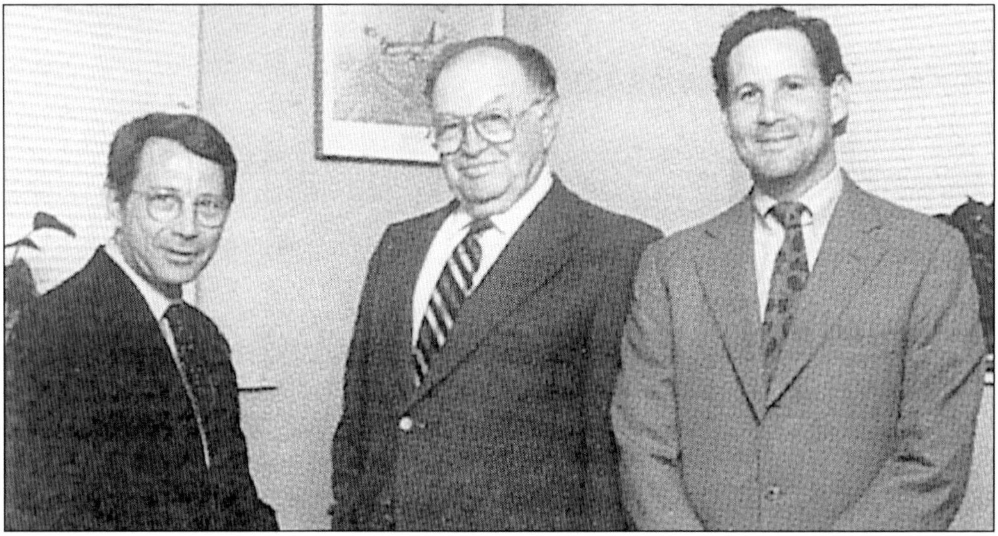

The Southern Foundry Supply, Inc. has been at the forefront of the recycling industry for over four decades. The corporate headquarters is in Chattanooga, with facilities in Knoxville and Atlanta. Julius Chazen, chairman of the board, founded the company in 1953 on the site of the Tennessee Valley Authority River Terminal. More than a scrap metal processor, the corporation is dedicated to improving and conserving our environment through total resource management. Pictured with their father in 1994 is Gary D. Chazen, president, on the right, and Robert G. Chazen, vice-president.

Youth group activities have always been a top priority in Chattanooga's congregations. In 1978, Andy Hodes, the son of Alvin and Elizabeth Hodes of the Mizpah Congregation, was elected president of the Southeastern Federation of Temple Youth. Following this, he was elected president of the National Federation of Temple Youth in 1979. Andy lives in Wayne, New Jersey. His sister is Leslie Swichkow of Marietta, Georgia. Andy's great-grandfather, Abraham, and his wife, Pauline, came to Chattanooga c. 1907. They had six children: Edna, Ella, Morris (Andy's grandfather), Ida, Sarah, and Philip. All but Ida are buried in B'nai Zion Cemetery.

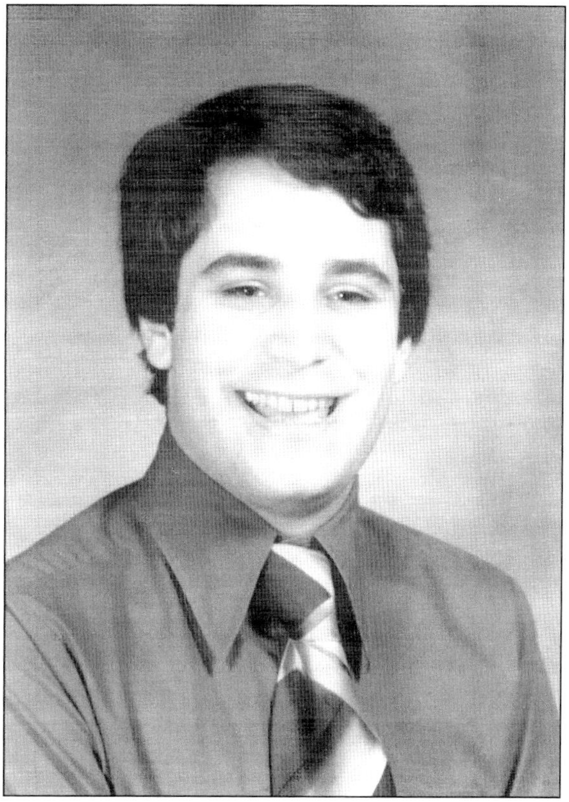

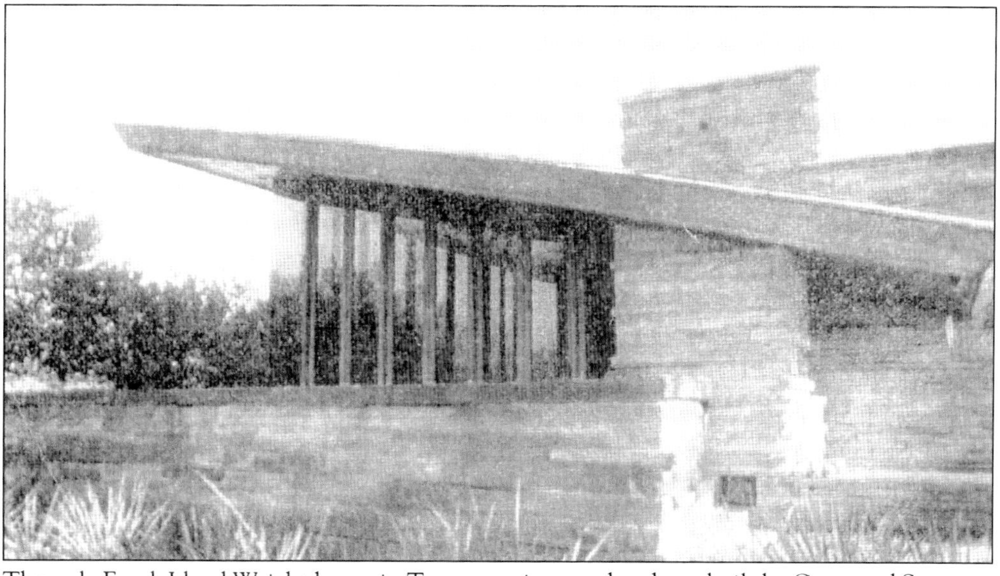

The only Frank Lloyd Wright home in Tennessee is owned and was built by Gerte and Seamour Shavin in the 1960s. It is located on North Crest Road on Missionary Ridge overlooking the city. It is finished in red cypress and Tennessee crab orchard stone in both the interior and exterior walls. It is called the "Usonion" house and has been placed on the National Register of Historic Places. The Shavins had three children: Karen, David, and Elliot. Gerte's sisters are Pauline (Irving Schulman) and Joyce (Saul Morris).

ACKNOWLEDGMENTS

I am deeply indebted to the families in the Chattanooga community who so graciously entrusted me with their treasured family images of children, parents, and grandparents for the creation of this book.

My special gratitude goes to the Board of the Chattanooga Jewish Community Federation, which funded the creation of the Chattanooga Jewish Reflections Exhibit in 1996. I am the curator of the exhibit and this book is based on it. I owe appreciation to Federation Directors Lori Myers, Irv Ginsburg, and Deborah Levine and Federation Presidents Pris Siskin, Helen Pregulman, and Claire Binder (in particular) for their help.

The exhibit was a project of the Federation's Chai Steppers Senior Coed Club, which encouraged me to go forward with this project after we had seen exhibits in other southern cities. Jane Leavey, director of the William Breman Jewish Heritage Museum of Atlanta, Georgia, was most helpful in initially getting us started on this project. Thanks are also extended to her for donating an immigration picture.

To my very dear and special friend, Barnetta Allen, who was constantly at my side, diligently telephoning, gathering, sorting, and arranging pictures for the exhibit every step of the way, I owe a deep and lasting debt of gratitude. I do appreciate the help and encouragement that my two sons, Lee and Richard Abelson, have given me. I extend thanks to my sister, Liz Raisin, for data about Dalton, Georgia.

Thanks are due to the rabbis and to the three congregations in Chattanooga: Beth Sholom, B'nai Zion, and Mizpah, to the Chattanooga Jewish Federation, to the Chattanooga-Hamilton County Bicentennial Library, to author Charles Wilson, and to Curator Jerry Desmond of the Chattanooga Regional History Museum, for their help, information, and images.

To the staff of Arcadia Publishing Company, and to my publisher and special advisor, Mark Berry, I extend a very special thanks.

Any errors, omissions, or misrepresentations are unintentional. Space limitations forced me to limit the families and persons mentioned here. I compiled this book hoping to record some of the activities of our Jewish community over the last 130 years, so that future generations can understand that Chattanooga's earliest Jewish citizens were involved in preserving Judaism and bettering our lives, our community, and the world.

—Joy Effron Abelson Adams
January 29, 1999